Ketan,
Could not have done
this without you,
Paul

Are Americans Becoming More Peaceful?

Paul Joseph

Paradigm Publishers

Boulder • London

Copyright © 2007 Paradigm Publishers

Published in the United States by Paradigm Publishers, 3360 Mitchell Lane Suite E, Boulder, CO 80301 USA.

Paradigm Publishers is the trade name of Birkenkamp & Company, LLC, Dean Birkenkamp, President and Publisher.

Library of Congress Cataloging-in-Publication Data

Joseph, Paul, 1948–
  Are Americans becoming more peaceful? / Paul Joseph.
    p. cm.
  Includes bibliographical references and index.
  ISBN-13: 978-1-59451-299-5 (hc : alk. paper)
  ISBN-10: 1-59451-299-X (hc : alk. paper)
  1. United States—Foreign relations.   2. Terrorism.   3. Iraq War,
2003–   4. Peace.   5. Television and war.   I. Title.
  JZ1480.A3J67 2007
  303.6'60973—dc22

               2006021981

Printed and bound in the United States of America on acid-free paper that meets the standards of the American National Standard for Permanence of Paper for Printed Library Materials.

This book was designed and typeset in ITC Bookman Light by Straight Creek Bookmakers.

11 10 09 08 07   1 2 3 4 5

Contents

Preface

"A book," I'd answer.

"What is it called?"

"'Are Americans Becoming More Peaceful?'"

"You must be kidding." At least that is what many of my friends and colleagues said after I told them the title of my project. Many chuckled, shook their heads ruefully, or just looked the other way. One or two even punched me on the shoulder, thinking that I must be joking.

I could see their point. After all, the United States is currently engaged in one medium-sized conflict in Afghanistan and a major war in Iraq. Its military forces are active in the Philippines and Colombia and are stationed at dozens of bases around the world. North Korea and Iran are the subjects of intense debate over the possible use of deadly force. The Pentagon has 1.5 million troops in uniform and officially spends more than $400 billion a year. Unofficially, it spends at least another $100 billion more. Measured by dollars or combat capability, no other country comes even remotely close.

Stepping back even slightly from the present, we can see the Pentagon fighting in Somalia and Kosovo, intervening in Haiti and Bosnia, and launching cruise missiles against targets in Sudan and Afghanistan. In 1991, the Pentagon mounted a major effort in the Persian Gulf War and continued to bomb Iraq intermittently until the start of the current war. And that list covers only the end of the cold war. Military force might or might not have been justified, but it was certainly used again and again. How could one possibly create an argument that Americans are becoming more peaceful?

My thesis concerns the American people, not the American government, an institution that is certainly not becoming more peaceful. In focusing on the public, I argue that a significant minority rejects war on principle, and that even more are becoming sensitive to war costs such as casualties to U.S. troops and to civilians on the other side. War opposition is multisided: some explicitly oppose armed conflict as a way for the United States to make policy, and some of these will resist war by participating in antiwar movements or through another form of direct disagreement. Another, larger proportion of the public can be characterized by its nonacceptance of war. These individuals' opposition is more muted; it lies beneath the political surface and emerges only when the concrete results of people killing other people become apparent. This nonacceptance of war can be more potential than actual, and government officials seek ways to manage opinion so that prospective opposition remains beneath the surface. War management is carried out by the White House and the Pentagon and involves public rhetoric, a media strategy, and drawing upon popular beliefs and opinions that are decidedly not peaceful. The tension between the still uneven tendency of Americans to become more peaceful and the management of opinion to produce war support forms the organizational backbone of this book.

The strength of opposition to war fluctuates and is not always sufficiently influential to prevent war. But the need of administration officials to dampen potential opposition has changed the way that war is organized and conducted. Costs must appear low. If they do not, the negative memories of Vietnam will quickly emerge and principled opposition to war will be joined by the now many who think that the intervention is a "quagmire" with no "light at the end of the tunnel." Conversely, successful war management will evoke more positive narratives from World War II. These competing memory sites, World War II and Vietnam, form one element of the broad collision between war opposition and war support.

While this framework is developed further in chapter 1, "From Mobilized to Conditional War," I can already anticipate some objections. In March 2003, the Bush administration launched Operation Iraqi Freedom, which received the support of more than two-thirds of the population. Saddam and the Ba'ath regime were quickly overthrown and President Bush declared "mission accomplished." Despite a growing insurgency and casualties, the failure to find weapons of mass destruction, and a prison scandal at Abu Ghraib, a war president was reelected in November 2004. What is so peaceful about that?

One answer is that the tendency of Americans to become more peaceful is at least partially countered by public fear, especially following the dramatic and devastating attacks against the World Trade Center and the Pentagon on September 11, 2001. Chapter 2, "Managing Fear," reviews the record and impact of the Bush administration with respect to fear messages. But there is another side to September 11. Many academics and journalists predicted a broad set of changes in personal habits and civic life. Henceforth, Americans would read more books, give more to charity, spend more time with family and friends, follow the news more closely, and make decisions about flying, vacations, and use of public spaces with a new sense of (in)security in mind. I review those claims using evidence as diverse as smoking patterns, post–traumatic stress syndrome and television watching, travel plans, and public responses to changes in the color-coded alert level announced by the Department of Homeland Security.

After the initial overthrow of Saddam's regime, the U.S. military presence in Iraq became a military occupation. A long search failed to find weapons of mass destruction or support for the other principal claim in support of the war, namely, that Saddam was connected to international terrorism. Prominent whistle-blowers and a series of official reports seemed to repudiate the factual claims of the administration's case. Yet a substantial minority of the public continued to believe that Saddam not only had weapons before the war began but that WMD had actually been found in Iraq. Many also thought that he was connected to terrorist groups or involved with September 11. These views certainly challenge my argument. How could Americans be becoming more peaceful when so many were failing the simplest entrance exam? Chapter 3, "Managing Information," considers the knowledge base of the American public and the shape of its eventual "learning curve" on the claims advanced by the Bush administration. I also trace the implications of the public's "war smarts" for the quality of democracy and civic society in the country.

One possible explanation for the public's initial low grades was the failure of the media to scrutinize the administration's case for war. The public had to first unlearn what it had already been taught. In February 2003, Secretary of State Colin Powell presented the administration's position before the United Nations to rave reviews. No major newspaper or media outlet challenged the argument. Later it was determined that many of his arguments rested on the thinnest evidence. Some were straight-out fabrications. Powell even based part of this speech on British intelligence sources who in turn had copied it from an unclassified academic paper written several years before. Yet the press, particularly the *New York Times* and the *Washington Post,* was largely complicit. It is certainly difficult for Americans to become more peaceful when the institution that is so key to the check-and-balance theory of democracy had failed so completely.

Chapter 4, "Managing the Media," reviews recent changes in the organization of the industry including the increasingly important shift from print to television and, within television, from the traditional three networks to cable and the twenty-four-hour news cycle. I also consider more critical media coverage, such as the frequently charged relationship between journalists and the military during the Vietnam War and the emergence of more accurate coverage of Iraq as the war went on. Using a series of interviews conducted with public relations managers in the Pentagon, I also discuss the impact of embedded reporting in producing war support. Anonymity was promised for all original interviews conducted for this book. These interviews are indicated in the text by the phrase "in an interview," but otherwise no source is provided.

It is often said that we are becoming a more visual culture. Photography, what Americans see of armed conflict, forms another key collision point between war constraints and war enablers. Chapter 5, "Managing Photographs," provides a brief history of combat photojournalism, examines the impact of pictures of humanitarian emergencies, and compares the photographs used by the *Boston Globe*, *New York Post*, and *London Times* in March–April 2003 (a triumphal period) with April 2004 (a more sober period culminating in Abu Ghraib). I also look at shifting understandings of "good taste" employed by editors to decide what should and what should not be placed before the public. The chapter includes interviews with a photography director of the *Boston Globe* and, to include more explicit antiwar efforts, the editor responsible for selecting the pictures used in the *Anti-Personnel Landmines Monitor.*

Since the establishment of the all-volunteer military in 1973, women have made up an increasingly large proportion of the armed forces. In both Afghanistan and Iraq, both female and male service members were directly involved in the war effort. Both sexes fought, killed, died, were wounded, and came home with psychological traumas including post–traumatic stress disorder. What did the public think about the new proximity of women to harm despite the formal ban on their participation in combat? What about the continued record of sexual violence within the military itself? Or the efforts of the administration to defend its war policies by arguing that it was protecting vulnerable women from repressive patriarchies? One vulnerable American woman, Private Jessica Lynch, was "rescued" by a Special Forces team during a critical stage in the march toward Baghdad, and the warm feelings generated by the event cast a positive glow on the entire operation. But another woman, Private Lynndie England, became the public face for the sexual abuse and humiliation of Iraqi prisoners at Abu Ghraib. The relationship between gender and the changing organization of war is pursued in chapter 6, "Managing Gender."

A nationalist surge followed the September 11 attacks, and unlikely segments of the public, including some college students, liberals and former anti–Vietnam War activists gave enthusiastic support to military intervention in Afghanistan. The lead singer of the Dixie Chicks questioned President Bush's policies on the eve of the 2003 war with Iraq, and many radio stations and country-and-western fans organized a boycott of their music. "Saddam's Angels" read one bumper sticker. "Dixie Sluts" was another. Despite this support for war and an increasingly urgent need for additional military personnel, the public continued to oppose a resumption of the draft. Increased hate crimes against Muslims were another consequence of September 11, and polls captured a broad pattern of prejudice that weighs against the thesis that Americans are becoming more peaceful. But much of the population continued to uphold the importance of cultural and religious tolerance, thus creating a more positive counterforce. The cultural currents surrounding patriotism, the draft, multiculturalism, and celebrity blacklisting are discussed in chapter 7, "Managing Militarism."

Since Vietnam and its fifty-eight thousand U.S. dead, the public has been especially concerned with casualties to its own troops. Until Iraq, most post-Vietnam military commitments resulted in deaths measured in the dozens. In the Persian Gulf War more died from accidents than from hostile fire. Yet, as this book was written, casualties in Afghanistan and Iraq continued to mount. How have these losses affected the public? How have they been managed by government officials? How have they been treated by the press and media? Most importantly, how have they affected the military itself? The top military leadership remained publicly loyal to the White House, and there has been no fundamental loss of will such as that shown by ground troops in Vietnam after 1968. But lower recruitment rates, third and fourth tours of duty, and problems with supplying armor for soldiers and Humvees pointed toward an extremely difficult occupation. In December 2005, Representative John Murtha, former marine and conservative Democrat, issued a striking call for withdrawal from Iraq within six months. Chapter 8, "Managing Casualties," examines the claim that the U.S. military must fight in ways that keep casualties "small" and prevent—or at least reduce—civilian losses in the battle zone. The chapter also reviews the record of the U.S. military with respect to "collateral damage" during the Gulf War, Somalia, Kosovo, Afghanistan, and the current war in Iraq.

The concluding chapter, chapter 9, "From Managing War to Making Peace," examines the implications of the tendency for Americans to become more peaceful for the future use of U.S. military force and to transform Washington's policies so that they too can become more peaceful. Despite the violent record taken in their name, I am optimistic about the current opinions held by the American public. And the potential is even better. But I have some explaining to do.

Acknowledgments

The book started a long time ago and I have acquired many debts along the way. I first started to think about this project during a yearlong sabbatical in New Zealand and I am grateful to Geoff Fougere and the sociology department at the University of Canterbury for their collegiality. I spent another year buried in the Brandeis University library, where Lisa Hatch and other members of the staff helped with various requests. Carmen Sirianni, Gordie Fellman, Judy Hanley, and others in the Brandeis sociology department helped make my stay productive and enjoyable.

My treatment of war and the American public starts from two intellectual bases: my own discipline of sociology and the interdisciplinary field of peace studies. But I also roam through the rest of the social sciences and into areas as diverse as gender studies, communications and media, international relations, and even community health. Inevitably, I have made mistakes along the way. My arguments have been clarified and some of the early missteps corrected through conversations and/or readings provided by Karlyn Bowman, Dale Bryan, Carl Conetta, Donna Dean, Michael Denning, Charlie Derber, Paul Devlin, Richard Eichenberg, Cynthia Enloe, Matthew Farrelly, Bill Fried, John Gianino, Mark Grandstaff, Jim Green, Matthew Gregory, Anne Joseph, Andrew Katz, Jim Robbins, Gabriel Rossman, Fred Rothbaum, Lydia Saad, Michael Schneider, Kathleen Weiler, and Maryanne Wolf.

Although I never had a chance to talk with the late Susan Sontag, her book *Regarding the Pain of Others* has been extremely valuable in the development of this project.

The essays and final examinations of students in my course "Sociology of War and Peace" also gave me many ideas and leads, as did the e-mailed articles that I also received from them. Their messages often began with "Thought this might be of interest" and they were almost always right. In fall 2004, I was lucky to have a small group of capable and eager first-year students who in an experimental advising program called "Windows-on-Research" helped with various parts of the project. Their names are: Monica Camacho, Alexandra Dunk, Bruni Hirsch, Megan Chang, Michael Rausch, Peter Shaeffer,

Adam Levy, Ketan Gajria, Chryssa Rask, and Matthew Weinberg. Their individual contributions are noted in the text. They didn't always agree with what I had to say and many of them still don't, but I always enjoyed working with them.

The Tufts University Faculty Research Awards Committee provided key assistance with portions of this project.

Interviews with national security officials play a major role in this book. Tony Banbury provided some early leads for whom to contact for interviews, and Maxine Issacs gave valuable advice on how to conduct them. I admired the open-minded spirit demonstrated by Colonel Robert D'Amico and Colonel Paula Thornhill, whom I met at an Oxford University conference, "War and Virtual War." Colonel D'Amico set up a series of valuable Pentagon interviews that I would never have been able to arrange on my own. My appreciation as well to the former and current officials who made themselves available but who cannot be thanked by name. And I must not forget Alexander Wendt, who under only slight pressure from his parents, Jim and Katherine, graciously allowed the use of his bedroom when I visited Washington, D.C.

Two work-study students in the Tufts sociology department, Cathy Serrano and Dorothy Bandura, helped with some of the nuts and bolts. Adam Levy was extraordinarily patient in his preparation of two key figures. Tanya Connolly helped prepare many of the tables, and Lynn Wiles was not only of immense administrative value in the collection of the images used in this book but also contributed her own considerable talent as a photographer to the selection and editing process. When things became truly desperate, Melody Ko, Jeff Weiner, and Andrea Daley provided last-minute technical assistance.

At Paradigm Publishers, comments from an anonymous reviewer helped clarify the main argument, and Patricia Gimenez helped prepare the manuscript with skill and diligence. Cheryl Hoffman copyedited the manuscript with expertise and saved me from many mistakes. Melanie Stafford and Jason Potter produced an accurate and eye-pleasing book. My editor, Jennifer Knerr, read the chapters carefully, knew how and when to push, and knew how and when to back off. I won't say that the final revision of the manuscript was pain free but Jennifer's professionalism and commitment made the outcome much better.

My three children, Ian, Sara, and Danny, knew how important this book was to me. My wife, Linda Schiffman, herself an active and principled critic of war with our local community group, was always supportive, especially during the last two months of writing, when I needed the most help.

Paul Joseph

From Mobilized to Conditional War

In March 2003, the United States invaded Iraq in an operation supported by more than 70 percent of the public. Despite Bush administration claims of a quick victory, the occupation grew more difficult. Antiwar protests and large demonstrations had always challenged Washington's policy on Iraq. Now broader public opinion also started to move against the war. By the beginning of 2006, significantly less than half the country continued to support the Bush administration's handling of Iraq. This chapter tracks two different types of opposition to war, balances this opposition against continuing administration efforts to manage public perceptions in ways that produce war support, and explores changes in the social organization of war itself.

Two Types of Opposition to War

Americans are becoming more peaceful in two distinct ways. The first and most proactive trend toward peace opposes war in principle and favors instead more emphasis on diplomacy, negotiation, mediation, conflict resolution, and other methods of grappling with international problems without resort to violence. This position advocates reducing the role of armed force in international affairs significantly by making it—genuinely—a last resort. For the United States, the defense budget could be reduced by at least $100 billion, and the military could be reorganized to make it less of an interventionary force. This position recasts patriotism so that it is no longer identified with unconditional support of government policy. Love of country fits within the broad recognition that peace and security rest on a new, more positive role for the United States in world affairs rather than on the preparation and actual use of military force. I call this attitude toward peace a "Type I" opposition to war.

A Type I peace policy would include the reduction of nuclear weapons to fewer than a thousand, with Washington issuing a declaration that it would not use those weapons first. The State Department would also make a stronger commitment to multilateralism in sanctioning the use of force, especially by allowing the UN Security Council to become the principal site for making decisions about when and where war might be ultimately necessary. The United States would also recognize the importance of reciprocity in its relations with other countries, especially in important arenas such as arms control, nonproliferation, and the international trade of military weapons. One of the most important steps in this set of revamped policies would be recognition of the International Criminal Court and a commitment to build its organizational capacities.

This current of thought would link changes in military policy to a reformed foreign policy. Washington would side more consistently with the hopes for greater equality, human rights, and opposition to the authoritarian regimes throughout the world. Energy policy would also change, substituting conservation and renewable resources for the current overdependence on foreign oil. The current "war on terrorism" would be replaced by more focused international police activities aimed more precisely against terrorist networks. These changes would also begin to alter the current image of the U.S. government abroad, particularly among those who regard Washington as the defender of a status quo that is all too frequently unjust and repressive. Long-term security is best achieved not by targeting and intimidating opponents but by building cooperative relationships connected to the struggle for stronger human rights and social development. Indeed, it is hard to think of a world as "peaceful" where almost half of the population attempts to live on less than $2 a day. (The same argument can be applied within the United States, where the poverty rate for children remains close to 20 percent. For a country with so much wealth and resources, this level of "structural violence" can also be said to fall far short of peace.)

Some of the savings acquired from the shrinking of the war system would provide a peace dividend that could be applied to support other social projects. For example, by the end of 2005, the cost of the war in Iraq was nearly $200 million a day, more than enough to provide sufficient food for every starving child on the planet. Funds could also be devoted to development projects that would prevent poverty and the subsequent need for assistance in the first place. This agenda suggests the possibilities of extending war prevention, often called negative peace in the field of peace studies, into a more ambitious program of positive peace, or reducing inequality, creating a stronger human rights regime, and building a more just social order.

Many of these policies, including the reduction of nuclear weapons, multilateral approaches to global threats, support for the International Criminal Court, and rigorous efforts to control the international arms trade are already supported by a considerable majority of Americans. Taken piece by policy piece, Americans are significantly more reformist than government officials and the media recognize. But the size of the dove constituency willing to put the pieces together and mold them into a self-conscious, alternative approach to the problems of global violence and security is about 15 to 20 percent of the population. For example, nearly this proportion opposed even the post–September 11 military intervention in Afghanistan, a mission that one would expect to receive the greatest level of support. The explicit peace sentiment can be found in all parts of the country and among all occupations and demographic groups but tends, regionally, to be found more on the two coasts than in the South and Midwest. Institutionally, it is encountered more in universities, churches, and labor unions than in business. And this sentiment is shared more by African Americans, women, and younger and older adults than by their demographic opposites.

At the core of this constituency lies an activist component—those willing to participate in social movement opposition to war policies. Activism includes local rallies, national demonstrations, lobbying, petition drives, and dramatic forms of nonviolent protest such as the 1994 hunger strike by TransAfrica director Randall Robinson, which was aimed at reversing the Clinton administration's initial reluctance to restore deposed Jean-Bertrand Aristide to his position as the elected president of Haiti. The size of the peace activism component varies, but this group never disappears entirely. During the peak resistance to the Vietnam War, the organized peace movement numbered more than three million. In early 2003, roughly the same number participated in protests against the war in Iraq.[1] A *Nation* editorial noted three weeks after the war began:

> We have created the largest, most broadly based peace movement in history—a movement that has engaged missions of people here

and around the world. Never before have U.S. churches, from the Conference of Catholic Bishops to the National Council of Churches, spoken so resolutely against the war. Never before have so many trade unions supported the antiwar movement. In practically every sector of society—business executives, women's groups, environmentalists, artists, musicians, African-Americans, Latinos—a strong antiwar voice has emerged. Antiwar rallies and vigils have occurred in thousands of communities, and many cities have passed antiwar declarations.[2]

The impact of this activist core far outdistances the numbers that it is able to gather together in one place. Movement actions often gain media attention, thereby communicating an oppositional presence to politicians and other citizens. Peace movements can place policy alternatives on the political agenda, forcing political and military leaders to confront issues that they would otherwise ignore. Movements also influence key third parties such as editors, journalists, business leaders, and members of Congress, who in turn influence members of the administration. Activists have been able to establish important working relations with movements in other countries and thus contribute to an international synergy that sustains motivation and commitment. A different, more complex message about the political and cultural inclinations of the American public is conveyed to the rest of the world. All of these measures contribute to the antiwar oppositional legacy. Indeed, many of the conditions explored in these pages are in part a response to the arguments and political influence of the peace movement tradition.[3]

Type I opposition has concluded that in almost every case war is a misguided policy and that following other, nonviolent alternatives will consistently bring better outcomes. Americans are also becoming more peaceful in their increased sensitivity toward the costs of war. In what I call "Type II" opposition, the public does not oppose war out of principle but recoils in response to costs once these become visible. Conscription, taxes, and other sacrifices that require mobilization behind the war effort are now more difficult to obtain. There are fewer types of war that are considered legitimate; war must appear as immediate self-defense or opposition to concentrated forms of evil such as terrorist groups or authoritarian regimes. Military interventions that seem to target entire peoples or that are fought for geopolitical motives will meet disapproval. Where war carries only low costs, efforts to maintain public approval may be temporarily successful. But as military intervention becomes longer or more intense, or if the outcome appears inconclusive, sensitivities that lie beneath initial public support will surface. Evidence of damage, such as casualties, collateral damage, or photographs of the wounded, will limit support for military action. The pain of war continues to be felt acutely in private, especially by families whose loved ones have been killed or injured. But the leaders who made the decisions to go to war will do little to draw attention to this sacrifice.

Besides the dove constituency, Type II opposition can be found in an additional 50 to 60 percent of the population. Taken together, actual and potential opposition found in approximately three-quarters of the population force political and military leaders to manage the public face of war. Management means generating war support either by covering up the costs of war or by balancing them with competing war enablers. Examples include the strong desire to support the president in the midst of a crisis, fear of being attacked, and a determination to support the country's troops once they are committed to a danger zone. In practical terms, this "yellow ribbon" effect usually means initial support for the policy that placed the military in harm's way. The considerable respect enjoyed by the military, which is higher than for any other institution, including Congress, the media, and the corporate sector, plays an important background role. But while there is no great enthusiasm for war in the large second group, neither is there any significant appreciation that there might be alternative methods of coping with external threats. Military actions may be approved that are seen as successful, do not appear to carry significant costs, and are supported by the president and Congress. In short, the second group straddles a tension between Type II sensitivity to war costs and support for military intervention once the government declares that such a course of action is necessary. The fluidity contained within the second group allows for both strong war support in 2003 and the (bare) reelection of a war president, as well as for the widespread opposition to the war policies of that same president that emerged in 2004 and became stronger throughout 2005 and early 2006. Type II opposition became more important than the coexisting tendencies that provide war support.

The clash between the features of popular culture that constrain war and those that make war possible underscores fundamental uncertainty toward war as an instrument of policy. Of the two peaceful currents, Type I opponents may be more likely to vote Democratic than Republican—or even to look toward the possibility of building a third party. But Type II opposition cannot be linked as easily to political parties or particular locations on the ideological spectrum. On the whole, Republicans may be somewhat more loyal in their adherence to those features of popular culture that provide war support but many are also unwilling to embrace the tangible costs of war. In this respect, Type II opposition is not merely an expression of left or liberal political sentiments. In fact, in an uneven but occasionally strong and distinct manner, war sensitivity can be traced within the military itself.

A third group, constituting perhaps 25 to 30 percent of the population, provides consistent war support for the Pentagon.[4] For this group, the United States must confront a world that contains significant evil, and these threats can be deterred or defeated only through the use of armed force. Currently, this group is somewhat larger than Type I opposition located among the doves. Even as the majority of the public turned against the Vietnam War, a core of about one-third would have supported further escalation or other efforts to continue to try to win. Even as a majority turned against the war in Iraq, a similar one-third continued to support the military effort despite the costs. War support may be sustained by family military traditions, traditionally understood patriotism, and the belief that traits such as heroism, duty, loyalty, and masculinity are well expressed in the conduct of war. (Many of these elements also operate in the second group but are counterbalanced by Type II sensitivities.) Military force is often seen as the most appropriate way to respond to the security challenges that confront the United States, and there is little inclination to be skeptical of government or media explanations of why war is necessary. Furthermore, once military force is committed, it is important to see the job through to the end.

Taken together, Type I and Type II opposition form a significant pool of resistance whose precise impact varies in different contexts but whose overall influence has made it more difficult to enter certain types of war and has changed the behavior of the United States in the wars that it does fight. The result is a cautiously optimistic reading of the public, meaning that a significant majority, perhaps as high as 75 percent, either rejects war as an acceptable policy or is becoming more sensitive to the actual costs of war. Wars that appear to have a traditional geopolitical motive, such as preserving access to scarce resources like oil, supporting a presumed balance of power, or overthrowing ideological opponents will not gain easy support. The public is less likely to make wholesale enemies out of other people and nations. Instead, enemy status is focused more narrowly on individuals and regimes that embody evil or carry out criminal acts. The public is more likely to be critical of situations where there are large casualties, not only to its own soldiers but also to civilians in combat areas. Where concrete pictures of war and combat are available, the public is more likely to reject than embrace the need for sacrifice. Tangible reminders of these costs may not quickly lead to demands for withdrawal but do erode support for the more heroic story lines of war.

The two forms of opposition have not yet created an absolute barrier against war. Type II sensitivities coexist with themes that provide war support, thus allowing for considerable fluctuation. Since the end of the cold war, Washington has used military force many times, often with the support of a majority of the public. But conflicts that appear on the surface to embody "the good fight" are more easily punctured by relatively small doses of pessimism. Within situations that initially evoke the more positive memories of World War II lurk more negative Vietnam images and narratives—even where these interventions appear initially to be justifiable and successful. In their recognition and rejection of the costs of war, Americans are, in an uneven and often contradictory manner, becoming more peaceful.

Militarism

The tendency of Americans to become more peaceful collides with militarism or the "attitude and a set of institutions which regard war and the preparation for war as a normal and desirable social activity."[5] Militarism contains several key components: the belief that the country should maintain a strong military and be prepared to use it to promote national interests; support for military values within the overall culture of a society; and militarization, or the influence of preparations to make war on the social institutions of society as a whole. Militarization deepens when specific arrangements—recruitment, training, acquisitions of weapons, and legitimation of the use of force—simultaneously modify the economic, political, cultural, and psychological dimensions of society.

Militarism can also include the more direct participation of military officers in governing structures such as occurred in Germany under National Socialism, in imperial Japan, and in Greece, Argentina, Chile, Burma, and other countries where the military has played a dominant role in the administration of society. For the United States, this particular feature of militarism has been largely absent. The Constitution calls for presidential or civilian control over the uniformed military leadership; what is distinct, especially in the conduct of foreign policy after World War II, is how consistently civilian officials, even those without personal experience in the military, can nonetheless advocate and enact policies that reflect what C. Wright Mills called "the military definition of reality."[6] Under the influence of the cold war, professional diplomacy and negotiation skills have been weakened relative to realpolitik backed by calculations of military might. Civilians still make the main decisions but the policies themselves, be they conceived in the Pentagon or the

State Department and White House, typically rest on the projection of military force.

After the end of the cold war, many commentators predicted a peace dividend in which the defense budget and the role of the military in Washington's global policies would both be reduced dramatically. But in the 1990s, the absolute size of the Pentagon shrank only slightly. It then started to increase again in 2001 after the Bush administration assumed office.

Military force was used in many different circumstances. Between the 1991 Operation Desert Storm against Iraqi forces occupying Kuwait and Operation Iraqi Freedom, which began in 2003, Washington used air power against the Serbs, first in Bosnia and later in Kosovo, and different combinations of air and ground troops in Somalia, Haiti, and Afghanistan. On a smaller scale, the Pentagon has been engaged in Colombia and the Philippines, against targets in the Sudan, and in several armed peacekeeping missions, including in the Balkans. Importantly, the United States did not intervene in several cases of humanitarian emergency, including the 1994 genocide in Rwanda in which eight hundred thousand died in six weeks, and East Timor, where a series of organized killing sprees over the 1990s took the lives of more than a third of the population.

During this time, neither the senior Bush nor the Clinton administration did much to restructure the traditional primacy of military force. The George W. Bush administration actually rededicated itself to strengthening military force so that it might be used more easily and effectively in the pursuit of its own foreign policy objectives. The *National Security Strategy of the United States of America*, released one year after the September 11 attacks, outlined a strategy of preventive war in which the United States would have to "act against emerging threats before they are fully formed."[7] After noting the unprecedented strength and influence of the country in world affairs, the document declared the right to "dissuade potential adversaries from pursuing a military buildup in the hopes of surpassing, or equaling, the power of the United States." Washington's dominance was to be permanent. Simple deterrence, or preventing war by threatening retaliation, was seen as less likely to work against rogue and failed states that were more likely to take risks. The conclusion called for "anticipatory action to defend ourselves—even if uncertainty remains as to the time and place of the enemy's attack. To forestall or prevent such hostile acts by our adversaries, the United States will, if necessary, act preemptively."

Many of the programs of weapons modernization and preemptive military strategies that were now pursued with determination were not really new. In many respects, the Bush administration's steps only reinforced the Pentagon's long-standing goal of preparing a broad range of military options to be used in different circumstances. The Pentagon had more money, newer and better weapons, and more sophisticated means for communication, but the distinctive feature of the *National Security Strategy* was a determination not only to plan to use but actually to use the military more often. Moreover, the United States would attempt to do so unilaterally, without the need for ratification from the United Nations or from European allies. The White House and Department of Defense followed its military commitment in Afghanistan with an even larger intervention in Iraq. Detainees captured by U.S. forces were brought to Guantánamo Bay and other secret facilities, where they were held in legal limbo and often mistreated. Leading officials in the Bush administration seemed to support the use of torture, and the Patriot Act provided for new surveillance measures, even against U.S. citizens. Secret military bases were set up in several countries and some suspects were snatched (through "extraordinary renditions") by CIA operatives and brought to violent interrogation sessions. Spending for all of these activities also increased, although often through surreptitious procedures that made it difficult to know exactly how much was being spent. The "global war on terror" (GWOT) was now in full swing.

After September 11, the initial international reaction to the United States was one of sympathy. Many people throughout the world expressed their grief and many countries indicated their willingness to help track down the perpetrators and bring them to justice. But as additional information regarding Washington's intentions became known, international alarm grew. Within the United States a critique of the militaristic policies pursued by the Bush administration also emerged. Frances Fox Piven attributed the war in Iraq and Afghanistan to a desire first to buttress George W. Bush's political base at home and then to enact a series of domestic policies that transferred resources from middle- and lower-income Americans to the wealthy. Her book, *The War at Home,* describes the weakening of many progressive social programs, a more regressive tax structure, an erosion of democratic rights, and the dismantling of many environmental regulations—all made possible by the political context of prosecuting the GWOT. Chalmers Johnson's *Sorrows of Empire* reviewed the vast system of overseas military bases that the United States has established as well as the threat to democracy of the military-industrial complex and rising secrecy. Michael Klare's *Blood and Oil* documented the dependence of the United States on petroleum resources and client regimes in the Middle East—and how this dependency underscored recurring military engagement in the region. Noam Chomsky's *Hegemony or Survival* provided an even more sweeping indictment of Washington's desire to establish "full-spectrum dominance" throughout the globe. Chomsky's critique focused on the hypocrisy of U.S. claims to represent human rights and to assume the main responsibility for combating terror when the country was itself responsible for many violations of human rights and support for state-sponsored terror. He also castigated the media for its general subservience to those in power and its role in "manufacturing consent." Benjamin Barber paid special attention to the manipulation of fear to obtain public acceptance of a foreign policy that supported dictatorships regarded as loyal to the United States, and for the limitations (and hubris) of efforts to impose a thin form of democracy that actually served as cover for Washington's self-interests.[8]

Other authors focused on cultural beliefs that helped explain why the American population seemed so unaware of (or unconcerned about) the impact of their country on the world's poor and repressed. Andrew Bacevich's *New American Militarism* argued that the new, more aggressive military strategy was cloaked in long-standing historical assumptions that Americans are "chosen people" on a mission to establish a more benign world.[9] The United States is exceptional compared to other interventionary powers because of its fundamentally moral inclinations and the overriding purpose of promoting good rather than selfish pursuits. The popular perception of much of the public is that the United States acts abroad only at its own expense and to provide redemption, salvation, and, most of all, freedom. Nearly a hundred years ago, President Woodrow Wilson argued in support of the treaty establishing the League of Nations by declaring, "For nothing less depends on this decision, nothing less than the liberation and salvation of the world."[10] In 2002, President Bush's preamble to the *National Security Strategy* echoed Wilson's rhetoric by claiming a "single sustainable model for national success: freedom, democracy, and free enterprise" as well as America's "responsibility to lead in the great mission" to apply this model everywhere on the face of the earth.[11] Bacevich then demonstrated how diverse cultural streams—the intellectual currents surrounding neoconservative political journals, feature films produced in Hollywood, the resonance of "morning in America" (rebirth) in political life, and the evangelical movement in conservative Christianity—find common ground in their preparation of the public to accept militarism. The subtitle of his book is *How Americans Are Seduced by War.*

Washington's policies *are* largely militarized, and there *are* powerful cultural forces that both blind and bind many Americans to the war system. But there are also important countercurrents. The explicit rejection of war by many citizens and the increasingly ambivalent stance toward war displayed by still more have created significant cracks in the system. Militarism encourages war preparations to be seen as "natural." But this process collides with competing developments that cause war preparation to be seen as decidedly "unnatural." War acceptance clashes with the tendency of Americans to become more peaceful. The tension between the two underlies a fundamental change in the social organization of war itself.

Mobilized and Conditional War

The two types of opposition are not always strong enough to prevent war. Nor are they sufficiently potent to ensure that the public will disagree with every war policy and example of military intervention. But the potential of withdrawn support is of sufficient influence that the social relationships contained in the war system have undergone a fundamental transformation. War may still occur but the sociological rules and understandings governing its conduct have changed. "Mobilized" war has been replaced by "conditional" war.

Mobilized war contains a high level of militarization; the number and density of connections between the military sector and the rest of society is large and significant. Examples include war taxes, a significant economic effect from defense spending, required military service (especially in the form of the draft), and the spread of enemy images in the popular culture. Mobilized war tends to be an expensive, demanding enterprise that involves significant casualties and compels citizen participation in many areas. Mobilized war also tends toward escalation until one side wins a war of materiel and human attrition. World War II provides a good example.

Societies with relatively low war mobilization devote fewer resources to war preparation, usually rely on a volunteer or professional army rather than conscription, and generally do not require a significant level of sacrifice—or even direct engagement—from most citizens other than those in the military and their families. War measures exert less influence on the economy and culture. Low mobilization is not incompatible with patriotism and concern for military personnel. Indeed, in the United States the flag remains a very powerful symbol, as is the impulse to rally behind a president during a crisis and the desire to support the troops. But war, when it does occur, tends to use weapons and strategies that promise a low number of casualties ("force protection"). Military force reflects the need to keep perceived collateral damage low and must be framed in the media so that graphic images or other messages that portray war damage are largely avoided. Casualties are relatively less numerous than in mobilized war, and the conflict does not inevitably escalate into an all-out war of attrition. In general, the Pentagon's level of lethality and damage is significantly less than what it could achieve. Some of these changes have been made possible by improvements in technology, particularly the development of precision-guided munitions, but the most important explanation of this strategy lies in the reluctance of the public to accept the costs of mobilized war. Conditional war has two interrelated meanings: First, it contains a different set of social relationships between the public and war that embody a transition from mobilized war. Second, the public will withdraw approval unless certain conditions are met. Conditional war has become more contingent.

The change from mobilized to conditional war can be summarized through the answers to a short series of questions: Who fights in these wars? Who is the enemy? Who dies? What are the social consequences of the fighting? How does the public see war? And how is the war covered in the media?

Who Fights?

In mobilized war, the demand for national service tends to be universal. During World War II, every male of appropriate age was expected to serve in the military or in a substitute activity that still supported the war effort. The personnel demands of the Vietnam War, which serves as a transition toward conditional war, were also large and could only have been met with a system of conscription. This system was not always fair, particularly because the policy of allowing student deferments helped ensure that those actually fighting in Vietnam were drawn disproportionately from the working class and minorities. But the threat of being drafted applied to everyone and provided an important stimulus to the antiwar movement. A more equitable lottery system was started in 1969, just as the withdrawal from Vietnam began and the need for new soldiers started to decline. Even so, the Pentagon determined that the avoidance and resistance that surrounded the draft were not worth the trouble and sought other ways to attract recruits to the armed forces.

Since 1973 the United States has relied on an all-volunteer professional force that now numbers approximately 1.5 million, plus a reserve force that is almost as large. Until 2005, when the increased dangers of serving in Iraq began to have an impact, better pay, educational credits, less expensive housing, more congenial family policies, and other career benefits generally enabled the Pentagon to attract sufficient numbers without relying upon conscription. Clever advertising campaigns and well-organized recruiters also helped. The professional military still does not reflect the country as a whole. The middle and upper classes are underrepresented, as are those from the Northeast and urban areas. Latinos are replacing African Americans as the largest minority serving in the military. Another significant development is the higher proportion of women, who now make up almost 15 percent of the armed forces, up from only 2 percent in 1973. Questions surrounding waste continue to be asked of the Pentagon, particularly in weapons procurement and the duplication of effort among the different military services. Other critics ask whether the military, especially the army, is taking full advantage of new technology or if the traditional division is the best organizational unit in a world dramatically different from that of the standing armies of the Napoleonic period. But the military is better educated than in the past and few would challenge the conclusion that it is also well trained and well led.

While conscription remains a legal and political possibility, a key difference in the transition to conditional war is that most of the public no longer expect to serve in the military. In the period immediately following the September 11 attacks, many newspaper stories tracked the rediscovery of patriotism among college students and found new, higher levels of support for the military. (It is also important to note that college students were also at the forefront of the modest 2001 movement that opposed intervention in Afghanistan and the more significant 2002–2003 movement opposed to the invasion of Iraq.) An October 2001 poll of students at the University of Houston found 90 percent favoring military intervention in Afghanistan to overthrow the Taliban, while a national survey of 634 college students conducted in May 2002 found 79 percent supporting the removal of Saddam Hussein from power.[12] Yet only 20 percent of the students at the University of Houston favored the reinstitution of the draft, even in circumstances where the national leadership was arguing that terrorism threatened the very core of U.S. society. Remarkably, 37 percent of the students in the national survey said that they would be "likely to evade the draft." Barely a third said that they would be "willing to serve and fight anywhere." While it is difficult to imagine millions of college students actually resisting a legal compulsion to serve, their responses underscore the continued sensitivity of the draft and the reluctance of many civilians to risk the possibility of combat even in circumstances when the traditional sense of patriotism was on the rise. In fact, in February 2003, Representatives John Conyers (D-Mich.) and Charles Rangel (D-N.Y.) coupled their opposition to the forthcoming war on Iraq with a call to reinstitute the draft. The congressmen felt that making the potential costs of intervention more tangible and shared among the entire population would be both more democratic and a possible method of galvanizing opposition. Realizing the consequences, Secretary of Defense Donald Rumsfeld was quick to oppose the proposal, arguing that draftees added "no value, no advantage" to the military. These comments provoked a series of negative reactions among many veterans' groups, especially among those who had served in World War I, World War II, Korea, and Vietnam. Rumsfeld was later forced to issue a clarification of his remarks that some suggested came as close to apology as one could possibly expect from this particular secretary of defense.[13] Meanwhile, young men and women do not anticipate that they will be required to serve in the military. In fact, before Iraq many volunteers in the armed forces, and especially those in the National Guard and reserve, did not anticipate that they would actually have to go to war. These fault lines between soldiers and civilians and between those who do expect to fight and the many more who do not, form key boundary lines of conditional war and underscore divisions that contain profound political and cultural repercussions for the United States as a whole.[14]

Who Is the Enemy?

One of the most important cultural practices of mobilized war is the construction of an enemy who is subhuman or otherwise different from oneself.[15] It is easier to wage war against faceless people who appear fundamentally evil, irrational, barbaric, and capable of torture and rape. Germans and Japanese during World War II and the Vietnamese during the Indochina War became demonized Others who not only opposed U.S. forces on the battlefield but posed a cultural and psychological threat to American life as well. (The fact that this degradation was not quite as pronounced for Germans also signifies that race plays a critical role in the construction of the enemy.) The emergence of a threatening Other was a key step in justifying the use of force against those who would normally be regarded as innocent civilians. Carpet bombing cities in Germany, setting them on fire in Japan, and using atomic weapons that killed hundreds of thousands of civilians in Hiroshima and Nagasaki were easier because these acts were carried out against people who were thought to be different. All of Japan had become a "legitimate" military target. Everyone living there was an enemy. In mobilized war, the enemy-making function is reciprocal. The Nazis regarded Jews as subhuman and the Japanese referred to the victims of their infamous medical experiments as *maruta*, or logs.

Similar processes occurred during both the Korean and Indochina wars. The political motivations and cultural practices of those opposing the United States remained mysterious in the public mind. Washington was fighting "gooks" rather than people, a label that opened the door to battlefield practices that eventually killed more than 2 million Koreans and another two to three million Vietnamese, Laotians, and Cambodians. These numbers defy rational comprehension. Except for the antiwar movement, few in the United States were aware of or cared about the scale of these catastrophes.

Another important feature of mobilized war was the targeting of presumed internal enemies: Jews, gypsies, homosexuals, and labor union leaders in the case of the Nazis, anyone of Japanese descent, including its own citizens, in the case of the United States. Key distinctions still take place within mobilized war, such as the difference between the Nazi practice of systematically killing internal enemies in death camps and the practice of the United States, which "merely" ordered its domestic enemy to detention camps for the duration of the war.

The legitimation process for conditional war is different. The practice of making a full-scale enemy out of the Other is now more difficult to achieve. Military force can only be targeted against repressive, criminal regimes, not an entire culture or nationality. The public recognizes that there are actually people on the other side who continue to hold the status of being human. This makes it more difficult to use military force indiscriminately. In the late 1980s, one sign that the cold war was beginning to wind down was the appearance in U.S. media of ordinary Russians engaged in everyday activities. Instead of goose-stepping soldiers in Red Square, Russians could be seen on newscasts bundling up against the cold, shopping for consumer products, and laughing along with their children. Suddenly, "the enemy" was more or less similar to Americans. As NATO planes bombed Belgrade in 1999, it was simultaneously possible to see footage of Serbs continuing to follow their daily routines. It is more difficult to make a full-fledged enemy out of someone whose picture appears in a newspaper drinking coffee in an outdoor café.

This is not to suggest that prejudice has disappeared from American society. Serbs, Bosnians, and Croats may look European, and thus it is relatively easy to sympathize with their losses. Iraqis and Afghans are less familiar but are still deserving of support where they appear as victims of repressive regimes. Africans are at a still further remove. More than a hundred times as many people have died in the Sudan than were killed during Milosevic's campaign of ethnic cleansing in Kosovo, yet the plight of many Sudanese remained largely invisible until late 2004. The 1994 genocide in Rwanda did not produce much concern in the United States, but it would be difficult to imagine standing by while eight hundred thousand Europeans were being murdered. Yet, where the media and political leaders have focused on the problem, humanitarian emergencies in Africa have elicited compassion. The plight of children in the famine in Somalia compelled intervention with food and other forms of assistance. A similar record was established during the early 2005 outpouring of support for the victims of the tsunami that wreaked destruction throughout the Indian Ocean. Despite continued differences in the public's valuing of other people's lives, conditional war has yet to produce a full-scale Other in a way that permits wholesale destruction. The obligation to protect innocent people remains present among the public even if imperfectly carried out by the government and its military forces.

A similar argument holds true with respect to internal enemies. Even as Washington launched Operation Enduring Freedom in Afghanistan, key members of the administration, including President Bush himself, warned against waging a war against the Muslim religion. (The Pentagon's original name for the mission, Operation Infinite Justice, was rejected after Islamic scholars criticized its insensitivity. Muslims believe that only Allah can be responsible for "infinite justice.") In many cities, religious leaders organized interfaith services to memorialize the victims of the September 11 attacks, and Oprah Winfrey devoted several television shows to explaining the fundamentals of Islam and remembering the innocent victims of violence in both the United States and Afghanistan. The United States still harbors racial and religious tensions. Immigration authorities and local police have continued to display discriminatory behavior toward people of Middle East descent—and even toward South Asians who are mistakenly thought to be of Middle East descent. Some of the public participated in this behavior as well. But the hate crimes that followed both Operation Desert Storm in 1991 and September 11, 2001, were committed by a small minority of the population; the vast majority of Americans disagreed with these actions. The Patriot Act and the incarceration of terrorist suspects at Guantánamo Bay have raised many issues regarding civil liberties and probably contributed to a modest increase in anti-Arab bias among the population. But these questionable legal measures have yet to use national or religious identity to mobilize enemy images on a significant scale. The result is a series of contradictions in which prejudicial and discriminatory behaviors continue and yet the need for tolerance and mutual respect is also recognized. Conditional war tends to minimize the demonization of entire social categories and instead encourages more limited, focused definitions of the enemy. But the process is not perfect.

How Many Die?

Mobilized war produced many casualties because the main military strategy was attrition, or wearing down the enemy's human and materiel resources so that the political will and capacity to fight were destroyed and surrender became the only possible outcome. The fundamental logic of mobilized war was escalation, which produced casualties on a scale that is now very difficult to comprehend. During World War II, millions died in Germany, Japan, France, China, Vietnam, and England, in part because the distinction between soldiers and noncombatants continued to erode and had almost completely dissolved by the war's end. The Soviet Union alone lost more than twenty million people. Both sides deliberately tried to kill civilians—although at that point it was far easier for the Allies to accomplish this goal than it was for Germany or Japan. The concept of collateral damage did not exist either; attempting to break the enemy's will by destroying as many people and as much of society as possible was precisely the point. The number of civilians killed during both the Korean and Vietnam wars was also large. The granite wall of the Vietnam Memorial that runs along a section of the Reflecting Pool in Washington holds the names of the fifty-eight thousand Americans killed in that conflict. Visitors to the site are usually overwhelmed by the scale of the loss. But if a similar wall were to be constructed with the names of all the Vietnamese who died, it would be forty times longer and stretch almost the entire way from the Lincoln Memorial to the Capitol.

The expectation of a low number of deaths has accompanied every post-Vietnam intervention. "Force protection" has emerged as a principal and sometimes primary goal governing military operations. President Clinton coupled his announcement of the start of Operation Just Cause, NATO's 1999 air campaign against Serbia, with a promise that no ground troops would be used in the conflict. General Wesley Clark ordered his aircraft to fly above fifteen thousand feet to avoid Milosevic's air defenses and minimize the chances of being shot down.[16] Operation Just Cause also established an important standard because the hostilities resulted in exactly zero combat casualties to NATO forces. Conditional wars contain the expectation that U.S. military casualties will remain "small."

Conditional war also contains an expectation that casualties on the other side will be kept low. As one Pentagon official said in an interview:

Usually, we want our guys not to get hurt. We want to win the war, which means you want to beat the bejesus out of them. The more we beat the bejesus out of them the more quickly they're likely to surrender and it'll be over. So, hey, if there's a lot of carnage on the other side, there's a lot of carnage on the other side. Before Vietnam, certainly in Korea and World War II, the higher the enemy casualties and, I dare say, civilian, the better. But that's not the way we thought of the war in Iraq.

Recent military actions undertaken by Washington have certainly included collateral damage. Despite the use of new, more accurate weapons during Operation Iraqi Freedom, the number of civilians killed was at least thirty thousand by the end of 2005.[17] But some of the mistakes in recent wars, such as bombing the Chinese embassy in Belgrade, strafing an Afghan wedding party, and killing an Iraqi family as its van approached a checkpoint, made the front pages. In Vietnam, the unintended killing of several dozen villagers, or even a hundred or more Cambodians by a B-52 bombing raid, typically would not have appeared in the paper at all. Even as concern mounted for the rising number of U.S. casualties in the Indochina War, very few paid attention to what was happening to "them." The loss of Vietnamese lives went down the memory sinkhole. But now, the obligation felt by the public to avoid killing innocents affects policymakers. The Pentagon cannot take actions that make the costs of war transparent, even to people on the other side, without risking the desertion of public support. As one former Pentagon official observed in an interview: "In Vietnam, an officer said, 'We have to destroy the village in order to save it.' Well, that's just not on anymore. You are going to get the picture of the damage we've done and the human cost of it, and because we keep setting the bar higher by showing the world how precise we can be. If you have this precise capability you're expected to perform to it."

To prevent this erosion of support for a war, the numbers on both sides must be managed so that they appear low. Low can be an actual number achieved by minimizing the risk to U.S. soldiers and collateral damage on the other side. Low can also be a perceived number achieved by keeping both types of losses out of the newspapers and off television. The Bush administration has attempted to enforce a ban on photographs of flag-draped body containers as they arrived at Dover Air Force Base. The thousands of wounded in that conflict, many of whom clogged the military's Walter Reed Hospital, were also kept from view, in part by scheduling arriving planes so that they landed at night. Civilians accidentally killed during Operation Iraqi Freedom have occasionally been highlighted in the media but have also often been ignored. This inconsistency has made it more difficult for the public to fathom the true nature of the costs involved. Civilians still die in conditional war. But unlike in mobilized war, they are not expected to die on a significant scale.

What Are the Consequences of War for Society?

World War II mobilized an enormous proportion of the country's resources. Approximately 40 percent of the gross national product (GNP) was devoted to the war, and it would be difficult to find an industry or region unaffected by military spending. For most of the cold war, including the Vietnam period, military spending was still significant, ranging from 8 to 10 percent of GNP. Many industries, such as aerospace and electronics, continued to rely on military spending, and the manufacturing sector as a whole experienced an important and sometimes critical stimulus from Pentagon demand. Similarly, many important regions such as southern California and the Route 128 belt around Boston and cities such as Seattle and Charleston relied on the direct and trickle-down effects of defense expenditures.

For most of the twentieth century, mobilization for war carried other types of influences that continued to affect society long after the war was over. During World War II many women left their homemaker role and worked in the war industry. While most returned home when the war was over, the experience became one of the critical reference points for the movement for equal rights in the years that followed. In the name of freedom, African American and Japanese American soldiers fought in an army that remained segregated. The memory of their sacrifice became a springboard for their own respective postwar drives for greater equality. After the war, a strong obligation was felt toward veterans, and postwar housing and education loans to them boosted major expansions of each industry. Thus the end of the war was not only a victory over fascism but also an opportunity to expand government programs and add another chapter to the long record of minority contribution to the country's economic growth and cultural enrichment.

This is not to suggest that war is, by itself, a positive social project. One could hope that the occasional progress achieved in its wake could come to pass without the killing. But it is also true that the mobilization of society behind the war effort during World War II created a more activist state and new opportunities. The state needed loyalty, productive potential, and destructive capacity. Some movements were able to capitalize.

The Vietnam War had an additional major social impact because it stimulated a broad range of social movements. Along with the civil rights movement, resistance to the war encouraged other forms of social activism that challenged prevailing gender, racial, environmental, and cultural structures. The cold war also carried social influence, in part by creating and shaping the world's main political divide, but also by providing themes for the entertainment industry, inspiring action figures and other objects for children's play, stoking public fears, and dominating the nation's sense of (in)security. In short, mobilized war was a complex enterprise with unanticipated but often profound consequences that extended well beyond the military measures themselves. War and society were closely intertwined.

During the transition toward conditional war, the overall economic impact of defense spending has declined and now hovers at close to 4 percent of GNP. Because of significant increases in the overall economy, the absolute level is still large, approximately $500 billion. The United States spends more than all of its NATO allies combined, more than seven times China's expenditures and more than ten times the total of all the "rogue states." Actual military spending is even higher than official figures indicate because some categories of spending, such as military aid to other countries, do not appear in the budget of the Department of Defense. Allocations for nuclear warhead production are actually a component of the Department of Energy's budget and do not even show up as an official military expenditure. Despite the shrinking of the Pentagon in relative terms, when these additional costs are included, U.S. military spending is roughly equal to that of the rest of the world combined.

Supplemental military expenditures for Afghanistan and Iraq are still another impact not included in official calculations of the economic size of the Pentagon. The cost of both wars totaled $66 billion in 2003 and $80 billion in 2004. In late 2005, the Congressional Research Service estimated that an extra $357 billion had already been spent on military operations since September 11, 2001, and that the cost through 2006 would reach $500 billion.[18] In early 2006, the White House asked Congress for an additional $70 billion for fiscal 2006, bringing the total for the year to $120 billion.[19] A full accounting, including care for the injured, increases in the price of oil attributed to instability in the Middle East, interest payments, disability payments, wear and tear on military equipment, reenlistment bonuses, and losses in productivity to businesses whose employees served overseas could be more than $2 trillion.[20] The $46 million bill for just a single hour of the war in Iraq in 2003 equals the cost of improving, repairing, and modernizing twenty public schools. The $2.1 billion cost of a single Stealth bomber is the equivalent of the annual salary and benefits for 38,000 elementary school teachers.[21]

The still-increasing bill for Afghanistan and Iraq is significant and to some degree weighs against the overall thesis that militarization is receding in the United States. The economic cost of the war has added to the federal deficit and come at the expense of important civilian projects. To take but one example, funding for needed repairs to the Mississippi River levees that had been recommended by the Army Corps of Engineers was cut by two-thirds, in part due to the competing priority of Iraq. The failure to make the necessary improvement to the dikes then contributed to the disastrous 2005 flooding of New Orleans during Hurricane Katrina. As of early 2006, the cost of the Bush administration's military interventions approached that of the Vietnam War, and special interests clustered around its appropriations. Private contractors provided services, often at inflated prices, that used to be carried out by soldiers.[22] Corruption increasingly surrounded expenditures in Iraq. Specialized firms provided new weapons and tools such as handheld devices capable of translating fifteen thousand phrases into Arabic and modular armor that enables soldiers to add or subtract pieces depending on the particular mission. The public continues to pay taxes, at a higher level than most realize, for the war effort.

The economic impact of recent military spending raises the possibility of remobilization on some dimensions of social militarization. The transition from mobilized to conditional war is not inevitable and selective reversals may occur as overall costs continue to mount. Nonetheless, fewer in the United States are dependent, either directly or indirectly, on military spending for their livelihood than at any other time since the Depression. Business firms in metropolitan areas such as San Diego and Boston that were once heavily dependent on the Pentagon have been forced to find other customers for specialized manufacturing and high-tech employment previously tied to defense. Despite Afghanistan and Iraq, the costs of individual military operations tend to be lower in conditional war. Figure 1.1 provides the estimated price tag of military missions after the end of the cold war other than for the two major interventions. Their cumulative expenditures are about $40 billion, certainly a significant amount of money yet also equal to only the approximate value of the GNP produced in a single day. The requirements of conditional war are also reflected in the method of funding the two more expensive efforts. Despite continued difficulties in the U.S. economy, many measures of mobilized war—rationing, wage and price controls, conversion of civilian factories to military production, and a government-sponsored public relations campaign to buy war bonds—are difficult to imagine

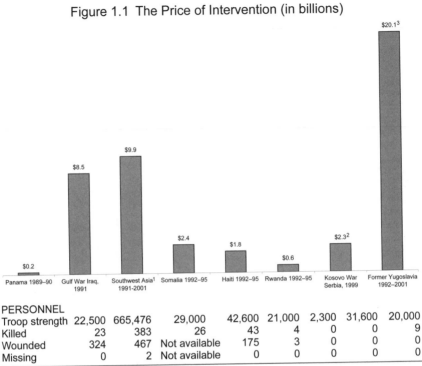

Figure 1.1 The Price of Intervention (in billions)

PERSONNEL								
	Panama 1989–90	Gulf War Iraq, 1991	Southwest Asia[1] 1991-2001	Somalia 1992–95	Haiti 1992–95	Rwanda 1992–95	Kosovo War Serbia, 1999	Former Yugoslavia 1992–2001
Troop strength	22,500	665,476	29,000	42,600	21,000	2,300	31,600	20,000
Killed	23	383	26	43	4	0	0	9
Wounded	324	467	Not available	175	3	0	0	0
Missing	0	2	Not available	0	0	0	0	0

Notes:
[1]Operation Provide Comfort, Northern Watch, Southern Watch Vigilant Warrior, Desert Strike, Desert Fox, United Nations Special Commission and UN Iraq-Kuwait Observation Mission.
[2]Does not include $7.1 billion for peacekeeping operations from 1999 to 2001.
[3]Amount includes US participation in NATO peacekeeping but not UN Interim Administrative Mission.
Sources: Center for Defense Information; Congressional Budget Office; news reports. Adapted from the *Boston Globe.*

today. No administration can deliberately raise taxes to support war. Approval depends on leaving the home front undisturbed; measures that would place the country on economic war footing must be avoided. No true accounting can take place.

How Does the Public Experience War?

The public participated in mobilized war in many ways. Most important-ly, parents had to feel that war, while unfortunate, was also necessary and that the military's use of their children was legitimate. This family "approval" is often assumed, yet the willingness of parents to have their children enter the military and to be exposed to risk varies over time and circumstance. The conditions of mobilized war facilitate this approval; those of conditional war make it more problematic. During World War II, citizens also paid higher taxes, contributed scrap metal, rationed vital goods, and volunteered in social agencies connected to the war effort. The country's entertainment often revolved around the war. Psychologically, a significant proportion of daily worry, hope, and reflection were caught up in the progress of the war. The terms of this engagement might be heroic, tragic, or some combination of both. But mobilization required participation and often sacrifice. Putting society on a war footing had an impact on the daily life of a majority of the population. Conditional war has not eliminated all connections between society and the war effort but it has reduced and transformed them in significant ways. For example, the relationship between most citizens and war has changed from participant to spectator.

The term "spectator" suggests that armed conflicts are fought at a distance and carry only a limited impact on civilian life. The fact that the public has in its relationship to war become more like sports fans than mobilized participants was first made clear after small expeditionary conflicts, such as British military action in the Falklands and the U.S. invasion of Grenada, elicited media hype, popular enthusiasm, and political gain for Prime Minister Margaret Thatcher and President Ronald Reagan. The relatively small losses associated with the Kosovo conflict also contributed to the thesis that war could arouse emotions but usually in a temporary manner. Michael Ignatieff described war events for citizens in the West as "remote from their essential concerns as a football game, and even though the game was in deadly earnest, the deaths were mostly hidden, and above all, someone else's."[23]

The public continues to feel connected with their soldiers and may send e-mail, gifts, videograms, and other measures of support. Particularly after 9/11 and in contrast to the alleged rejection of returning Vietnam veterans, citizens have welcomed soldiers by applauding them at airports, giving up a seat on public transportation, or offering to buy them a meal at a local restaurant. Spectators are involved in other ways as well. They may follow the events closely, read the papers, watch television, and reflect on the commentary offered by retired generals and former government officials. Colin McInnes has compared sports fans with consumers of war news:

> There are those who watch, unmoved, seeing little of interest or relevance. There are those who are moved for the moment, who share in the transitory joy or sorrow, but soon forget as more direct and immediate stimuli appear. Still others may become knowledgeable in the tactics, strategies, and personalities but are devoid of the direct experience. Then there are those for whom the conflict becomes an all-encompassing obsession, involving travel to be near the event but never actual participation.[24]

As in sports, spectators of war are able to contribute to a moral dialogue about the way that the game should be played. By expressing their judgments, they influence codes of behavior and shape understandings of community, loyalty, and national identity. Rather than being completely passive, spectators react in ways that carry some weight. At the same time, the relationship between the public and war now takes place at further remove. Importantly, this statement does not apply to those who are actually fighting or to their families. It would be the height of insensitivity to fail to recognize that some still make the ultimate sacrifice and that families and friends deeply worry about the fate of their loved ones who are deployed in combat. These people *are* engaged in the classic sense. But most of the public, in their relationship to the war experience, are more like witnesses than participants.

How Do We See War?

Since the invention of photography, militaries have been concerned about the impact of war visuals on public attitudes. Television and video—and ever quicker ways to distribute images via satellite and over the Internet—have done little to change the belief of most war managers that the public should be shielded from the more explicit images of the battlefield. Their main fear is that the heroic story lines of war will dissolve when combat appears squarely in the public field of vision. As a result, the first impulse of political and military leaders has always been to attempt to control journalists so that the more graphic costs of war are not communicated to the population. Coverage of World War II was censored, although most journalists quickly internalized the guidelines and monitored their own reporting to comply so direct management was usually not necessary. As the war went on and casualties continued to mount, Washington eased some of the restrictions. Codes governing the presentation of war still existed but by 1943 it became possible to see pictures of bodies from both sides of the battlefield. Contemporary readers of issues of *Life* from that period are likely to be shocked by the graphic pictures that appeared in the magazine during the second half of the war. One reason for the appearance of these photographs is that the nation's leaders were confident in the public's support for the war effort and felt that making the sacrifice explicit could advance mobilization for the war.

The relative independence of print and television journalists during the Vietnam War posed a different problem for the Pentagon. Many reporters were able to move freely throughout the country. As the war progressed, their reports provided dramatic combat footage.

Television viewers back in the United States felt that they could "see" the war. Most journalists did not explicitly disagree with the anticommunist effort but by conveying the drama and costs of the fighting they contributed to the growing feeling that the war could not be won in a short amount of time. At its daily Saigon press briefing, the Johnson administration still tried to impose its own optimistic view of the progress allegedly being made in the war. But these efforts were increasingly dismissed by the press as the "Five o'Clock Follies." Washington's goal remained complete control over the war story, but prevailing journalist practices made this impossible. Vietnam provides a key transition in the movement from mobilized to conditional war. Like World War II, sacrifice was called for; unlike World War II, this sacrifice was not accepted. Many conservative postwar retrospectives held the media responsible for the loss of civilian and congressional political will. For the White House and the Pentagon, a key question emerged: how could journalists be allowed to cover future wars when censorship or other forms of total control were no longer possible?

Washington would still like to control the media directly—even in the more limited circumstances of conditional war. In many post-Vietnam conflicts, the press has been organized into pools whose membership and movement were closely supervised by the Pentagon. This emphasis on control provides one of the continuities between mobilized and conditional war. But the explicit reminders of sacrifice that were present in mobilized war are no longer acceptable, so a media strategy other than censorship or embracing the loss is required. Where direct control is not possible, administrations try to develop a substitute form of media coverage that shapes public perceptions and provides support while avoiding the charge of censorship. The best example is the practice of embedded reporters during the 2003 war in Iraq, which produced favorable coverage during the march to Baghdad. But the presence of a (somewhat) independent media on the ground also led to "postwar" reporting that challenged many of the claims of the Bush administration. Pentagon officials with responsibility for working with journalists fumed at what they saw as a failure to tell the more positive side of Operation Iraqi Freedom.

Washington recognizes that media coverage can be as important as—and perhaps even more important than—the battlefield in determining the perception of who wins and loses. Conditional wars are fought—and also spun. Every key government agency, including the White House, State Department, Department of Defense, and the various branches of the armed forces have either hired outside expertise from the advertising and public relations industry or developed internal career tracks to promote the same skills. Many of the generals responsible for commanding U.S. forces—Norman Schwarzkopf for the Gulf War, Wesley Clark during NATO's campaign over Kosovo, and Tommy Franks during the 2003 war with Iraq—knew how to use the media to make their points to Congress, U.S. allies, and the public at large. Great care has been devoted to trying to forge a war story that the public will accept. The costs of actual war cannot become transparent.

Yet conditional war has not become a virtual world where images and representation trump reality so that it becomes difficult to distinguish between what one sees and the underlying authentic experience. In 1991, French philosopher Jean Baudrillard argued "that the Gulf War did not take place."[25] What he meant by that provocative statement is that the war of pictures and signs waged in the media, such as videos of precision-guided munitions allegedly striking their targets with remarkable accuracy, images of Patriot II anti-missile missiles knocking down incoming Iraqi Scuds, and even up-close-and-personal coverage of soldiers at rest, had become more important than political goals or events on the battlefield. What could be seen on television had displaced the "real" war. While images and presentation *are* a critical element of conditional war, and political and military leaders must have a media strategy if they are going to retain public support, Baudrillard is mistaken in one crucial respect: The transformation from mobilized war has not prevented people from dying or their families from feeling the loss. There is nothing virtual about those pains. At key moments, either through modified coverage by mainstream media or via independent sources that are increasingly able to distribute visuals across the Internet, a more critical message comes through. Conditional war differs from mobilized war but it is not cost free. When those costs appear, latent Type II opposition will rise to the surface and join with already existing Type I rejection to form a strong challenge to war management.

Intervention in Humanitarian Emergencies

The movement from mobilized to conditional war, summarized in table 1.1, encompasses new sensitivities toward the cost of war (Type II opposition) that augment direct policy-based resistance (Type I opposition). Americans are becoming more peaceful. But there is an important twist to this argument. Wars that appear to have geostrategic motivations will not gain significant support. But what should be the response to widespread killing of innocent

Table 1.1 Comparing Mobilized and Conditional War

	Mobilized War	Conditional War
Who fights?	Conscription	Volunteer/professional military
Who is the enemy?	Nations; enemy-making of other people	Evil Regime; enemy-making function reduced
Who dies?	Escalation; many soldiers and civilians on both sides	Lower casualties (actual and/or perceived)
What is the social impact?	Major economic and social effects	Minimal effects
What is the relationship between the public and war?	Participation	Spectator, witness
Media coverage?	First control, then possibility of seeing sacrifice	First control, then reshaping perceptions

people? Should the United States use its military forces to intervene in humanitarian emergencies?

The post–cold war period has seen many wars where civilians have been the main victims of the fighting. In some cases, the number killed has been in the hundreds of thousands. These wars have frequently raised the question of what Washington decision makers and the public feel should be the proper response to the devastating loss of life. The usual answer offered by the traditional managers of U.S. power is to do nothing. In defense of the Bush (senior) administration's policy of nonresponse to the increasing savagery afflicting Bosnia in the early 1990s, former secretary of state James Baker famously claimed that "We don't have a dog in that fight." The implication was that Washington should stay far away from places, such as the Balkans, where it was difficult to identify traditional national security interests.

A majority of the public disagrees. Many are compassionate toward refugees, those threatened by "ethnic cleansing," those maimed or killed by anti-personnel landmines, and other victims of war and violence. When photographs and other evidence of their plight are presented consistently, the public is willing to support clearly explained plans to alleviate the suffering of people, be they oppressed Afghan women, starving Somali children, or Haitian political victims. In 1994, leading officials in the Clinton administration were ordered to avoid using the term "genocide" to describe the massacre of Tutsis and moderate Hutus by Hutu militia. The Clinton administration recognized that the country would be ashamed of the fact that their government had stood by while a holocaust was occurring—even if the United States had no conventional "national interests" in Rwanda. Public awareness that Washington was choosing a nonresponse to genocide might have also increased the vulnerability of the administration in the forthcoming congressional elections.[26] The reaction to the strife in Rwanda, as well as to crisis moments in the Sudan, Bosnia, Haiti, and Somalia, indicate that when it comes to protecting other human beings whose security is threatened on an epic scale, the public would seem to indeed have "a dog in the fight."

But public support for humanitarian intervention is more complex than recognizing an underlying desire to come to the aid of others. This sympathy must be expressed in a concrete, effective policy if it is to be sustained over time. Yet the decision to engage humanitarian emergencies often means calling on military forces that are not particularly well suited for the job.[27] Peacekeeping requires training in policing more than in soldiering, working in tandem with nongovernmental organizations that may have greater experience in supplying aid and coordinating with local groups and leaders who already command respect and authority. This is not to suggest the existence of a civilian magic wand that can easily be substituted for well-intentioned but inappropriate military measures. The recent history of civil wars has shown how difficult it can be to end the fighting even where there is well-meaning outside intervention. But other than traditional diplomacy, Washington has not cultivated peacekeeping skills and organizational resources other than using the Special Forces or military units trained primarily for offensive missions against other armies.[28] Nor has Washington shown much interest in developing early warning systems that would call quick attention to human rights violations or building UN capacities that might prevent the need for intervention, no matter its form, in the first place.

Another complication is the fact that the military does not like to intervene in situations that the Pentagon calls MOOTW, or "Military Operations Other Than War." ("Real men don't do MOOTW" is an expression that sometimes accompanies intramilitary debate on the subject.) Peacekeeping missions are often expensive, not only in terms of dollars but also because of the training and disruption of normal tours of duty that follow the commitment. As a Clinton official on the national security staff who was deeply involved in peacekeeping efforts noted in an interview:

> I know from personal experience that the Pentagon doesn't want to have resources committed to one particular place where they acquire

semi-permanent status, such as in the Sinai. Then we get stuck. Instead they prefer to retain the capacity to fight wars on our terms against "real enemies." They worry that the United States will get strategically frozen in various parts of the world without the flexibility to move around from one place to another. For the military, there are considerable opportunity costs to humanitarian missions.

Peacekeeping missions can also be quite dangerous. Indeed, as far as the public—and the military—is concerned, peacekeeping may look and feel like war. A former intelligence official speculated in an interview on the difficulties of militarized peacekeeping:

> With the exception of South Korea it has been an extraordinary humbling experience. No one has a particularly clear sense of exactly how you do it. If you shoot people, people get angry and shoot you in return. If, on the other hand, you don't shoot people, people might still shoot you. If you patrol aggressively, even more people get angry and try to shoot you. But if you don't knock down doors, people will regard you as a paper tiger.

The U.S. military has been successful in some peacekeeping operations and there are specialized niches within the armed forces that recognize the need to be better prepared to confront a broader range of missions than fighting conventional wars. Many individual officers and soldiers do take pride in trying to improve security for civilians. But the military is not particularly equipped or trained for these missions and as an institution has done little to change this state of affairs. Its fundamental job is still to win wars, not serve as peacekeepers. Where preferred civilian options are either absent or ineffective, the process of becoming more peaceful may necessitate support for selective intervention when lives are being snuffed out on a large scale. As one former Clinton official noted in an interview, "It is almost as though one needs to shine two frequencies of light on the question of public support for military deployment. One model works addressing classical strategic interests—such as Iraq—but you get a reversal when it comes to humanitarian ventures." The relatively thin majorities of public support for humanitarian intervention currently shown in opinion polls should be balanced by a crucial consideration: The public has never had an opportunity to register its views in a context of a policy and capacity truly dedicated to that purpose. Such a policy might not require military force, or it might not require U.S. troops but rather a stronger and more permanent capacity at the UN Security Council. But given the current limitations of these two options, the only way to make good on a "never again" ethical stand may be to approve a military interven-

tion that may look like and be governed by the understandings of
conditional war.

World War II versus Vietnam

The process by which the American public is becoming more
peaceful is uneven and sometimes contradictory. Type I and Type
II opposition is making it more difficult to engage in traditional
geostrategic conflicts. But the public may still support military interventions where they are seen as meeting humanitarian concerns
or for strict self-defense. And war can often be managed to appear
effective and low cost. "Manage" and "appear" are key words for
understanding conditional war because they imply both the possibility that public support can be secured and that this support may
erode relatively quickly. Management operates through presidential
power, rhetoric, and the public relations strategies that influence
media coverage. An adept administration will know how to draw
upon war enablers that resonate with much of the public. But as
every manager knows, there are limits to their control. Managing
conditional war with its many reservations, tighter rules, and quali-
fying conditions can be particularly difficult, and management can
also fail. A type of structural hesitation toward the use of armed
force runs through the major institutions, places of work, education
systems, and individual hearts and minds. War exists in political
and cultural limbo.

Two photographs capture the tension over war that currently exists in popular culture. The first shows the power of patriotism as
well as the influence of a familiar and well-crafted commercial message. At a 2001 United We Stand concert in Washington, D.C., that
raised money for 9/11 victims, parking cost $10, five tickets $375,
and food and drinks $100. But being an American is "priceless."
Spectators at the concert were no doubt genuine in their desire to
help and the viewer can sense the emotional power of being in the
stadium and feeling outrage against the terrorist attacks. But it is
also not difficult to connect the meaning of the many flags and the
determined looks in the picture with support for military force.

The second photograph shows a 2005 sign in a Duluth, Minnesota,
office window that keeps track of American casualties in Iraq. The
office is located immediately adjacent to an army recruiting station.
The sign is not particularly critical. It reads, "Iraq: Remember the
Fallen Heroes." Yet the army requested that it be taken down. The
man responsible for posting it, a veteran wounded in Vietnam, claims
that he was not trying to discourage recruiting efforts but only to

Participants carry a patriotic message at an October 2001 United We Stand Concert at RFK Stadium in Washington, D.C. (Paul J. Richards/Getty Images).

A poster keeping count of American casualties in Iraq is displayed near a U.S. Army recruiting center in Duluth, Minnesota (Julia Cheng/AP Photo).

remind passing pedestrians that there was a definite human cost to the conflict.[29] The sign evokes Type II opposition.

Patriotism is an especially important quality for Americans. The U.S. public scores higher on surveys designed to measure the strength of patriotism than the citizens of any other high-income country in the world. In the United States, patriotism is often linked to positive perceptions of Washington's international role—and support for its defense policy. The identification of the flag with freedom is especially powerful. The poster in the office window is not explicitly antiwar, yet the Army's irritated response generated national attention. Important questions are raised by the juxtaposition of the two photographs. Is it patriotic to call attention to the cost of war? Why should a factual tally of the killed and wounded be so controversial? How would a participant in the patriotic rally in RFK stadium react, four years later, to evidence calling attention to real sacrifice?

The uncertainty of the public is captured in two different story lines about war. Stories select and shape memories, provide morality plays for judging events, and help audiences approve or reject behavior. Stories furnish lessons and contribute guidelines for the future. Those told about World War II are largely positive: The nation entered only under duress and with comparative weaknesses. But the country ended up winning and in the process made the world a better place. The stories told about Vietnam are mainly negative: It was a mistake to intervene, many things went wrong, and identifying a positive legacy is extremely difficult. Successful management of conditional war will invoke the more satisfying qualities of World War II; Type I and emerging Type II sensitivities will bring forth the more critical memories of Vietnam.

World War II is remembered as a heroic and necessary effort to stop fascism. Americans wanted peace but war became inevitable after Hitler started to dominate Europe and Japan launched a vicious sneak attack at Pearl Harbor. The war entailed enormous sacrifice but was conducted with the help of cooperating allies. Leadership, both in Washington and on the battlefield, was of high quality and many of the social assets of the country, including technology and the industrial base, were effectively mobilized to defeat the Axis powers. Virtually every male, whether working class, middle class, or a member of the elite, became a soldier or joined the war effort in some other way. Those who could not serve directly usually had a very good reason for their alternative form of service. The sacrifice was shared. Soldiers fought well and the home front came together to contribute in whatever way it could. Women worked in war factories, Hollywood churned out supportive entertainment, scientists made new weapons, and journalists reported favorably on the war effort. All were loyal members of the team. It was relatively easy to chart progress during the war, whether island hopping in the Pacific or invading Normandy and marching toward Germany. The war ended in joyous celebration and the soldiers were welcomed home with parades and heartfelt thanks for a job well done. Afterward, an enlightened policy in both Europe and Japan strengthened democracy and brought prosperity to both areas. These developments contributed to postwar security and economic growth of the United States as well.

Vietnam carries an entirely different set of memories. World War II brought unity but military intervention in Indochina led to disagreements over the necessity and wisdom of the original commitment that only became more acute as the war went on. The country's technology may have been superior but was also of little meaning where the battlefield counted less than the political will of Vietnam's revolutionary forces. The Saigon government, Washington's ally in the conflict, was almost useless because its politicians were corrupt and many of its soldiers deserted. Most U.S. soldiers fought bravely but the search-and-destroy missions and bombing strategies were often misdirected and ineffective. Body counts turned out to be a dumb way of measuring progress and Vietnam quickly became a very expensive stalemate. After the My Lai massacre in which U.S. soldiers killed hundreds of Vietnamese civilians and raped dozens of women and girls, charges of war crimes were repeated with increased regularity. As the war ground on, more soldiers started to use drugs or go AWOL. Some even attacked unpopular officers in what became known as "fragging" (rolling a fragmentation grenade under the tent flap of a commander who took unnecessary risks with his men). Many soldiers came home physically wounded or psychologically damaged by post–traumatic stress syndrome. While the idea that returning veterans had to pass through a gauntlet of spitting antiwar protesters is a myth, certainly there was no welcoming committee organized by the home front.[30] In World War II, fascism was a clearly understood evil but in Vietnam the nature of the enemy was mysterious. Were they communists or nationalists? Guerrillas or regular soldiers? And how could a movement that the Pentagon fought in the name of democracy nonetheless mange to enjoy so much popular support among the Vietnamese? Unlike in World War II, military service was distributed unfairly due to class and racial privilege. The impact of the media was particularly controversial, with charges and countercharges surrounding the claim that journalists were responsible for turning military victory into political defeat. And unlike the difficult but ultimately successful recovery from World War II, the Vietnam War left the United States

with economic troubles and social unrest and mired in the ignomini-
ous Watergate political scandal. Meanwhile, Indochina's population
and ecology were left devastated. World War II was "the good fight."
Vietnam was a mess.

Vietnam casts a long shadow over current military operations,
and the comparison between the Indochina debacle and the Bush
administration's military invasion of Iraq has been offered by Democrats, newspaper columnists, security analysts, and even some
retired military officers. The Vietnam metaphor cannot be taken
literally. There are crucial differences in political goals, geography,
type of opposition, and level of technology. But the critical themes
of Vietnam—the possibilities of stalemate, the death, injury, and
psychological toil on American soldiers, opposition at home, unfath-
omable and unfixable chaos, a more critical press, loss of virtue,
and self-defeat—will be raised more quickly in conditional war. As
Americans become more peaceful, war costs and failed war management will more quickly conjure Vietnam. The power of Vietnam
memories operate for much of the military as well as for the public.
As a member of the Clinton administration National Security Council
noted in an interview, "The impact of Vietnam is hard to overstate,
even, or perhaps even especially, on the military. Living through
Vietnam permeated every level, and there are incredible effects on
the military and military leadership running right up to the chair and
vice-chair of the Joint Chiefs of Staff. Even now Vietnam is part of
the underlying psychology." Retired General Anthony Zinni, former
commander in chief of the United States Central Command, noted in
a speech before members of the U.S. Naval Institute and the Marine
Corps Association that examined the Bush administration's policies
in Iraq: "My contemporaries, our feelings and sensitivities were forged
on the battlefield of Vietnam, where we heard the garbage and the
lies, and we saw the sacrifice. I ask you, is it happening again?"[31]

Iraq: Good War or Quagmire?

Operation Iraqi Freedom began with strong public support. Type I
principled opposition to war could certainly be found in the dove
constituency and in the many examples of antiwar activism that
flourished just before the war. But for most of the public, the war
in Iraq could be easily justified. Like World War II, there appeared
to be a clear sense of purpose, a coalition of allies, a popular leader,
and support for the troops. The war would bring freedom to an oppressed people and make the United States more secure. But as
the war went on and carried more costs, these perceptions began to

change. Saddam was overthrown but weapons of mass destruction could not be found and the purpose of the mission was no longer clear. Many countries withdrew from the coalition or left only a paper-thin commitment of forces. Support for the troops remained but the political leader became less and less popular. As in Vietnam, the original promise to bring freedom to the local population was contradicted by the emergence of well-organized armed opposition and smoldering resentments among much of the population. In name, the war was fought against terror but as the conflict went on terror attacks within Iraq and throughout the world actually increased. The economic costs of the war grew steadily and even eclipsed those of the decade-long effort in Indochina. Increasingly, the war seemed self-defeating. As the costs mounted and became more apparent, Iraq became an example of a conditional war passing beyond the limits of public acceptability. Type II opposition had become stronger.

Iraq's desert does not equal Vietnam's jungle and the precise circumstances of the two wars differed in other ways. But underlying themes in each war were very similar. In both, a major effort seemed to bring about only a quagmire. In each case, it became difficult to measure progress, and soldiers were being killed and wounded for no substantial purpose. Distinguishing between friend and foe was difficult, and many locals who were trained and armed to fight with the Pentagon ended up deserting. Even from within the U.S. ranks, finding enough people to fight became increasingly difficult. International opinion turned against both interventions. In its relationship to the press, the administration seemed to think that anything other than publishing good news was disloyalty. The local populations increasingly resented the U.S. presence. At home, more and more people thought that the original decision to intervene was a mistake. Criticisms also emerged from unlikely places such as mainstream security analysts, former government officials, and from within the military itself. Whistleblowers and scandals embarrassed administration officials. In Iraq, U.S. war managers tried hard to avoid Vietnam images and comparisons. But the tendency of Americans to become more peaceful and the fragile nature of support for conditional war have made it more difficult to achieve that goal. In its main story lines, conditional war is more likely to be like Vietnam than like World War II.

Chapter 2

Managing Fear

On September 11, 2001, terrorists hijacked two planes and slammed them into New York City's World Trade Center, bringing the two towers crashing to the ground. Another seized jet was flown into the Pentagon. Still another heading for Washington was forced down into a Pennsylvania field. All told, three thousand people died. The day saw extraordinary acts of heroism and sacrifice, particularly by rescue personnel in New York City and by the passengers who brought down the Pennsylvania plane before it could do any further damage. The site of the World Trade Center became known as "Ground Zero," a label that invoked the scale of the atomic bombing of Hiroshima and Nagasaki at the end of World War II. Americans were angered by these attacks, the loss of life, and the destroyed symbols of economic, political, and military power. But Americans were not only angry; many also feared that it might happen again.

Then an anthrax scare moved through the United States. Several well-publicized deaths followed and even the mail no longer seemed safe. Though al Qaeda was not responsible for this particular threat, the scale of the terrorism threat now seemed enormous. Much of the public felt vulnerable and some observers predicted that rapidly accumulating public fear would transform American life. Travel would never be the same, suspicion would trump trust, and strangers would automatically be regarded as a threat. Many thought that the measures necessary to protect against another attack would induce deep-seated changes ranging from military restructuring and intensified government surveillance to new vacation habits and less participation in public spaces.

This chapter examines the tension between the opportunities for managing war that are provided by public fear. The understandable fear—and anger—that followed the September 11 attacks was successfully managed by the Bush administration so that most of the public supported not only military intervention in Afghanistan but also the subsequent invasion of Iraq. Revenge also played a part, as did the tendency to rally around the president in a time of crisis and the desire to support troops deployed overseas. Though substantial majorities initially supported both military operations, the requirements of low-cost conditional war remained in place. Most of the public endorsed Operation Iraqi Freedom only because the Bush administration was able to connect, in public perceptions, Saddam Hussein to September 11 and other forms of terrorism that threatened the United States. At the same time, the emotional side of public politics with regard to war and the personal habits of most Americans did not change significantly after September 11. The public could not be mobilized to support measures that would have violated the boundaries of conditional war. Steps that would have systematically encouraged the population to participate in the war effort were largely ignored. Fear did affect support on a policy level but did not fundamentally alter the public's relationship to war.

The Structure of Public Fear

For most of human history, people feared supernatural forces. Volcanic eruptions, eclipses, and major storms were seen as signs of divine unhappiness. It seemed impossible to do anything about them other than to try to be as pious as possible. Modernization has brought more rational understandings of the causes of these phenomena as well as the expectation of protection from them. Most no longer think that a hurricane is a form of God's punishment. Pat Robertson is an exception.

Modern society now expects to be secure. Going to work or school, shopping, visiting friends, even traveling significant distances, all are supposed to be free from the threat of harm. Government regulations and science help keep food and medicine safe. Firefighters, police, and other officials maintain the security of our buildings and public spaces. Life expectancy continues to increase. Traffic accidents may claim close to fifty thousand lives a year but Americans still feel reasonably confident as they drive. Automobiles are manufactured to certain specifications, new safety devices are always being introduced, and the rules of the road are largely shared by other drivers. Individuals are free to engage each other without fear of violence, and strangers can conduct impersonal transactions without becoming enemies. Some may seek (carefully regulated) risk sports, amusement parks, and adventure travel. But the attraction to these activities lies precisely in their status as alternatives to the calm waters of "normal" existence. They are safe even though they may not appear to be. The public expects to be protected.

But fear also persists in public life, at times acutely so. In his *Culture of Fear: Why Americans Are Afraid of the Wrong Things*, Barry Glassner suggests that we have acquired a type of social investment in fear so that a certain level will persist even where the objective basis for this feeling is not sustained by actual threats. For example, the rate of violent crime dropped dramatically over the 1990s, but surveys taken at the end of the decade found two-thirds of the country believing that crime was still on the rise. Sixty-two percent called themselves "truly desperate" when describing their attitude toward the problem, more than double the level of the late 1980s, when the crime rate was actually higher.[1] Similarly, by 2000, the number of drug users had decreased by half and a majority of high school seniors reported that they had never used an illegal drug. Yet nine of ten adults believed that the drug situation in the country was out of control, and only a few thought that the country was making progress on the drug problem. Violent deaths in schools are extremely rare. Yet a few tragic and well-publicized cases helped create the impression that children are in constant risk from deranged, raincoated goths ready to pull the trigger at a moment's notice. Waves of public fear rippled across any number of identified risks: contaminants in apple juice, asbestos in children's play sand, flesh-eating bacteria, and killer bees moving up from South America. Meanwhile, other threats to public well-being such as underfunded schools, SUVs, and stressful lifestyles are largely ignored.

Why so much, often misplaced, fear? Glassner suggests two answers. First, many find it easier to convert general unease about life uncertainties to a more tangible threat that can be identified and confronted. It has always been difficult to understand an underlying and perhaps permanent malaise within one's social and personal universe. Understanding a concrete danger is not as hard. The process of transposing deep-seated but nebulous discomforts to a definite external source helps individuals make sense of their world, even where the chosen threat is misperceived and the compensating strategy is ineffective. Confronting a specific, concrete challenge is easier than grappling with abstract problems that do not lend themselves to simple solutions. Visible threats can be "understood" and may seem amenable to effective countermeasures. Punishment and other coercive measures often seem to present a straightforward answer, which is why they are often the most favored approach for providing reassurance and coping with perceived danger. Something is being done.

U.S. popular culture may carry a particularly large dose of unease due to the mix of individualism, fluidity, and mobility that has characterized its history from the colonial period. The United States has been a comparatively dynamic, optimistic society that has provided multiple opportunities for personal success. Yet generalized apprehension, insecurity, and cultural disquiet also serve as parallel stories in this history. A persistent anxiety has stamped the "first new nation," and one result has been an aggressive focus on enemies, both external and internal, real and imagined. Progress and change have been strong themes, but creating a vital sense of community has not. English poet John Donne may have recognized that "no man is an island," but many Americans feel themselves isolated and surrounded by dangerous waters. For all the growth and accumulation of wealth, some measure of fear has also been a constant presence.

The influence of the media and other fear entrepreneurs is a second reason that the public misreads threats. The system capitalizes on and stokes fear to improve media circulation and enhance audience ratings. While discussing the nation's morbid fear of crime, Glassner notes that "between 1990 and 1998, when the nation's murder rate declined by 20 percent, the number of murder stories on network newscasts increased 600 percent—and that's not counting the O. J. Simpson case."[2] The media call attention to dangerous viruses, school murders, workers run amok, pedophiles, and road-rage killers in part because it is possible to turn fear into a commodity. In one of the most egregious examples, the U.S. news media responded to a British tabloid headline, "Killer Bug Ate My Face," by publishing several lurid stories about "flesh-eating bacteria" that produced gross disfigurement and occasional death (a disease known as necrotizing fasciitis). Medical experts discounted the scale of the threat—only 500 to 1,500 suffer from the syndrome each year—yet news stories continued to appear. Some papers published horrifying pictures of the victims. The spring 2003 SARS (severe acute respiratory syndrome) panic, which coincided with the war in Iraq, is another example of media hype. The newscasts were full of breathless commentary, erroneous comparisons to the spread of HIV, and backgrounded doom music. But the response of the World Health Organization and most national governments was prompt and effective. Still, even after the identification of the responsible coronavirus and the complete mapping of its genetic structure, the media insisted on calling SARS a "mystery disease." During the duration of the panic, garden varieties of flu contributed to the deaths of 1,800 people in the United States. Around the world, more than 180,000 died from tuberculosis. Neither disease enjoyed the fanfare of SARS, which was not linked to a single death in the United States.[3]

Other organizational and commercial interests sustain public fear. The National Rifle Association uses the relatively rare invasion of private homes by armed intruders to guard against gun control legislation, and real estate agents sell property in "gated communities" because residents will feel better protected against unwanted outsiders.

Threats, risk, and fear are constructed. Social agents call attention to particular problems and in the process shape perceptions of danger and appropriate response. Perceived threats can be real. More people in the United States do become murder victims than in any other developed country. SARS did kill people. The fear of African Americans that they will be the targets of racial profiling by the police is supported by studies showing that black drivers are more likely to be pulled over and arrested than whites and are more likely to be physically abused once they enter the judicial system.[4] But these "realities" should not be read in a simpleminded way. One year after 9/11, the odds of a civilian dying in a terrorist attack were 1 in 9 million while the chances of dying in a traffic accident were just under 1 in 7,000. Yet some people switched their preferred mode of transport from airplanes to cars because they thought it safer. Twenty percent of these drivers continue to operate their vehicles without seatbelts. Many drivers also use cell phones while driving, a practice that a University of Utah study compared to operating an automobile while intoxicated and one that increases fourfold the chances of ending a trip in an emergency room.[5] Solar exposure causes an estimated 1.3 million cases of skin cancer a year and the Center for Risk Analysis at Harvard University estimates that 7,800 people in the United States died from solar radiation in 2000. Yet the Bush administration has shown little commitment to slowing global warming or to strengthening international treaties that would control the depletion of the ozone layer, which provides protection against ultraviolet radiation. Medical and pharmaceutical errors, smoking, and obesity are all more dangerous—and more immediately treatable—than terrorism.[6] Yet the perceived risk from these threats, and a commitment to do something about them, lags behind. Threats, including genuine threats, are managed and important agendas are embedded in the chosen response. The public is not always wrong in its choice of threats. But it is not always aware of the implications of what it has learned to fear and how other, more powerful actors have determined what should be the strategic reply.

Organizing Fear

The terrorist network that organized the September 11 attacks is a real threat by any definition, and in the aftermath of the attacks people feared a repeat performance. The fact that home territory has been spared from war remains one of the most distinctive features of the American experience. Save for the attack against Pearl Harbor, a war has not been fought on U.S. territory for more than 150 years. War was something that took place "over there." Now it was over here. Something had to be done.

The Bush administration chose to wage war against terror, a decision that carried enormous consequences for foreign policy, domestic policy, and the long-term security of Americans. But different responses were possible. September 11 could have been treated as a crime, terrible in its proportion and choice of target, that required an international police investigation into the organization and funding of terrorist networks as well as the identification and capture of those responsible. The United States would have had a leading role in this investigation, special responsibilities in the prosecution, and perhaps the ultimate threat of military force would have had to remain in place. But the main front of justice would have favored legal accountability over a violent retribution that itself inflicted costs on innocent people.

Additionally, the attack by al Qaeda could have been seen both as reprehensible and as a warning about the troubled relationship between the West and Islam. Without excusing the murder of three thousand, a program of providing better security would include ending Washington's support for repressive regimes in the Middle East and strengthening moderate Muslim voices. This strategy would require a new respect for cultural and religious differences, removing obstacles to needed reform in the region, and an energy policy that reduced U.S. dependency on foreign oil. This approach would not have excused September 11. But an effective approach to combating terrorism would have recognized the negative consequences of existing policy, particularly with regard to the lack of respect that is frequently communicated to peoples of the Middle East. A December 2002 poll of global attitudes toward the United States provides one indicator of this problem. About 75 percent of the publics in Europe gave the United States a favorable rating.

But the respective proportions were: for Lebanon only 35 percent, Turkey 30 percent, Jordan 25 percent, Pakistan 10 percent, and Egypt only 6 percent.[7] (After the initiation of the war in Iraq, many of the relatively favorable European attitudes fell as well.)

In its "global war on terror," the Bush administration expanded its target list well beyond al Qaeda. Justice meant the process in which its military forces identified, hunted down, and killed these enemies. The same would apply to any government or other organization that harbored terrorism. Post–September 11 fear was successfully managed by the Bush administration to promote important changes in domestic policy and to leverage the public's original desire for payback against al Qaeda into initial support for a broader military campaign against Iraq. As a member of the Clinton administration later observed in an interview: "The public harbors a natural desire to have a commander-in-chief in situations where you feel you are in peril. The sense of the American people that they were under siege or at threat that prevailed post 9/11 is absolutely capitalized on for Iraq."

George W. Bush's first words after the September 11 attacks did not promise a military response. "The full resources of the federal government," the president said at a Florida elementary school, forty-five minutes after the first tower crumbled, "[will] go to help the victims and their families, and to conduct a full-scale investigation to hunt down and to find those folks who committed this act."[8] "Hunting down and finding the folks" promises strong measures that include the possibility of military action but not yet a commitment to it.

By the evening of the same day, the government's promised response was far more ambitious. In his address to the nation, the president declared that that day "our way of life, our very freedom came under attack in a series of deliberate and deadly terrorist acts."[9] The speech spread a wide net of responsibility ("we make no distinction between the terrorists who committed these acts and those who harbor them") and went on to promise that America and its friends and allies would join with all who want peace and security "to win the war against terrorism." That war would soon include military intervention in Afghanistan, covert operations elsewhere in the world, a significant increase in the defense budget, new military bases in Central Asia, the Patriot Act, the Department of Homeland Security, and another war in Iraq.

In fact, plans for creating a more substantial military force in the Persian Gulf had been developed by key members of the Bush administration well before they assumed office. Vice President Dick Cheney, Secretary of Defense Donald Rumsfeld, Deputy Secretary of Defense Paul Wolfowitz, and Cheney chief of staff Lewis Libby helped draft *Rebuilding America's Defenses: Strategies, Forces, and Resources for a New Century*, written in September 2000 for the Project for the New American Century (PNAC). The report noted that "while the unresolved conflict with Iraq provides the immediate justification, the need for a substantial American force presence in the Gulf transcends the issue of the regime of Saddam Hussein."[10] The PNAC report echoes an even earlier document written by Libby and Wolfowitz that argued that the United States must "discourage advanced industrial nations from challenging our leadership or even aspiring to a larger regional or global role."

In defining the appropriate response to terrorism as "a war," the Bush administration tried to weaken post-Vietnam constraints on military force among the public. One step in this process was Bush's use of rhetoric that was remarkably similar to that employed by President Roosevelt in the immediate aftermath of Pearl Harbor. Two examples follow:

December 8, 1941: Yesterday, December 7, 1941, a date that will live in infamy, the United States of America was suddenly and deliberately attacked.
September 11, 2001: Today, our fellow citizens, our very freedom came under attack in a series of deliberate and deadly terrorist acts.

And:

December 8, 1941: With confidence in our armed forces—with the unbounded determination of our people—we will gain the inevitable triumph so help us God.
October 7, 2001: We will not waver; we will not tire; we will not falter; and we will not fail. Peace and freedom will prevail. May God continue to bless America.[11]

With the stakes now defined in maximal terms, the administration also challenged a key axiom of conditional war, namely, that combat would involve only few to no casualties to U.S. forces. The war, Bush told the nation on September 20, would not be short and it might be costly:

This war will not be like the war against Iraq a decade ago, with a decisive liberation of territory and a swift conclusion. It will not look like the air war above Kosovo two years ago, where no ground troops were used and not a single American was lost in combat.

Our response involves far more than instant retaliation and isolated strikes. Americans should not expect one battle, but a lengthy campaign, unlike any other we have ever seen. It may include dramatic strikes, visible on TV, and covert operations, secret in success.[12]

One of the key targets of the Bush administration's strategy was the public, particularly its hesitation to accept the necessity of a war environment. When asked by a reporter to define victory in the new post-9/11 context, Secretary of Defense Donald Rumsfeld's reply was telling. "That's a good question," Rumsfeld said. "Now, what is victory? I say that victory is persuading the American people and the rest of the world that this is not a quick matter that's going to be over in a month or a year or even five years. It is something that we need to do so that we can continue to live in a world with powerful weapons and with people who are willing to use those powerful weapons. And we can do that as a country. And that would be victory, in my view."[13] One measure of success would be the remobilization of the population into support for a semipermanent state of war.

Bush's January 29, 2002, State of the Union address opened with the assertion that "our nation is at war" and used the words "terror," "terrorist," and "bioterrorism" thirty times. "Thousands of dangerous killers," he warned, "schooled in the methods of murder, often supported by outlaw regimes, are now spread throughout the world like ticking time bombs, set to go off without warning." A color-coded national threat system was established, and on the eve of the first anniversary of September 11 the level was raised from yellow (elevated) to orange (high). Attorney General John Ashcroft said: "Information indicates that al Qaeda cells have been established in several South Asian countries in order to conduct car bomb and other attacks on U.S. facilities." Two days later, President Bush's speech at the United Nations pointed to a specific target: "In cells and camps, terrorists are plotting further destruction and building new bases for their war against civilization. . . . In one place, in one regime, we find all these dangers in their most lethal and aggressive forms. . . . Saddam Hussein's regime is a grave and gathering danger."[14]

The Bush administration consistently argued that Iraq and al Qaeda were cooperating with each other. Republican pollster Frank Luntz advised Republicans that no speech on Iraq should begin without reference to 9/11. In late 2001, Vice President Cheney said that it was "pretty well confirmed" that Mohammed Atta, the individual believed to be responsible for masterminding the 9/11 attacks, met with an Iraqi intelligence official in Prague in April 2000. The Czechs denied that the meeting ever took place, and a congressional report of summer 2003 stated that "The CIA has been unable to establish that [Atta] left the United States or entered Europe in

April under his true name or any known alias."[15] Using cell phone records, government investigators placed Atta in Florida, where he was taking flight training, at that time.[16]

Bush himself continuously juxtaposed Iraq and al Qaeda, saying on October 7, 2002: "We know that Iraq and the al Qaeda terrorist network share a common enemy, the United States of America. We know that Iraq and al Qaeda have had high-level contacts that go back a decade," and "we've learned that Iraq has trained al Qaeda members in bomb-making and poisons and deadly gases." In his January 28, 2003, State of the Union address Bush maintained that "evidence from intelligence sources, secret communications, and statements by people now in custody reveal that Saddam Hussein aids and protects terrorists including members of al Qaeda." His March 2003 speech on the eve of war stated, "If the world fails to confront the threat posed by the Iraqi regime, refusing to use force, even as a last resort, free nations would assume immense and unacceptable risks. The attacks of September the 11th, 2001, showed what the enemies of America did with four airplanes. We will not wait to see what terrorist states could do with weapons of mass destruction." His 2003 letter to Congress announcing the start of the Iraq war declared the need "to take the necessary actions against international terrorists and terrorist organizations, including those nations, organizations, or persons who planned, authorized, committed, or aided the terrorist attacks that occurred on September 11, 2001."

Bush and his speechwriters became adept at using linguistic techniques aimed at quelling potential public opposition to their policies. According to Renana Brooks, "Bush creates and maintains negative frameworks in his listeners' minds with a number of linguistic techniques borrowed from advertising and hypnosis to instill the image of a dark and evil world around us. Catastrophic words and phrases are repeatedly drilled into the listener's head until the opposition feels such a high level of anxiety that it appears pointless to do anything other than cower."[17] Bush himself offered a simpler description of his mission: "See, in my line of work you got to keep repeating things over and over and over again for the truth to sink in, to kind of catapult the propaganda."[18] Either way, pessimistic language and bleak descriptions of the world underscored the status of the United States as victim while simultaneously reinforcing the dependency of the public on the administration to organize a response.

Spain follows an alternative approach. Following a terror attack, the public gathers together in a demonstration of unity against the taking of innocent life. Many participants paint their palms white in a symbolic rejection of violence. Everyone is encouraged to take an active part, together, in opposition. The public itself becomes a resource. This practice has been followed in response to ETA attacks and has contributed greatly to the moderation of Basque protest strategies. Massive rallies also followed the March 11, 2004, Madrid train bombings. Collective assertions of the value of human life trump fear. The police certainly are a key instrument in the fight against terror and many arrests of suspected terrorists have been made in Spain. But populist measures play an important part as well.

Meanwhile, in the United States, administration rhetoric continued to link Saddam Hussein to weapons of mass destruction, international terrorism, and September 11. In the absence of an alternative approach to combating terror, and given the understandable need to do something, most of the public became convinced that an attack on Iraq was justified retribution for the attack on American soil. Type I explicit opposition to war was present but included at most 15 percent of the population. Potential Type II sensitivity to war costs lay submerged within support for a war that appeared to be the only option. Opinion polls confirmed the role of fear, especially in demonstrating that those who believed in the alleged link between Saddam Hussein and terrorism also tended to support an invasion of Iraq. A CNN/*USA Today*/Gallup Poll conducted in March 2003, just before the launch of Operation Iraqi Freedom, found about two-thirds of the country favoring an invasion of Iraq with ground troops to remove Saddam Hussein. A majority thought that Saddam was personally involved in the September 11 attacks. Almost 90 percent believed that the Iraqi leader supported terrorist groups that had plans to attack the United States. Table 2.1 shows that among those holding the view that Saddam supported terror,

Table 2.1 Public Support and Opposition to Invading
Iraq with Ground Troops in Order to Remove Saddam
Hussein from Power, March 14–15, 2003

		Saddam Hussein involved in supporting terrorist groups planning to attack the U.S.		
		Yes, involved	No, not involved	Don't know	Total #
Favor or Oppose Invasion of Iraq	Favor	70.2%	15.6%	30.8%	305
	Oppose	26.7%	84.4%	61.5%	158
	Don't know	3.1%		7.7%	14
	Total number	419	45	13	477

Source: CNN/*USA Today*/Gallup Poll, March 14–15, 2003.

Table 2.2 Public Support and Opposition to Invading Iraq with Ground Troops in Order to Remove Saddam Hussein from Power, March 14–15, 2003

		Saddam Hussein involved in 9/11 terrorist attacks			
		Yes, involved	No, not involved	Don't know	Total #
Favor or oppose invasion of Iraq	Favor	72.0%	42.7%	46.3%	308
	Oppose	26.2%	56.0%	41.5%	210
	Don't know	1.8%	1.4%	12.2%	13
	Total number	271	218	42	531

Source: CNN/*USA Today*/Gallup Poll, March 14–15, 2003.

70.2 percent favored an invasion and 26.7 percent opposed it. But among those thinking that he was not involved, only 15.6 percent supported an invasion while 84.4 percent opposed it. Table 2.2 shows a similar pattern for the question of whether Saddam was involved in the September 11 attacks. Among those believing that he was involved, 72 percent supported an invasion and 26.2 percent opposed it. Among those who thought he was not involved, a majority disagreed with the planned military operation. The Bush administration's rhetoric was able to link the Iraqi leadership to an ongoing threat to the United States even though firm evidence of this connection was never provided.

Did September 11 Increase War Mobilization?

Public fear had a significant impact on policy but how much influence did administration rhetoric and the prospect of another attack have on the underlying relationship between the public and war? Did Americans undergo any fundamental change as a result of September 11 and the government's subsequent declaration of a war against terrorism? Did the population become remobilized to any significant degree so that the Bush administration could claim success in its campaign to once again make the threat of war appear constant?

In the week after the disaster, members of the public were more likely to display an American flag, show more affection, pray, and cry (see table 2.3). Many also gave generously. According to a survey conducted by the Independent Sector, 70 percent of Americans contributed either time or money to charities that provided assistance to the victims of September 11.[19] The National Opinion Research Center (NORC) found that about half reported contribut-

Table 2.3 Responses of Americans to the September 11, 2001, Attacks

Within the past two weeks, have you, personally, done any of the following as a direct result of September 11? How about....

	Yes	No
Display an American flag		
September 14–15, 2001	82	18
March 8–9, 2002	68	32
September 2–4, 2002	66	34
Show more affection for your loved ones than you do normally do		
September 14–15, 2001	77	22
March 8–9, 2002	48	51
September 2–4, 2002	47	53
Pray more than you usually do		
September 14–15, 2001	74	25
March 8–9, 2002	37	63
September 2–4, 2002	41	58
Cry		
September 14–15, 2001	70	30
March 8–9, 2002	21	79
September 2–4, 2002	22	78

Source: Gallup/*USA Today*/CNN poll.

ing to charities immediately following the attacks. A quarter said that they either donated or attempted to donate blood, and about 8 percent said that they were doing extra volunteer work. Four out of five people displayed a flag on their home or car, and trust in major institutions including the federal government, Congress, organized religion, and leading economic organizations rose. The already high level of national pride typically exhibited by Americans increased still further following September 11. In the midst of considerable and understandable anger, the percentage of Americans who felt that others were basically "fair" or "helpful" actually increased after 9/11, possibly in response to the well-publicized acts of rescue and relief in New York City and the largely sympathetic response from the rest of the world.[20]

The significant charitable giving that followed September 11 confirmed the fundamental decency and generous spirit of much of the public. Initially, the impressive examples of citizen contributions and public spirit led to speculation that this civic engagement might, as in other periods of national mobilization, produce new types of membership organizations and encourage citizen involvement in many areas of public life. Some even expressed the hope that the self-interested individualism that forms such a significant component of popular culture might begin to be replaced by a new, more participatory civic society.

Unfortunately, many post–September 11 changes in personal habits turned out to be short-lived. Increased contributions were temporary and often substituted for donations to other agencies such as community organizations and local food banks. In early 2002, Robert Putnam noted that "occasional volunteering is up slightly, but regular volunteering (at least twice a month) remains unchanged at about one in every seven Americans. Compared with figures from immediately after the tragedy, our data suggest that much of the measurable increase in generosity spent itself within a few weeks."[21] On the more positive side, the emotional reactions to the attacks summarized in table 2.3 all show significant recovery. Similarly, a survey specifically designed to measure women's response to September 11 noted: "Women have not radically changed their lives in response to the terrorist and anthrax attacks. In the aftermath of the attacks, they donated money and went to religious services, and to a lesser degree attended memorials and rallies. A significant number of women report spending more time with friends and family. But the attacks did not lead women to change their travel plans, stock up on gas masks and Cipro, socialize differently or change their children's routines."[22]

In U.S. history, war has often had the effect of stimulating volunteerism and new forms of civic organizing extending beyond the conflict itself. The Revolutionary War, for example, was fought by committees of correspondence and volunteer militias—and set the stage for the rapid expansion of the voluntary organizations that Alexis de Tocqueville found such a distinguishing feature of the new nation. Similarly, the Civil War was fought for the most part by volunteers and the North's victory brought a new set of associations that built on war mobilization. The enormous social efforts connected to World Wars I and II also generated new kinds of connections between the federal government and civic organizations as varied as the Red Cross, the YMCA, the General Federation of Women's Clubs, and the PTA. But more recently, civic organizations that previously rested on multiple forms of involvement from their membership have become reliant upon professional staff and virtual forms of mobilization.[23] The war against terrorism enlisted security professionals rather than volunteers and sought better organizational coordination instead of direct citizen engagement.

New York City itself deserves special attention in this inventory of reactions and recovery to September 11. The NORC found that those from the city were twice as likely to take special precautions with their mail, to have canceled a scheduled trip, and to have asked for "medicine to calm themselves down." Sixty percent of the population as a whole but three-quarters of New York residents said that they had cried immediately after the attacks. This reaction dropped significantly in the months that followed. A similar trajectory can be traced for those reporting that they felt very nervous or tense, or "sort of dazed and numb." The most common lingering effect was difficulty sleeping and feeling more tired than usual, both in the country and in New York City, although here too there were signs of relatively quick recovery. Interestingly, the NORC found, on the whole, more pronounced reactions to the Kennedy assassination than to September 11.[24]

Polls conducted for the Pew Research Center traced a similar pattern of initial reaction and subsequent recovery. When respondents were asked, during the week after September 11, if they felt "depressed because of [their] concerns about terrorists attacks or the war against terrorism," 71 percent answered in the affirmative. A month later, only a third of he population felt that way. When asked in that first week they had "any trouble sleeping" because of worries about terrorism, a third answered yes. A month later, that figure had been cut in half. Finally, in the week following the attack, almost 60 percent answered in the affirmative when asked if they "had any difficulty concentrating on [their] job or [their] normal activities." Less than a month later, that figure had also dropped by almost half.

Self-reported post–traumatic stress disorder (PTSD) symptoms in New York were almost three times the national average. Interestingly, among those who watched four hours of television a day or less, 7.5 percent reported significant forms of clinical psychological distress. Among those who watched television for twelve hours or more, 18 percent reported the same symptoms.[25] The correlation between television watching and post–traumatic stress syndrome is similar to a finding from the researchers who probed children's reactions to televised accounts of the bombing of the federal building in Oklahoma City in 1995. Dr. Randall Marshall, director of Trauma Studies for the New York State Office of Mental Health, said that "we're seeing [watching television] as a trauma. It led people to react as if they were present."[26] The NORC also applied a standard inventory of questions designed to diagnose PTSD and found about 15 percent of New Yorkers and 8 percent of the rest of country experiencing this form of distress in the first week after

9/11. For PTSD and other negative physical and emotional symptoms, Hispanics, African Americans, and those with less education, lower income, and poor health tended to be more vulnerable and to recover more slowly.

Elevated levels of smoking can be taken as another sign of an emotional reaction to September 11. The NORC survey did find about 20 percent of the public reporting that they smoked more than usual, and the American Cancer Society found that after nearly a decade of decline, cigarette sales jumped 13 percent in Massachusetts during the last three months of 2001.[27] Another study, of Manhattan residents living below 110th Street, found small but measurable increases in smoking and alcohol and marijuana use after the attacks. A more significant increase was found among those who already smoked, with 41.2 percent in this category increasing their frequency of use. The overall rise in cigarette smoking was 9.7 percent. A survey by the New York City fire department's Bureau of Health Services found that 29 percent of firefighters and emergency medical technicians had increased their smoking, and 23 percent of former smokers in the fire department had started again.[28] At least some of this increase in smoking may be attributable to the practices of the tobacco companies that gave out cartons of free cigarettes at Ground Zero to American Red Cross and other volunteers.[29] Yet, as with the other reactions reviewed in this chapter, the impact on smoking subsided as time passed. By the beginning of 2002, according to the NORC survey, those reporting increased smoking fell to 10 percent.

President Bush encouraged civic commitment in name, and his 2002 State of the Union address promised to expand AmeriCorps, the national service program, by 50 percent. But his administration failed to come to the support of the program when House Republicans stripped it of $100 million in emergency funds later in the year. Despite the shrinking of two major programs—the number of participants in Teach for America dropped from 2,400 to 575 and City Year saw its membership fall from 1,010 to 347 and shut down operations in five of thirteen cities—a White House spokesman declared that the AmeriCorps situation is "not considered a disaster or an emergency."[30] Some of these programs, particularly City Year, were at least partially restored, but even after Hurricane Katrina in 2005, the Bush administration called for cuts to the National Civilian Community Corps, a group of 1,100 volunteers specially trained for disaster relief. After September 11, Bush did not call for any major effort, such as a required period of national service for younger citizens. Instead, the preference of his administration was for the return of normal commercial routines. Civic engagement meant spending money, buying houses, and resuming shopping. According to the Travel Industry Association of America, an estimated two-thirds of the country saw the president's television advertisement calling on people to express their "courage" by resuming business travel and going somewhere for their vacations. Some private companies followed suit. In an advertisement published immediately after September 11, the Ford Motor Company said: "In an instant everything can change. Yet everywhere you look the spirit of America is alive. That spirit makes us what we are today and what we will be tomorrow. We at Ford want to celebrate that spirit with the Ford Drives America Program, to help America move forward with interest-free financing on all new Fords." The *Wall Street Journal* noted that "during World War II, patriotic citizens planted cabbage, collected scrap, and lent their money to 'Uncle Sam.' Since the World Trade Center attack, it has been suggested that our patriotic duty now consists of investing in the stock market."[31] A month later, the House of Representatives passed a law creating a new round of national bonds but the Treasury Department was reluctant to support the measure because it encouraged saving rather than spending. A *New York Times* article noted that "while calling the bill a good patriotic gesture, the Bush administration is not going out of its way to promote the legislation, arguing that in today's economy it is important to encourage consumers to spend."[32] These messages are reflected in a cartoon of Uncle Sam pointing his finger and asking Americans to go shopping.

Not surprisingly, in the weeks following September 11, the public considered terrorism to be the country's most important problem. By January 2002, however, only a quarter of the population continued to do so. Within two years of 9/11, more than twice as many thought it more important for Bush to focus on the economy than on the war on terror.[33] Save for immediate downturns in the airline industry and on Wall Street, September 11 had only a minimal impact on the economy. Americans did become more fearful of travel after September 11. Airline revenue declined and the number of domestic and international travelers fell by over 5 percent. Many air carriers went into bankruptcy. The number of passports issued fell by almost three hundred thousand between 2001 and 2002.[34] The number of visitors at Florida's Epcot Center in 2002 declined 8 percent from the previous year, and travel to national parks fell from 290 million a year before the attacks to 266 million the year after.[35] At the same time, the overall pattern was one of recovery and growth. While economic conditions continued to hamper the airline industry, the number of passports issued by the State Department rebounded to previous levels, as did the number of visitors to all of

The original version of this poster was created by James Montgomery Flagg and published in the July 6, 1916, issue of Leslie's Weekly.

the Disney theme parks including Epcot Center. Fears of economic doomsday—a meltdown of consumer confidence, a precipitous drop in the stock market, much lower levels of world trade, and capital flight from the United States—did not materialize. Problems in these areas were largely the result of market conditions and irresponsible business behavior that predated the attacks. As noted by Jessica Mathews, "So far Kenneth Lay, Bernie Ebbers & Co. have been responsible for more damage to the U.S. economy than has Osama bin Laden."[36]

In the immediate aftermath of the destruction of the World Trade Center, a section of the Pentagon, and the downing of Flight 93 in a Pennsylvania field, many people did start to reconsider what they held to be most important in life. Perhaps what was most stirring about New York City's response to the tragedy was the newfound focus on the heroic behavior of ordinary men and women. Instead of world-class athletes, politicians, and celebrities, respect and appreciation for the contribution of working people were often acknowledged in the various ceremonies that took place in the months after the attacks. But this rare attention to the importance of noncommercial values soon faded. The strategy of bringing citizens together to express their shared opposition to terrorism (and other forms of violence) remains strikingly absent among U.S. political leaders.

Instead, the public was encouraged to take private measures that few believed would be effective. The Department of Homeland Security recommended stockpiling a three-day supply of food, water, and medicine. The Federal Emergency Management Agency prepared a new, post-9/11 edition of its pamphlet *Are You Ready?* which contained directions for preparing a disaster supply kit, emergency planning for people with disabilities, steps for locating the closest shelter, and even contingency planning for family pets. The public was encouraged to purchase duct tape and plastic sheeting to be used to seal windows and doors against chemical and biological attacks. While newspapers and television often showed pictures of Americans purchasing emergency equipment in response to an increased level of terrorist alert, the vast majority of Americans ignored the calls. By March 2002, only 13 percent reported that they had stockpiled supplies or purchased a "domestic preparedness kit" containing a gas mask, gloves, flashlight, tools, an alarm, and a chemical protection suit. About a quarter of the population indicated that they had changed some aspect of their personal life or activities to reduce their chances of being a victim of a terrorist attack. But even this modest response receded in the following months. During the February 2003 orange alert immediately preceding the war in Iraq, only 8 percent made special provisions or purchased duct tape.[37] Ninety percent reported that they and their family went about their day-to-day life as usual.[38] In these respects, the public's response is similar to the largely ineffective cold war efforts to encourage the construction of private shelters, which the government claimed would be able to protect against atomic bombs and subsequent radioactive fallout.[39]

A majority of the public did report that the warnings "were useful," and at least two-thirds thought that it was a "good idea" for Washington to issue warnings about possible terrorist attacks even without specific information.[40] At the same time, few people did anything to alter their daily habits because of the alerts. The workplace was largely unchanged as well. More than three-quarters of the population reported that their company took no action in response to the February 2003 orange alert.[41] In January 2004, the population made a similar (non)response. In its own way, the Bush administration has also been reluctant to make major changes. Airport security has certainly been strengthened but the medical system has not been given the resources to prepare for chemical or biological attacks. Many large cities have been forced to fund special training programs and the purchase of equipment for first responders from their own budgets rather than from grants promised from the federal government. Little has been done to guard the railway system or nuclear facilities. The continued vulnerability of the nation's ports also reflects the largely rhetorical nature of the Bush administration's security policy toward civilian infrastructure. Better methods of coordination between the Department of Homeland Security and the Nuclear Regulatory Commission (NRC) are still lacking. On one occasion, the NRC official responsible for notifying power plants learned from a CNN broadcast that a change in alert level had been issued.

Fear and Conditional War

In a country that harbors as much baseline fear as the United States, the relatively muted response to September 11 points toward normalcy and recovery. Hiroshima and Nagasaki managed to reestablish an atmosphere of civic pride and a strong record of urban development following the atomic devastation at the end of World War II, and the return of New York City and the rest of the nation to more normal routines is a similar sign of strength.[42] The memories of both Ground Zeros will remain but neither has become a springboard for social remilitarization.

After September 11, many Americans were understandably afraid. They wanted justice and they wanted to lower if not eliminate the chances of another attack. The Bush administration stoked this fear and used it to further its own domestic and international agenda. At times, it appeared that there was no other alternative method of responding than to wage a "global war." Part of the Bush agenda was the lowering if not elimination of the public's hesitation to use military force. Victory in the war against terror would be not only against rogue states and terror networks but also greater public acceptance of the need for a more permanent military campaign. A global war on terror would be easier to manage if the public was more willing to accept—or at least turn a blind eye toward—the costs. War could also be fought more easily if the public could be convinced of the need for urgent measures that pointed toward remobilization. Some steps, such as a resumption of the draft or increased war taxes, were off the table. But an atmosphere of fear and dependence on the government were not.

September 11 did not remobilize the public into a new period of wartime urgency. Anger certainly followed the attacks and the immediate aftermath saw changes as varied as flying the flag, more charitable giving, and different expressions of anxiety such as increased smoking. But there is little evidence of a durable impact on the daily activities and psyches of most Americans. Fear of terrorism has had considerable impact at the policy level but not on the emotional structure of the public's reluctance to accept the costs of war. The Bush administration organized military intervention in Afghanistan and a campaign that would eventually culminate in an invasion of Iraq. However, the strong support that Americans gave to the overthrow of the Taliban and the effort to shut down al Qaeda's network did not change the boundary lines of conditional war.

As Operation Enduring Freedom began, Washington organized well-publicized drops of ready-to-eat meals. Most Afghanis did not like the food, and the deliveries were far fewer and less efficient than could be provided by civilian relief agencies already on the ground. The drops were made in areas of Afghanistan that were less in need—but safer to fly over. The food packages were similar in color to antipersonnel bombs, leading to a number of unfortunate and deadly mistakes. Yet the operation helped manage public expectations that the military was engaged in a humanitarian mission. It is difficult to resist the conclusion that the American public was the true target of the food drop.

Combat operations conformed to the conditional war requirement that perceived casualties be kept low. The Pentagon placed Special Forces and other elite troops on the ground but relied largely on local troops to do most of the fighting against the Taliban. Washington leveraged CIA money to manipulate various ethnic and regional groups and to patch together a confederated fighting force that overthrew the government in Kabul. But the members of this thin coalition held competing agendas. Following the fall of the Taliban, Washington was unable to achieve coordination sufficient to create adequate security elsewhere in the country. Warlords, some profiting from renewed poppy cultivation and a dramatic increase in drug trafficking, continue to dominate the different regions. In early 2006, Afghan president Hamid Karzai called the drug trade, which by some estimates had reached 50 percent of the country's GNP, a greater threat than terrorism to the country's stability. Women have not been liberated, democracy was not been imported, and the country remains balkanized. International commitments to develop Afghanistan's civilian infrastructure, including those made by the United States, have fallen short of initial pledges. Meanwhile, force protection has remained the top priority for the United States. The substitute, airpower, while often devastatingly accurate, also led to a series of catastrophic mistakes that produced civilian casualties at levels that soon surpassed the number of people killed in New York, the Pentagon, and Pennsylvania. Peace activists such as Families for a Peaceful Tomorrow visited the families of the Afghan victims to deliver a message about the universal value of human life. But most of these casualties remained invisible to the U.S. public.

Fear of terrorism continues in the United States. In fact, as polls indicated weakening support for Bush over the second half of 2005, combating terror remained the only issue on which the president continued to receive favorable marks. This fear has yet to transform or remobilize the American public into an acceptance of militarism. On the other hand, this reluctance has not yet set in motion a concentrated search for alternative antiwar policies. For that to occur, fear will have to be both moderated and coupled to a new, stronger, and more deeply felt program of hope.

Chapter 3

Managing Information

Before the start of Operation Iraqi Freedom, the Bush administration claimed that Saddam Hussein's regime was an overwhelming security threat because it possessed weapons of mass destruction (WMD) and was linked to international terrorist groups. Even if Iraq had no present intentions to use weapons directly, a preemptive military intervention was necessary to prevent the possibility that WMD might be passed to terrorists. The administration asserted that Iraq had been given plenty of time to disarm but that Saddam continued to deceive the United Nations inspectors. In February 2003, Secretary of State Colin Powell presented the administration's case before the United Nations and a prime-time television audience in the United States. Other members of the Security Council, especially France and Russia, wanted to delay a resolution that would unambiguously approve the use of force until it was clear that Iraq did in fact have WMD and was unwilling to disarm. But Bush and his main ally, British prime minister Tony Blair, decided that the time for waiting was over. Baghdad had to be disarmed by force.

Public opinion seemed to be behind the Bush administration. Before the war, 70 percent of the public supported the use of military force against Saddam's regime. Eighty percent thought that Iraq probably did have WMD and almost half believed that the Iraqi leader was directly involved in the September 11 attacks.[1] As the war began, Bush's job approval rating jumped almost 15 points.[2] One month into the war, more than three-quarters of the population approved of the way George Bush was handling the situation with Iraq.[3] How does a picture of a public that largely believed the administration's claims and that appeared strongly supportive of the war fit with the argument that Americans are becoming more peaceful?

One answer is that the public, given a different political leader, would have just as easily approved of a policy of continued deterrence toward Iraq. In the months immediately preceding the war, a significant majority continued to support multilateralism over unilateralism and giving UN inspectors additional time to conduct their investigations.[4] The percentage of the public favoring military action against Iraq dropped to less than 50 when polling questions referred to U.S. casualties, Iraqi casualties, or to the possibility of a long war. A different president would have received strong support if he had delivered the following message: "We're still not sure whether Iraq possesses weapons of mass destruction. We're going to keep looking and we're going to keep looking hard. Meanwhile, we've got Saddam Hussein contained. We don't like or trust him. But we are not going to start a war until the cause is absolutely clear. And we're not there yet." Many Republicans, as well as Democrats, former national security officials, and military leaders, continued to be skeptical of the case for military action. A peace movement that was rapidly increasing in strength staged large demonstrations in Washington, New York, San Francisco, and in many smaller communities throughout the country. The Internet enabled organizers to build an impressive network among antiwar movements throughout the world. Within the United States, a large number of trade unions, churches, municipalities, and professional organizations took a stand against going to war without United Nations approval. Many people previously uninvolved in direct political activity became engaged in these efforts. In fact, the activist component of Type I opposition was one of the largest to take place before a war actually began.

Despite demonstrations that attracted several hundred thousand, a broader desire to allow the inspection process to continue until conclusive evidence had been established, and the public's reluctance to initiate war unilaterally, the Bush administration launched Operation Iraqi Freedom. Relatively quickly, U.S. troops entered Baghdad and overthrew the Ba'ath regime. In early May, Bush declared, "mission accomplished." Major hostilities, the president said, were now over. Yet over the summer, the Iraqi insurgency gained strength, and the administration's original case for war began to erode. UN inspectors had looked for WMD in vain. Now Washington's own Iraq Survey Group failed to find any weapons. Nor was there any evidence of a connection between Saddam Hussein and international terrorism. "At various times al Qaeda people came through Baghdad and in some cases resided there," David McKay, head of the Survey Group, later said. But "we simply did not find any evidence of extensive links with al Qaeda, or for that matter any real links at all."[5] Nonetheless, in May 2003, 34 percent of the public said that they thought that the United States had actually found weapons of mass destruction (with another 7 percent saying that they were not sure).[6] In November 2003, and then again the following April, a majority still thought that Iraq possessed WMD before the war began. As for the purported link with international terrorism, as late as August 2003 a *Washington Post* poll found 69 percent of the public thinking that it was likely or very likely that Saddam Hussein had been connected to the September 11 attacks.

Where was the "learning curve" of the American public? Why did so many continue to believe, despite the evidence, in the original claims of the Bush administration? How can the American public be considered more peaceful when, despite an underlying tendency to oppose war, it was so easily swayed in an opposite direction?

Information and Democracy

Many critics of the Bush administration have been dismayed by the inability of the public to see through the distorted claims advanced by their political leaders. William Rivers Pitt provides an example:

> The astounding level of blunt ignorance within the American populace about the events surrounding the attacks of September 11 cannot be easily quantified. In a nation with thousands of newspapers, thousands of radio stations, and a ceaseless data stream from CNN, MSNBC, CNBC, Fox, NBC, ABC, CBS and PBS, some 70% of the population believed as late as a month ago [November 2003] that Saddam Hussein was centrally involved in and personally responsible for the attacks which destroyed the Towers and struck the Pentagon. Beyond that, what most people know about the single most important event in American history does not go much beyond "evildoers" who "hate our freedom."[7]

Similarly, literary critic Harold Bloom thought that the false claims made by President Bush were "extraordinary blatant, yet the American people seem benumbed, unable to read, think, or remember, and thus fit subjects for a president who shares their limitations."[8] Even some experienced national security officials expressed disbelief at the continued ability of the Bush administration to deceive the public about Iraq's alleged possession of weapons of mass destruction. As a former member of the CIA said in an interview conducted in July 2003:

> OFFICIAL: Given the amount of information that took place before the war about WMD, I don't know why so many Americans are willing to shrug their shoulders and say, "Oh, well."
>
> JOSEPH: In one poll, 41 percent thought either that the U.S. had actually found weapons of mass destruction or weren't sure whether the military had found them.
>
> OFFICIAL: The administration has been very clever about actually producing situations that can confuse people that way. Announcing the "discovery" of labs and so on. But finding a couple of trailers with little chemistry labs, given the amount of drum beating leading to the outbreak of war, is puny.

The limited knowledge base of the public extends to other issues. In early September 2001, only 14 percent of the public could identify the issue addressed by the Kyoto agreement and less than a quarter could name the Russian prime minister. When asked to estimate how much of every dollar spent by the federal government goes for foreign aid, the average answer was 20 cents. The actual amount is less than a penny.[9] Just before the 2004 presidential election, the National Annenberg Election Survey found that more than half of the public did not know that President Bush favored the creation of private accounts for some Social Security money. Roughly the same proportion mistakenly thought that Bush supported a change in federal law to allow for drug imports from Canada.[10]

What are the reasons for this low level of information, especially about foreign affairs? One possible explanation is geographic insularity. The United States is a continental power and, according to the Pew Global Attitudes Project, only 22 percent of Americans have traveled to another country in the last five years, compared with about 75 percent of Western Europeans. Before September 11, only 30 percent of Americans claimed to be "very interested" in news about other countries. A year later, a bare quarter of the population said that they were following foreign news "very closely."[11] In this view, Americans are poorly informed about the rest of the world and are inclined to take their leaders' explanations of how the world works at face value, not because they are dumb or deceived, but because of the nation's large landmass, which creates many opportunities but also an inward, generally optimistic focus that is unique among the major powers in history. Simon Schama described the impact of this experience:

When Alexis de Tocqueville came to America in the 1830's he was struck by the intensity with which Americans boasted of their singularity. He granted them their novelty, but immediately understood it was, above all, the product of their liberation from social and spatial claustrophobia. The happiness to which, apparently, Americans were entitled by birthright (and that Tocqueville saw with shocking clairvoyance actually meant the raw pursuit of material satisfactions) was conditional on perpetual motion. Happiness for Voltaire was cultivating one's garden. Happiness for Thomas Jefferson was rolling across the continent, gathering the millions of acres needed to make the American homestead.[12]

A strong democracy provides the public with accurate information and multiple forums for debate over the meaning of that information. The ideal is a nation of deliberating citizens engaged in what Jürgen Habermas calls "rational-critical discourse." A public that is not knowledgeable and receives its information from relatively few sources becomes more vulnerable to manipulation and spin. A public that is better informed, with access to multiple sources of information, carries greater potential for independent judgment. In a society with a functioning democracy, involved citizens are able to criticize without fear of persecution. They recognize a connection between their own activities and the creation of multiple sites of social power beyond state and corporate power. Significant differences may continue to exist but the democratic process of debate is essential. The result is a vital civil society that can be defined as a "complex and dynamic ensemble of legally protected non-governmental institutions that tend to be non-violent, self-organizing, self-reflexive, and permanently in tension with each other and with the state institutions that 'frame,' constrict and enable their activities."[13] The state may act in ways that generate tensions but in a healthy civil society, the public is able to participate in contested politics. Strong democracies respect laws and customs that enhance freedom of speech and other civil liberties, promote transparency and accountability, and limit the influence of money in determining social outcomes. The presence of multiple opinions and different perspectives reinforces the goal of informing and encouraging citizens to engage in debate and argument.

In addition to the inward focus of the country, critics often link the more disappointing aspects of the knowledge base held by the public to failures of the press and media and to the ability of administration officials to deceive and manipulate. Perhaps no recent example is as striking as that offered by Sheldon Wolin, one of the foremost political theorists of the postwar generation. Wolin calls current American politics an example of "inverted totalitarianism."[14]

In his view, the invasion of Iraq, taken in the name of democracy and to overthrow a totalitarian regime, has in fact undermined the former while bringing the United States closer to the latter. Wolin notes that the terms "empire" and "superpower," once used primarily by opponents of Washington's foreign policy, are now employed casually by a broad swatch of op-ed writers and media experts and convey an assumption that the terms win prima facie approval. There can be no intelligent questioning of the domineering role that the United States plays vis-à-vis the rest of the world. "Empire" and "superpower" indicate a concentration of power abroad and the absence of an effective system of checks and balances at home. The easy acceptance of the two terms, Wolin writes, "stand[s] for the surpassing of limits and the dwarfing of the citizenry."

Wolin argues that the Republican Party has emerged as a "fervently doctrinal party, zealous, ruthless, antidemocratic, and boasting a near majority." But Democrats are also part of the problem because they have rejected the liberal label and reformist constituencies and have thus failed to serve as an opposition party. When combined with the role of money and the disproportionate influence of privileged groups on the electoral system, the two-party system has been effectively subverted. "Elections," writes Wolin, "have become heavily subsidized non-events that typically attract at best merely half of an electorate whose information about foreign and domestic politics is filtered through corporate-dominated media." Wolin believes that the citizenry has been "manipulated into a nervous state by media reports of crime and terrorist networks" and by the expansion of government power that "discourages the citizenry and leaves them politically apathetic." Wolin contrasts apathy as a form of political control with the practices of totalitarian regimes that secured internal stability by mobilizing their citizens into more active forms of participation, such as opposing religious, ethnic, or political minorities, or in direct support of the war effort.

The "inversion" described by Wolin represents the downside of the demobilization process that has been such a key element of the public's altered relationship to war. The Nazis wanted a mobilized society that would support sacrifice, the expansion of Germany in the search for lebensraum, and war. The population provided support by engaging with the war effort and through periodic plebiscites. In contrast, the U.S. empire wants a uninterested population that prefers to not engage issues, take elections seriously, or accept any measures that would require sacrifice. For Wolin, demobilization has limited both participation and the knowledge necessary to challenge governmental policies. The legislative branch is weak, the courts and media are largely compliant, policy alternatives are limited by a de facto one-party system, and the corporate sector feeds itself through state power. The result is helplessness and political despair.

Nina Eliasoph's study of the way that people discuss social issues provides an interesting complement to Wolin's argument. She starts with a question, "How do Americans talk about politics?" but ends up with a substitute query: "How is it that so many Americans avoid talking about politics?"[15] In her view, the absence of a community centered on concrete physical space is partly responsible for the low level of empowering political talk and the substitution of other forms of conversation and interpersonal exchange that help limit participation and political power. People do talk, but about the weather, sports, traffic, celebrities, and each other. They don't discuss politics—or at least not as much as a healthy democracy would require. If true, this interpretation of the concentration of political power in the United States and of the inability of many Americans to understand what their government actually does also challenges the viewpoint that Americans are becoming more peaceful.

My own view is not as pessimistic. The Bush administration did adopt an aggressive stance toward the media and to some degree these efforts have intimidated journalists and their editors. In many ways, the public remains poorly informed about Iraq. Nonetheless, over time, and as the costs of the Iraqi military expedition have increased, the accuracy of the information held by the population has also improved. To some degree, this change reflects new information provided by the September 11 Commission (a report on the U.S. intelligence agencies' prewar intelligence assessments on Iraq prepared by the Senate Select Committee on Intelligence); high-profile figures such as David Kay, the former head of the U.S. government's Iraq Survey Group; Hans Blix, the head of the UN weapons inspection team before the war; former government officials such as Richard Clarke; and even Michael Moore's film *Fahrenheit 9/11*.[16] But the movement also reflects the transition of the Iraq conflict toward the boundaries of what is acceptable in conditional war. War costs allowed for more critical information to appear before the public and this information encouraged some members of the public to reassemble these facts into their own assessments of the entire enterprise. Many have become better informed despite the administration's continued efforts to shape opinion. This process has been all the more remarkable because it has occurred without the benefit of a political figure willing to refocus the debate around the war as a mistake. Certainly Democratic presidential candidate John Kerry had an opportunity to do so in 2004 and chose not to.

The public arena in the United States is still without a political party or prominent individual capable of reframing existing information into an alternative that would help the public make sense of the facts and counter the misinterpretations that continue to exist. The improvement shown by the public, including a greater willingness to see through the official justifications of the war, represents a modest but significant element of the overall tendency of Americans to become more peaceful. But short of a clearly and consistently articulated alternative that reassembles the "new" facts into an acceptable narrative, the still-incomplete knowledge base of the public signifies that the tendency of Americans to become more peaceful will continue to be uneven.

The Bush Administration's Case for War

When, exactly, did George W. Bush make his decision to go to war with Iraq? Officially, military attacks began on March 20, 2003, and only after the administration found the UN inspection process lacking. (CIA-led teams were actually operating within Iraq well before this date, and U.S. aircraft had bombed selected targets in Iraq during the Clinton administration.) But Bush had actually made a firm commitment to invade as early as that January, when he told first Secretary of Defense Donald Rumsfeld and Secretary of State Colin Powell, "Look, we're going to have to do this."[17] A good argument can be made that the firm decision to go to war had been made even earlier. A July 23, 2002, meeting between Tony Blair and his advisers discussed the Bush administration's policy on Iraq. The minutes taken at that meeting include the following sentence: "It seemed clear that Bush had made up his mind to take military action, even if the timing was not yet decided." Those minutes, now known as the Downing Street Memo, also noted a recent visit to Washington by Richard Dearlove, the head of MI6, the British intelligence agency. In the U.S. capital Dearlove found "a perceptible shift in attitude. Military action was now seen as inevitable. Bush wanted to remove Saddam, through military action, justified by the conjunction of terrorism and WMD. But the intelligence and facts were being fixed around the policy."[18] The actual decision to invade could have been as early as November 2001, seventy-two days after September 11, when Bush called Rumsfeld into his office and ordered a revision of the war plan for Iraq.[19]

The actual intent to overthrow Saddam emerged still earlier. Immediately following September 11, Vice President Dick Cheney asked Bush's war cabinet if this "would be a good time to go after Iraq." Policy papers and strategic concepts calling for regime change circulated among key officials well before the 2000 election. The presumed threat of weapons of mass destruction was not a particular concern at this time. Instead, the drive to overthrow Saddam was rooted in a combination of neoconservative strategic priorities. These included demonstrating the ability to use military force unilaterally rather than under a UN mandate, adding a compliant Iraq to the list of oil-rich states under the protectorate of Washington, and a messianic desire to spread U.S.-style democracy throughout the Middle East. Iraq was regarded as an opportunity to demonstrate how the preeminent world power could be freed from the constraints of multilateralism exercised by the "old Europe," or from the UN, which had become in the administration's view "a mere debating society." Iraq was also a chance to obtain more firm control of the resources and politics of the Middle East. But none of these rationales would have worked with the public. Despite the administration's desire to act unilaterally, the process leading to war had to involve allies (no matter how small the number) and run through the UN (no matter how much this step would ultimately be for show). The ambitious neoconservative concept of "vital interests" would not fly with public opinion because it called for constant war preparation. To gain public support the Bush administration had to manage information that supported the twin claims that Iraq possessed WMD and was linked to international terrorism. When these claims proved to be false, the rationale shifted to Saddam's brutal human rights record. Self-defense and humanitarian concerns can be managed as rationales for conditional war but the actual strategic agenda of the Bush administration cannot.

Another complication was that some State Department officials and parts of the military did not fully embrace the ambitious neoconservative strategies. Finding and eliminating WMD became useful for internal politics as well. As Paul Wolfowitz, the deputy secretary of defense, later put it, "The truth is that for reasons that have a lot to do with the U.S. government bureaucracy, we settled on the one issue that everyone could agree on—which was weapons of mass destruction—as the core reason."[20] In pushing these claims, the Bush administration was able to influence much of the public by painting a picture of looming, undifferentiated terrorism coming from both al Qaeda and Iraq.

Yet neither UN chief inspector Hans Blix, who stated that there were "no persuasive indications" of links, nor the CIA, nor the FBI was able to present evidence to support the allegations. U.S. intelligence officials reported that they were under tremendous pressure to provide documentation of Iraqi–al Qaeda ties, but some told the New York Times, "We just don't think it's there"[21] As Ray McGovern, an intelligence officer with twenty-seven years in the CIA, stated:

The day after 9/11, [Vice President] Dick Cheney, [Deputy Secretary of Defense] Wolfowitz, and [Secretary of Defense] Rumsfeld were saying, "Now let's go get Iraq." And so the push was on to find evidence that Iraq had some sort of connection with 9/11. And I am very sad to say that our president himself has in a subliminal way always made that connection. And that is why most Americans, pity them, tend to believe that Iraq did have something to do with 9/11, while the intelligence community is convinced it did not.[22]

Over the summer of 2003, and after Saddam had been overthrown, some Bush administration officials stopped making public claims of an Iraqi connection to September 11. "I'm not sure even now," Wolfowitz said on a radio show on August 1, "that I would say that Iraq had something to do with it."[23] But these disavowals were still coupled with reassertions of ties to the overall al Qaeda network, thus continuing to keep the specter of evil before the public. In January 2004, Cheney told National Public Radio, "There's overwhelming evidence there was a connection between al Qaeda and the Iraqi government. I am very confident that there was an established relationship there."[24]

In July 2004, the September 11 Commission report concluded that there is "no credible evidence" that the Iraqi regime collaborated with the al Qaeda network. The commission did find that al Qaeda members contacted Hussein seeking support but that the Iraqi leader did not respond. "There have been reports," the 9/11 Commission stated in its interim report, published a month earlier, "that contacts between Iraq and Al Qaeda also occurred after bin Laden returned to Afghanistan, but they do not appear to have resulted in a collaborative relationship."[25] The commission said al Qaeda had far more contacts with Iran and Pakistan than with Iraq. Many newspapers editorialized against the attempts of the Bush administration to make the link.[26] But the message of the commission, and even the belated criticism of Bush by the press, was blunted by the continued publication of front-page stories reflecting administration statements and sources reasserting the connection. The very day before the release of the interim report, President Bush stated that Hussein "had ties to terrorist organizations." The day after the report, Cheney appeared on CNBC, where the following exchange took place:

CHENEY: There clearly was a relationship. It's been testified to. The evidence is overwhelming.

CNBC CORRESPONDENT GLORIA BORGER: Do you know some things that the commission does not know?"

CHENEY: Probably.... There are realms of material here. Your show isn't long enough for me to read all the pieces of it.[27]

On the same day, Bush stated, "The reason I keep insisting that there was a relationship between Iraq and Saddam and al Qaeda is because there was a relationship between Iraq and al Qaeda."[28]

While this reasoning would not convince all audiences, the tenacity of the repetition, even at this late date, helped prevent a total collapse of the administration's claim that the war in Iraq was leveled against a direct threat to U.S. security. Bush and Cheney did their best to keep, in the words of one expert on public opinion and war, "a general fuzz going around: People know they don't like al Qaeda, they are horrified by September 11th, they know this guy [Saddam] is a bad guy, and it's not hard to put those things together."[29]

Mistaken public perceptions reflected in part the impact of an unrelenting message delivered through speeches, press conferences, and television appearances, which resonated with an emotional view among a large part of the public that the United States faced a world that harbored considerable threats.

The other principal claim made by the Bush administration was that Iraq possessed weapons of mass destruction. Many of their arguments had at least temporary effect but none mattered as much as Secretary of State Colin Powell's February speech before the UN Security Council. Powell's synthesis of satellite photographs, intercepted audiotapes, human intelligence sources, a show-and-tell vial of simulated anthrax, reference to human intelligence sources, and sketches of mobile labs made for effective television. The secretary of state maintained that Iraq had concealed its weapons programs and had successfully deceived the inspectors. Powell cited a "fine paper that the United Kingdom distributed ... which describes in exquisite detail Iraqi deception activities." It was later determined that large parts of that intelligence report had been plagiarized from previously published academic articles and that the British did not have an independent means to substantiate the claim.[30] In fact, many of Powell's arguments turned out to be erroneous. But as a public relations exercise seeking to make the case that Saddam was an immediate threat, Powell's presentation was a tremendous success. Mary McGrory, a liberal columnist for the *Washington Post*, wrote in her next day's op-ed column, "I can only say that he persuaded me, and I was as tough as France to convince."[31]

Before the war, the White House referred to documents supporting the administration's claim that Iraq had imported a form of uranium ore known as yellowcake from Niger that could be used in a nuclear weapons program. In his January 2003 State of the Union address,

Bush stated, "The British government has learned that Saddam Hussein recently sought significant quantities of uranium from Africa." The documents that Bush used to make his case turned out to be fabricated, and the administration was forced to retract its claim.[32] Mohamed ElBaradei, director general of the International Atomic Energy Agency, told the United Nations that Iraq had no current nuclear weapons program, and a formal estimate produced by the U.S. intelligence community concluded that Baghdad would not be able to produce an atomic bomb until the end of the decade. Yet, immediately prior to the war, Bush still claimed that Iraq could produce a nuclear weapon in one year. (This particular incident produced considerable political fallout, including the indictment of Cheney chief of staff Scooter Libby for leaking the name of Valerie Plame, a CIA official and wife of former ambassador Joseph Wilson, who investigated the alleged Niger-Iraq uranium connection, found that it unsubstantiated, and wrote a *New York Times* op-ed piece outlining the Bush administration's use of the false story.)

A report for the Carnegie Endowment for International Peace reviewed many of the other claims by the Bush administration that Iraq held WMD. The authors concluded that the Bush administration had ignored experts who could have provided more accurate information and downplayed the significance of conflicting assessments from within its own departments, particularly from state and energy.[33] Table 3.1 presents a summary of administration claims and a review of the evidence uncovered after the war began.

The Structure of Mistaken Beliefs

While a fuller treatment of the role of the press and media awaits the next chapter, any understanding of the public's information failures must also incorporate the failure of professional editors and journalists to provide solid, steady scrutiny of the administration's claims. In mid-March 2003, for example, one week before the initiation of the war, three separate sources told Bob Woodward of the *Washington Post* that the intelligence on WMD was not as conclusive as the administration had been arguing.[34] Walter Pincus, another reporter for the paper, had heard similar skepticism from his sources. Woodward then drafted a story with the following lead: "Some of the key U.S. intelligence that is the basis for the conclusion that Iraq has large caches of weapons of mass destruction looks increasingly circumstantial, and even shaky as it is further

Table 3.1 Prewar Bush Administration Statements
versus Evidence Uncovered after March 2003

	Bush administration prewar statements	Evidence uncovered since March 2003
Biological weapons	Iraq had a "massive stockpile" of biological weapons "capable of killing millions"	No weaponized biological agents found
Biological program	Iraq was producing several types of biological agents and developing more	No weaponized biological weapons program but some evidence of future plans
Mobile biological labs	Iraq had at least seven "mobile biological agents factories"	Two vans found did not test positive for biological agents and could have had alternative uses
Chemical weapons	Iraq had vast chemical weapons stockpiles, including mustard, sarin, and VX gases	No chemical weapons found and it appears none were produced after 1991
Covert production facilities	Iraq had hidden its chemical weapons program "within its legitimate civilian industry"	No chemical munitions or production facilities found but "dual-use" programs possible
Nuclear weapons	Hussein restarted Iraq's program and would acquire nuclear weapons "fairly soon"	No signs of any active program
Attempts to enrich uranium	Iraq procuring equipment to enrich uranium including "high strength tubes" and magnets	No evidence that the tubes or the magnets were meant for uranium enrichment
Attempts to buy uranium	Bush said that the British government learned that Hussein tried to buy uranium from Africa	U.S. officials were aware in July 2003 that the uranium claims were unfounded

Source: Carnegie Endowment for International Peace; table adapted from *Boston Globe*, January 9, 2004.

scrutinized, subjected to outside analysis and on-the-ground veri-
fication, according to informed sources." But the story that was
eventually published, under Pincus's byline, focused only on the
difficulty of finding corroborating evidence. Crucially, no skepticism
about the very existence of Iraq's weapons program was expressed.
Nor was the administration's conclusion about the need for war

really challenged. What emerged was the possibility of an internal dispute over facts. The possibility that Bush's very case for war was fundamentally flawed did not appear.

Another example of press failure concerns the circumstances in which international weapons inspectors (UNSCOM) left Iraq in 1998. In 2003, most newspaper readers could be forgiven for thinking that Saddam Hussein had kicked those inspectors out because that is exactly what their papers were telling them. But the circumstances surrounding the termination of the UNSCOM program were quite different. Some of the inspectors on the UN team were actually conducting a U.S. espionage program that had been piggybacked on the search for WMD. Later reports said that information collected through the inspection process was used to pick bombing targets in Iraq and to develop a system for tracking the movements of Saddam Hussein. The Iraqi leader naturally complained about this second purpose of the inspection process and began raising obstacles to the UNSCOM mission. The inspectors were then removed by program head Richard Butler just before the Clinton administration initiated a bombing campaign in December 1998 to punish Saddam for his alleged noncompliance with UNSCOM.

What did the public know about the dual use of the UNSCOM inspectors? Not much at the time, for the few stories that did appear were buried in the back pages. But in 1999, major newspapers ran stories detailing the CIA strategy of using weapons inspectors to spy on Iraq. The *Washington Post* said that the United States "infiltrated agents and espionage equipment for three years into United Nations arms control teams in Iraq to eavesdrop on the Iraqi military without the knowledge of the U.N. agency."[35] The *New York Times* reported that "United States officials said today that American spies had worked undercover on teams of United Nations arms inspectors."[36] But this crucial contamination of the inspection process soon fell into the memory sinkhole.

In October 2003, the *New York Times* repeated as fact a charge by Colin Powell, who in a "television appearance today, noted that the Iraqi leader threw weapons inspectors out in 1998, making it more difficult for intelligence agencies to get hard information." In a good example of Type I opposition, activists mobilized by FAIR (Fairness and Accuracy in Reporting) wrote to the newspaper in protest. In response the *Times* printed a correction that acknowledged that the inspectors had been withdrawn by the UN, not expelled by Saddam Hussein. FAIR's newsletter noted that "it's hard to avoid the impression that certain media outlets would rather that UNSCOM's covert espionage had never been exposed in the first place."[37] It is interesting to note that the *Times* seemed to be having difficulty believing what its own reporters had published in the paper four years earlier.

Judith Miller's reporting, also for the *New York Times*, provides yet another example of distorted press coverage of the Iraqi WMD threat. Miller, who served essentially as a "government stenographer" on its case for war, relied on Iraqi defectors for her sources, particularly Ahmed Chalabi, former head of the Iraqi National Congress and an exile favored by many in the Bush administration.[38] Miller's front-page story in September 2002 contained the mistaken statement that an intercepted shipment of aluminum tubes to Iraq was part of a program to acquire nuclear weapons. Her story was repeatedly cited as an example of exemplary reporting on the following Sunday morning talk shows by Condoleezza Rice, Colin Powell, and Dick Cheney. "The White House had a perfect deal with Miller," a former CIA analyst said later:

> Chalabi is providing the Bush people with the information they need to support their political objectives, and he is supplying the same material to Judy Miller. Chalabi tips her on something and then she goes to the White House, which has already heard the same thing from Chalabi, and she gets it corroborated. She also got the Pentagon to confirm things for her, which made sense, since they were working so closely with Chalabi. Too bad Judy didn't spend a little more time talking to those of us who had information that contradicted almost everything Chalabi said.[39]

Later, belatedly, many major newspapers acknowledged their mistakes.

An intriguing study carried out by the Program on International Policy Attitudes six months after the war began makes it possible to chart the location and sources of erroneous information that continued to circulate within the public. Three specific misperceptions regarding the war in Iraq were examined, each "demonstrably false, or at odds with the dominant view in the intelligence community."[40] The first concerned the purported connection between Saddam and al Qaeda. Summer 2003 polls found almost half of Americans believing that evidence of the connection had been found. The second misperception was the belief that weapons of mass destruction had been actually discovered. About a third of the public thought that weapons had been found. And the third issue involved perceived support among world opinion for the U.S.-initiated war. Large majorities in most countries opposed a war carried out without UN approval. But a substantial minority of the U.S. public nonetheless believed that world opinion supported Washington's use of military force.

While only a minority of the public held to any particular misperception, a solid majority believed in at least one of the three mistaken assertions.[41] As might be expected, belief in any of these misperceptions was strongly related to approval for the Bush administration's policies. For example, among those who said that they had *not* seen evidence of a connection between al Qaeda and Saddam, and who also thought that such a connection did not exist, only 9 percent supported unilateral action against Iraq. On the other hand, 58 percent of those who thought that Iraq was directly involved in September 11 supported military action even if such a measure was taken unilaterally. Among those correctly believing that world opinion was opposed to war without UN support, only slightly more than a quarter supported the Bush administration's policies. But among those who thought that world opinion agreed with the United States, 81 percent supported Washington's intervention. All told, among those with no misperceptions, only 23 percent supported the war. Among those holding to all three misperceptions, a remarkable 86 percent supported the war. Clearly, accuracy of information is linked to a tendency to reject Bush administration policies.

As one might expect, these misperceptions are distributed unevenly throughout the population. The choice of news source is a key factor in explaining the differences. Those obtaining their information largely from National Public Radio or from the Public Broadcasting System were the least likely to hold to mistaken beliefs. A significant majority did not have any misperceptions and hardly any believed in all three (see figure 3.1). Those who received most of their news from newspapers and magazines were more accurate in their assessments than those who relied upon television and the radio (only about 20 percent of the public get most of their news from print sources). Among those relying on television, viewers of Fox News were far more likely to hold to misperceptions than those who favored CNN, NBC, ABC, or CBS. In fact, Fox News watchers were more than twice as likely to believe in all three misperceptions than the next news source.

Unsurprisingly, Bush supporters were more likely to believe in one or more of the misperceptions than those who planned to support the 2004 nominee of the Democratic Party. But news source still had a significant impact within the two political constituencies. Seventy-eight percent of Bush supporters who watched Fox held to one or more misperceptions, but only 50 percent of Bush supporters who counted on NPR or PBS held to a mistaken belief. Forty-eight percent of Democrats who watched Fox believed in one or more of the misperceptions while the survey could not find a single person

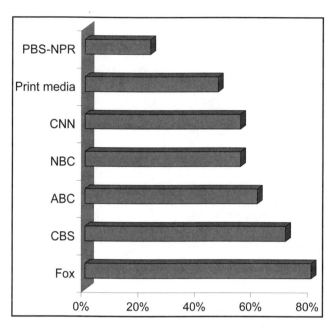

Figure 3.1 Frequency of Misperceptions:
Evidence of al-Qaeda Links, WMD Found, World Opinion Favorable
Source: PIPA/KN October 2003.

who relied upon PBS or NPR and planned to vote for the Democratic nominee who held to a mistaken belief.[42]

One redeeming element of this study of misinformation is that those who said they followed the news very closely had fewer mistakes than those who said that they did not. The media might not be perfect, but at least those who said they spent more time with it did better. But there was one exception to this statement: Fox News. Viewers of the cable station who reported that they followed the news closely were actually *more* likely to believe in one or more of the misperceptions. For example, in the Fox audience, among those who said that they were not following the news closely, 42 percent thought that there was clear evidence of a link between Saddam Hussein and al Qaeda. But among those who said that they followed the news very closely, that figure increased to 80 percent.

A National Teachable Moment?

Has Iraq provided a national "teachable moment" about the functioning of government and nature of war? As the war began, Emporia,

Kansas, seemed to provide a model civic forum. The Kiwanis Club discussed the news with a retired intelligence specialist, regulars at the Granada coffee house debated the territorial ambitions of the Kurds, a world history class at the high school reviewed the role of oil in the national economy, and the First Presbyterian Church studied the connections between the Protestant reform movement and the Middle East.[43] The town was quite patriotic. People supporting the troops bought three thousand yards of red, white, and blue ribbon from Dayton's Hobbies and Crafts Store. But local sources also reported that the flag-waving was more subdued than in the past and that educators were seeking ways to recognize the sacrifices of their soldiers without engaging in over-the-top boosterism. One school class had a moment of silence for the troops—and for the Iraqi people. The *Emporia Gazette*, one of the most famous small papers in the country, editorialized shortly after the war began, "If it turns out that there is no gas, no germs, no nuclear bomb laboratories, the United States will, at best, look foolish in the eyes of the world. At worst, America will look like an international bully that was trying to justify a war wanted for other reasons." In fact, weapons of mass destruction were never found. But did Emporia and the rest of country reach that crucial conclusion? Did the public see and absorb the information necessary to sustain the process of becoming more peaceful?

Any assessment of the public's information base must also consider the well-organized media strategy of the Bush administration and the general failure of journalists, especially during the prewar period, to examine the truth of official claims. Indeed, given the role played by government and media, it might be unusual to expect anything other than a poorly-informed public. Nonetheless, as the costs of the war in Iraq rose, the public not only became more peaceful, it also became smarter. Along with sensitivity to war costs, Americans began to have a better appreciation of the facts. The learning curve did not include everyone. Despite the availability of new information, a significant minority continued to support the administration—and continued to believe in the original sets of "facts." Americans were becoming more peaceful and more accurate, but not perfectly so.

Figure 3.2 tracks overall job approval for President Bush between mid-2001 and January 2006, and approval of his handling of Iraq between October 2002 and January 2006.[44] Bush enjoyed a huge jump in job approval following 9/11, then a steady decline over the next seventeen months. From a high of nearly 90 percent, Bush's approval level dropped to under 60 percent by February 2003. With the onset of the war, job approval increased significantly but declined once again throughout the remainder of 2003. Following a short-term boost after the capture of Saddam Hussein at the end of the year, the pattern then reverted yet again to overall decline and fell under 50 percent in early 2004. From that point to the end of 2005, Bush suffered another 10 point drop, most of that coming toward the end of the period when the administration was hurt by its handling of Hurricane Katrina and by rising oil prices. He hit a low of 37 percent around Thanksgiving but then rebounded slightly to 42 percent approval at the end of 2005. This is about 5 points lower than his rating during the crucial 2004 spring period.

The public's rating of Bush's handling of Iraq followed a similar pattern, although it tended to be a few percentage points under overall approval. In spring 2004, only slightly more than 40 percent approved of the president's handling of Iraq. Afterward, approval continued to erode, but not dramatically so. While the potential for further erosion certainly existed, the most significant decline occurred between May 2003 and May 2004. While a majority of the public thought that the president was doing a poor job, Bush also enjoyed an important resiliency that stemmed from his conservative base. Despite information that cast the administration's rationale for war into serious doubt, and rising costs, a significant minority continued to support the administration.

Figure 3.2 also tracks polling results on the question, "Do you think the result of the war was worth the loss of American life and the other costs of attacking Iraq or not?" The overall pattern of decline matched the other two questions but at a lower level due to the explicit reference to costs. In all three cases, the sharpest drop in approval came over the first few months of 2004, a period culminating in an aborted invasion of Fallujah and the exposure of the Abu Ghraib prison scandal.

Figure 3.3 contains polling results that demonstrate a distinct public "learning curve" on the war in Iraq. The months immediately following President Bush's declaration of victory continued to show that a considerable part of the public continued to believe in the stated rationale for war. But the population then demonstrated increasing skepticism, especially by early 2004. For example, when asked, "Do you believe Iraq actually had weapons of mass destruction when the war began?" about 70 percent answered in the affirmative. A year later, only half the country believed that Iraq was guilty of one of the Bush administration's key charges. During the immediate prewar period about half the population thought that Saddam was personally involved with September 11. Over the next year, this proportion dropped to just over a third. Of particular note are the June 2005 results of a Gallup poll showing a narrow majority believing that the administration deliberately misled the public before the war.[45] This was a change of more than 20 points from two

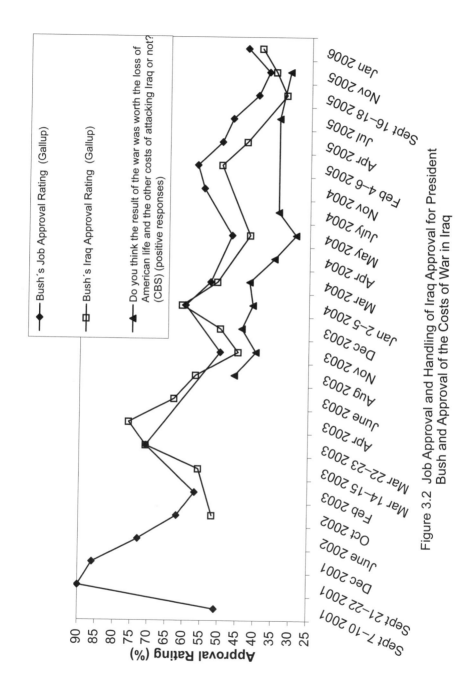

Figure 3.2 Job Approval and Handling of Iraq Approval for President
Bush and Approval of the Costs of War in Iraq

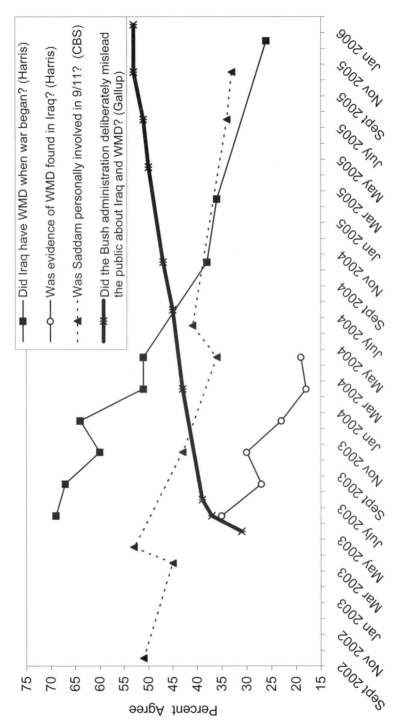

Figure 3.3 The Public's Learning Curve on the War in Iraq

years earlier, when approximately a third thought that U.S. leaders deceived the public. (In France, more than 80 percent said that U.S. and British leaders mostly lied in claiming that Iraq had weapons of mass destruction, and surveys conducted in Germany, Jordan, Turkey, Russia, Pakistan, and Morocco found those believing that U.S. political leaders lied outnumbering those believing that they were the victims of poor information by a better than three-to-one margin.) In fact, the end of 2005 found talk of impeachment entering the mainstream political arena, especially following the news that President Bush had wiretapped American citizens without judicial approval.

The information base possessed by the public and the processes by which Americans are becoming more peaceful are closely in-tertwined. The more accurate the information held by individual members of the public, the more likely they are to disagree with the policies of the Bush administration. Over time, more Americans have become able to pass the information exam, a process that sustains the tendency to become more peaceful. At the same time, some continue to fail the test. Why?

From the standpoint of developing stronger Type I and Type II opposition, the prospect of a national "teach-in" seems especially appealing. Standard professorial messages—read a good newspaper every day, listen to NPR while driving, consult different sources of information on the Internet —seem appropriate. But where and how one learns is not always easy to predict. The movement of facts from a source of information to the cognitive process in which an indi-vidual readjusts his or her construction of reality often requires an atmosphere of social or personal urgency. Changing one's mind is a challenge and there are many forms of resistance to the process. Some will continue to ignore the "inconvenient" facts.

Consider a recent, fascinating study that considered the perceived truth of certain incidents that the media said occurred during the Iraq war. Respondents from three countries—Germany, Australia, and the United States—were asked if the incidents actually took place.[46] Some of the stories were actually true, such as the killing of several women and children in a van as it approached a Bagh-dad checkpoint. Others were originally presented as true but then retracted by authorities as erroneous. An example was the civil-ian uprising in Basra against Saddam's rule in the early stages of the war. Both stories were initially covered by the news media but military officials later called the second false. There was no civilian uprising in Basra.

After being asked if the stories were true or false, those taking part in the study were asked if they thought that the story had been retracted after its initial publication. Germans and Australians tended to respond "logically": those that knew that a story had been called erroneous were more likely to think that the original event did not take pace. They no longer believed in stories that they later knew had been reported in error. Americans, however, responded differently. Once they heard of an incident in the war, they were more likely to think that it was true. Even those who remembered that the story had been retracted continued to think that the original story was true. In contrast to Germans and Australians, Americans were more likely to believe that civilians in Basra rose up against Saddam even though they had also heard subsequent reports saying that the incident did not take place. They continued to believe in the story even when they were aware of a retraction.

Are Germans and Australians smarter than Americans? There might be an argument in some quarters, but at the end of the day the answer is "probably not." The national differences are explained better by their respective political contexts, especially by the tendency of the non-U.S. publics to be skeptical of the overall case for war and by the inclination of American respondents to be more supportive. (The survey was conducted in May 2003, when most of the U.S. public still approved of military force in Iraq.) Each group "remembered" in ways that sustained its beliefs. The authors argue that "by the time they receive a retraction, the original misinformation has become an integral part of that mental model, or world view, and disregarding it would leave the world view in shambles." Facts are assembled by individuals in ways that are consistent with their own understanding of how the world works. Using information to change one's mind on basic issues is not easy. The study concludes, "People continue to rely on misinformation even if they demonstrably remember and understand a subsequent retraction."

Now let's go back to the question of why a considerable minority of the U.S. public continued to believe in specific claims that had been advanced by the Bush administration despite the appearance of so much information that called the veracity of these claims into question. Eighteen months after the start of the war, many had changed their minds and now recognized that the case for war was flawed. But many did not. What was remarkable was how strongly these perceptions were correlated with political affiliation. In a survey conducted in October 2004, after the release of the reports of the 9/11 Commission and the Iraq Survey Group that rejected the factual claims of the administration, almost three out of four Bush supporters continued to believe that Iraq had either actual WMD or a major program to produce them. Only one out of four respondents planning to vote for Democratic nominee John Kerry thought so.

Similar partisan results were found for perceptions of Saddam's alleged support for al Qaeda. A majority of Bush supporters thought that the United States should not have gone to war if intelligence concluded that Iraq did not have WMD or had not provided support to al Qaeda. But they thought that Iraq did have a WMD program and that there was a terror connection. "To support the president and to accept that he took the U.S. to war based on mistaken assumptions," said political psychologist Steven Kull, "likely creates substantial cognitive dissonance and leads Bush supporters to suppress awareness of unsettling information about pre-war Iraq."[47] Facts that challenge power can be difficult to accept because they seem to be inviting disloyalty or an uncomfortable judgment that the president must be deceptive. Another distressing conclusion is that the loss of the country's soldiers was actually unnecessary.

Prior to the war in Iraq, evidence that undermined the White House case was available but also overwhelmed by social constructions created by powerful individuals and legitimated by the media. Those who were already part of Type I opposition had no trouble finding facts that supported their case. As the war progressed and costs started to mount, new information became available and the public started to show a learning curve on issues that were central to the administration's case. The slope of that curve became steeper during dramatic incidents, such as the news of the abuse and torture at Abu Ghraib. Many did change their minds. At the same time, there have been limits to the transformation process. The public is not "dumb." The limited knowledge base is better explained by the behavior of two politically powerful institutions, the executive branch and the media, by the virtual absence of mainstream opposition, and by more private habits of mind exhibited by individuals for whom acceptance of more critical information would deeply challenge assumptions about the motivations of their country and president.

Chapter 4

Managing the Media

In August 1965, Morley Safer, then a thirty-five-year-old reporter for CBS News, accompanied a unit of U.S. Marines on a search-and-destroy mission to the Vietnamese village of Cam Ne.[1] A few weeks before, the military had been given the responsibility of taking offensive actions against the Vietnamese revolutionary forces and now Safer wanted a televised account of how well the troops performed in the field. After leaving their base in Danang, a marine lieutenant told Safer, "We've been taking fire every time we go by [that village] and the gook head honcho in these parts told us to go teach them a lesson." The soldiers entered Cam Ne and, using cigarette lighters and a flamethrower, proceeded to burn down 150 houses, wound three women, kill one child, and take four old men prisoner. Safer and his Vietnamese film crew caught it all on film. The military's later report claimed that the only structures damaged by U.S. troops in Cam Ne were "fortified Vietcong bunkers from which the marines received fire. Others ... were damaged by accident in the course of heated battle." But according to Safer's account, no pitched battle had taken place. The only death had been that of the village boy and not a single weapon had been uncovered. Safer later discovered that the province chief (the "gook head honcho") had wanted the village destroyed because the locals were refusing to pay the taxes that provided a portion of his personal income.

After a heated debate among CBS officials, Safer's film was shown on *The Evening News with Walter Cronkite.* The government's reaction to the footage was immediate and from the very top. "Frank," President Lyndon Johnson asked CBS president Frank Stanton early the next morning, "are you trying to fuck me?" Stanton had been awakened by the phone's ringing and didn't immediately recognize the caller. "Who is this?" he asked. "Frank, this is your president," came the reply, "and yesterday your boys shat on the American flag." The Pentagon was also furious because Safer's story challenged its own reports of many more enemy dead from the operation and of the ability of U.S. troops to distinguish the Vietcong from the local population. One of the marines whom Safer interviewed said that he had no doubts about burning the village. "You can't do your job and feel pity for these people," he told the correspondent.[2] The Marine Corps later claimed that the footage was a fake staged in a vacated village, and that the Zippo lighter used to set the roofs on fire had actually been borrowed and used by Safer himself. But Safer's images of soldiers setting roofs on fire became an icon for U.S. conduct in Vietnam, both among the troops, who now referred to the practice as "to Zippo a village," and in Hollywood, where setting a village on fire, as in Oliver Stone's *Platoon*, became de rigueur. Televised accounts of the battlefield had introduced more critical, disturbing, and unpredictable elements to the coverage of the Vietnam War.

Until Safer's account, the U.S. media had been a reliable partner in their government's military intervention in Vietnam. Consider the 1964 Gulf of Tonkin incident in which North Vietnamese patrol boats were said to have fired upon U.S. destroyers, an action that in turn prompted the passage of a congressional resolution that gave President Johnson the legal right to use military force in Indochina. Stanley Karnow summarizes the media's account of the incident:

> The American press published vivid eyewitness accounts of the incident, dramatized by news editors with inspiration from Pentagon officials. As "the night glowed eerily," wrote *Time*, the Communist "intruders boldly sped" toward the destroyers, firing with "automatic weapons," while *Life* had the American ships "under continuous torpedo attack" as they "weaved through the night sea, evading more torpedoes." Not to be outdone, *Newsweek* described "U.S. jets diving, strafing, flattening out . . . and diving again" at the enemy boats, one of which "burst into flames and sank." Now, having won the battle, *Newsweek* concluded, "it was time for American might to strike back."[3]

All of this was quite dramatic and interesting except for the fact that this attack never took place. The partnership between the press and the government that lay behind the falsified account of the battle was the only real element of the description. In the midst of the cold war, the press saw its first obligation as remaining loyal to Washington's policies. Vietnam would change that.

The Johnson administration feared—correctly, it would turn out—that televised reports showing less-than-honorable behavior on the part of the troops, or even the fundamental chaos of the battlefield, would undermine support for the war. But public reactions to Safer's Cam Ne story and to other examples of what became known as "the living room war" were neither simple nor straightforward. Many watched in fascination and increasing dismay. But other viewers thought it inappropriate to place the striking footage on the air. The CBS switchboard was flooded by calls arguing that Safer's story should never have been shown. Similarly, when Ronald Haeberle later published his devastating pictures of the 1968 My Lai massacre in the *Cleveland Plain Dealer*, some readers phoned in to protest the decision to carry them in the newspaper. Senator Peter Dominick (R-Colo.) claimed that the My Lai massacre was based on "unverified photographs" and argued that showing them did not serve a "public need to know." One implication, which carries through to current war coverage, is that authentic descriptions of the battlefield prompt visceral reactions. Much of the public will be dismayed by this vision, thus contributing to Type II opposition. But some of the public will prefer to avert their gaze so that they do not see at all.

Meanwhile, the Pentagon was thoroughly worried about the impact of the Cam Ne story and tried to prevent the recurrence of similar efforts. At first, the administration claimed that Safer was a communist and a KGB agent, but an internal investigation, which included reports from the Royal Canadian Mounted Police because the reporter was a Canadian, eventually showed that this was not the case. President Johnson, disappointed that the charge of left-wing treason could not be substantiated, had to satisfy himself with his initial assessment that a patriotic citizen could not have filed the Cam Ne story. "I knew that he was not an American," Johnson told one of his subordinates after being informed of Safer's nationality.

By 1968, a significant number of press and television reporters had become skeptical of the administration's optimistic claim that they were winning the war. During the Tet Offensive, Walter Cronkite, the undisputed dean of U.S. journalists, visited Vietnam and filed an influential assessment of the military's failure to make significant progress. Cronkite's report focused on the accuracy of government claims of a high Vietnamese "body count":

> The very preciseness of the figures brings them under suspicion. Anyone who has wandered through these ruins knows that an exact

count is impossible. Why, just a short while ago a little old man came and told us that two VC [Vietcong] were buried in a hastily dug grave up at the end of the block. Had they been counted? And what about these ruins? Have they gone through all of them for buried civilians and soldiers? And what about those 14 VC we found in the courtyard behind the post office at Hue? Had they been counted and tabulated? They certainly hadn't been buried....

We'd like to sum up our findings in Vietnam, an analysis that must be speculative, personal, subjective. Who won and who lost in the great Tet Offensive against the cities? I'm not sure....

To say that we are closer to victory today is to believe, in the face of the evidence, the optimists who have been wrong in the past. To suggest that we are on the edge of defeat is to yield to unreasonable pessimism. To say that we are mired in stalemate seems to be the realistic, yet unsatisfactory, conclusion.[4]

President Johnson later lamented, "If I've lost Cronkite, I've lost the country."

The contingent of journalists covering Vietnam never questioned the original anticommunist commitment that lay behind the intervention. Almost all were initially in favor of the war and very much wanted the United States to prevail. Walter Cronkite had visited Vietnam in July/August 1965 and reported that he was "impressed with our effort." ABC commentator Howard K. Smith concluded a July 1966 broadcast with the following assessment: "It's a good thing that we are doing." And Chet Huntley of NBC insisted in February 1966 that "there is no alternative in Vietnam to fighting it out."[5] Even as skepticism grew, the critique offered by mainstream journalists remained limited. Most importantly, they failed to provide the historical background that would have helped the public understand the popular appeal of the Vietnamese revolutionary forces. Instead, the movement remained faceless and mysterious, a classic example of the inscrutable Other. Nor did reporters raise fundamental questions such as the reasons for the corruption of Washington's Saigon allies, or why the task of getting the Saigon army to fight effectively was virtually hopeless. Instead, they wrote that they could not detect the same "light at the end of the tunnel" that Johnson and his advisers claimed to be seeing and that the combination of air strikes in South Vietnam, search-and-destroy missions, and sustained bombing of North Vietnam were not winning the war of attrition. At home, by showing only its more bizarre face and militant tactics, the press also distorted and helped undermine the message of the burgeoning antiwar movement.

Despite these limitations, by 1968, coverage of the Vietnam War had departed from what the government wanted the public to read and see in two significant ways: first, an increasing number of reports argued that the war was a costly stalemate; and second, disconcerting battlefield visuals began to appear on television with greater regularity. During the period immediately prior to the Tet Offensive, 22 percent of television footage was of actual combat, and 24 percent contained shots of dead or wounded.[6] The appearance of casualties contributed to growing public unease that the Pentagon was not making significant progress in its fight against the Vietnamese popular forces. Media opposition did not contain a reasoned and consistent critique of the government's intentions and strategy.[7] Nonetheless, the presentation of the chaos, uncertainty, and cost that surrounded the U.S. effort helped undermine public legitimacy in the war.

As the war wound down and defeat seemed unavoidable, conservatives began to hold journalists responsible for losing the war. One major retrospective on the Tet Offensive held television largely responsible for turning "a military victory into a political defeat."[8] In this view, journalists were panicked by the surge of the revolutionary forces during Tet and misread intensified fighting in the cities of South Vietnam as a victory for the National Liberation Front (NLF) and Hanoi rather than a major but ultimately fatal last gasp. Conservatives argued that journalists failed to realize that Tet was Vietnam's "Battle of the Bulge." Reporters had behaved irresponsibly and helped create an unwarranted shift in public opinion against the war. The result was a two-sided defeat for the United States: first on the battlefield, and second in the creation of a "Vietnam syndrome" that limited public approval of soldiers in overseas combat. For conservatives and those wanting to restore greater freedom to use military force in the post-Vietnam political climate, reporters had become a major problem.

Many in the military agreed with this retrospective. A survey of 173 U.S. Army generals conducted after the war found 38 percent agreeing that press coverage "on the whole tended to be irresponsible and disruptive to United States' efforts in Vietnam." Another 51 percent agreed that press coverage was "uneven. Some good but many irresponsible." Only 8 percent of the army generals found the press "generally responsible and playing an important role in keeping United States informed." Television fared even more poorly. Thirty-nine percent of the generals thought that television coverage was "probably not a good thing on balance because such coverage tends to be out of context." Another 52 percent agreed with the statement that television was "not a good thing since there was a tendency to go for the sensational, which was counterproductive to the war effort." Only 4 percent said that it was "good for American people to see actual scenes of fighting about when they occurred."[9]

Media watchdog groups such as Accuracy in Media were formed to counter the alleged liberal bias of the media. Dan Rather, Cronkite's replacement as anchor at CBS News, was a particularly favored target. One of the most important but unrecognized stages in the confrontation came in the aftermath of a documentary, *The Uncounted Enemy: A Vietnam Deception,* which CBS aired in 1982. The show skewered General William Westmoreland, Johnson's commander in chief for U.S. forces in Vietnam, for grossly miscalculating the "order of battle," or size and composition of the military forces arrayed against Washington and Saigon.[10] Westmoreland, supported by outside financial and legal resources, sued CBS for defamation of character. A long and expensive legal process followed, culminating in Westmoreland's withdrawal of the suit.[11] CBS did not apologize or pay damages but did promise to withhold further distribution of *The Uncounted Enemy.* In one way, the network secured a victory by staving off a legal judgment that would have required compensation to Westmoreland. But in the aftermath, CBS became less willing to offer critical documentaries that questioned the Pentagon. Independent analyses of Rather's newscasts have showed no political difference or ideological slant that would have placed him to the left of the other two networks. CBS might have won the battle with Westmoreland but conservatives had won the media war. Henceforth, the media understood that critical coverage of the Pentagon would be a battle. In many cases, executives and editors became more timid.

Media Coverage and Potential Opposition after Vietnam

After Vietnam, U.S. leaders became more worried about public attitudes toward the use of military force and many recognized the need for a more effective media strategy. Their first choice was to impose stricter control over the movement of journalists. Washington could no longer afford to let reporters run around the battlefield, going wherever they wanted and speaking to whomever they pleased. Guidelines had to be developed that could more effectively govern the queries, tone, and even very presence of reporters. Potentially critical questions, even if limited to pragmatic issues such as the pace and timing of victory or the actual performance of the troops and their equipment, had to be avoided if at all possible. In two 1980s operations, Grenada and Panama, and in the first Gulf War, the Pentagon organized journalists into small "pools" or teams with either no or only tightly controlled access to the battlefield. CNN's dramatic broadcasts from downtown Baghdad in the midst of Operation Desert Storm were considered subversive and unpatriotic by the Department of Defense, but not because the cable network actually criticized Washington's policy. It was the images of U.S. aircraft bombing a major city that by themselves were so unsettling. The audio track alone ran counter to the administration's preference for its own soundless footage of smart bombs unerringly guided to their military targets.

At the same time, Washington was unable to fully control the media. The increasingly critical coverage of the Vietnam conflict and the post-Watergate boost to investigative reporting left influential models of professional conduct—even as the industry often failed to measure up to its potential for critical reporting. Some journalists complained about the pool system used during the Gulf War and tried to strike out on their own. After the war, still more said that they would not, in future situations, submit to such close supervision.[12] The most astute media managers within the Pentagon recognized that censorship and other efforts to control the media directly were more likely to incite criticism and they sought other strategies to avoid negative coverage.

The potential of disturbing battlefield images and accurate pessimistic reporting to erode public support is one of the most important ways that conditional war carries an underlying tendency to become "like Vietnam." Administration officials will try to manage the public face of the battle and leverage their influence to prevent coverage that is likely to evoke Type II sensitivities to the costs of war. But the media cannot be fully manipulated. Indeed, the widespread availability of information and opinion is one of the key features of contemporary Type I opposition. War managers can do little to stop the diverse flow of reports and pictures from conflict areas to antiwar Internet sites and to home computers. But even more conventional professional media norms can burst the protective bubble of the sanitized presentation of war. Despite its many limitations, media coverage can frame war so that it appears like "another Vietnam." Both Type I and Type II opposition build on pessimism, chaos, the appearance of casualties, and exposure of the "credibility gap" between the statements of government officials and realities on the ground. Media management of the demands of conditional war substitutes for direct censorship and the unfiltered battlefield. Overt control will produce media and public opposition. But a Vietnam-evoking "living room war" also runs the risk that public support will erode. The Pentagon has preferred two replacements: first, a human-interest focus on the soldiers themselves; and second, the development of "embedded reporting" that seems to show combat but does so only through a lens that makes for coverage that is significantly different from that in Vietnam. Before examining each of these replacements, we will take a broader look at recent changes in the media industry to help measure the potential of Americans to become more peaceful.

Structure and Organization of the Industry

In a strong democracy, independent reporting contributes to a system of checks and balances that prevents a concentration of power. Journalistic detachment and scrutiny provide a constant review of claims made by government officials and contribute to a healthy debate over the motives, strategy, and abilities of those in charge. Good reporting helps the public to consider other policy alternatives—or at least provides the information so people can make their own assessment of the wisdom and effectiveness of existing policies. But how well has this system of checks and balances actually functioned?

In many ways, the newspaper and television industries have failed to meet the standard of independent investigators. On one level, they are themselves part of the structure of wealth and power and are restricted in the depth of their criticism by self-interest. The recent wave of media conglomeration and integration promotes homogenization in news coverage. Sustained critical coverage of controversial issues might prompt corporations to pull their advertising, thereby leading to a significant decline in revenue. Owners expect to make money and cutting costs can limit the size and priorities of the professional staff. A consistently skeptical stance can also make it difficult to have access to the sources investigative reporters need to do their job. As of January 2004, for example, President Bush had given interviews with ABC's Diane Sawyer, CBS's Scott Pelley, NBC's Tom Brokaw, and Brit Hume of Fox News. Yet he never agreed to meet with the late Peter Jennings, who had interviewed every president since Richard Nixon. Jennings later said of the pressure from the White House to conform: "I recently did an interview on a senior figure in the Bush White House and was told in advance, 'It better be good.' Which I thought was rather naked. It wasn't a threat, but it didn't sound like a joke. There is a feeling among some members of the press corps that you are either favored by the Administration or not, and that will have something to do with your access."[13]

Similarly, the White House was angered by a prewar article by *Washington Post* reporter Dana Milbank that appeared under the headline "For Bush, Facts Are Malleable." The story began:

President Bush, speaking to the nation this month about the need to challenge Saddam Hussein, warned that Iraq has a growing fleet of unmanned aircraft that could be used "for missions targeting the United States."

Last month, asked if there were new and conclusive evidence of Hussein's nuclear weapons capability, Bush cited a report by the International Atomic Energy Agency saying the Iraqis were "six months away from developing a weapon." And last week, the president said objections by a labor union to having customs officials wear radiation detectors have the potential to delay the policy "for a long period of time."

All three assertions were powerful arguments for the actions Bush sought. And all three statements were dubious, if not wrong.[14]

Milbank said that after the appearance of the story, the White House tried to freeze him out and for a while stopped returning his calls. Maralee Schwartz, the *Post*'s national editor, reported that press secretary Ari Fleischer, White House communication consultant Karen Hughes, and key administration adviser Karl Rove each complained to her about Milbank and even mentioned that he might not be a suitable person for his position. Schwartz thought that when Milbank started covering the White House, "there was a lot of attitude in his copy" but that this "got detoxed in the editing process and Dana has come to understand his role better." Perhaps it was a similar fear of retaliation that enabled Bush, in his March 6, 2003, press conference, called to explain the necessity of war with Iraq, to say that Saddam Hussein "has trained and financed al Qaeda–type organizations before, al Qaeda and other terrorist organizations," and to mention September 11 and al Qaeda no less than fourteen times in fifty-two minutes, without once being challenged on the implied connection between Iraq and the attacks on the World Trade Center and the Pentagon.[15]

Together with conservative political commentary, the Bush administration has also successfully stigmatized the press by labeling it "a special interest." This has the simultaneous effect of intimidating journalists and encouraging the public to discount the more critical stories that do appear. ABC News political director Mark Halperin concludes: "It is that a President surrounded by advisers who understand that a public that perceives the media as a special interest, rather than as guardians of the public interest, can manipulate us forever and set the press schedule, access, and agenda that he wants."[16] Conservatives often stigmatize the media in the same manner. For example, MSNBC host Joe Scarborough told his viewers that "some of the most powerful media players in America don't want America to succeed in Iraq. . . . American soldiers have told me that the biggest morale challenge that they are facing is not Saddam and Osama's thugs, but, rather, it's dealing with the biased, slanted reports that they're getting from American news organizations."[17] Since Vietnam, journalists have had to work under the fear of being branded as "liberal." Avoiding their presumed bias has made it more difficult for journalists to challenge the reasoning of government officials.

Administration officials can take a punitive approach toward media outlets that publish stories that are not to their liking. On May 9, 2005, *Newsweek* ran an account of conditions in Guantánamo Bay that included the accusation that investigators had flushed a copy of the Qur'an down a toilet in front of Islamic detainees. The sensitivities violated by the desecration illustrates one of the key boundaries of conditional war, namely, that large social groups such as an entire ethnic group or a particular religion cannot be targeted. The Bush administration maintained that the story was based on a single, anonymous, and erroneous source. The magazine issued first an apology and then a retraction. Talk radio and cable television jumped on *Newsweek* for shoddy journalism. Some commentators even suggested that the editors were responsible for the deaths of U.S. soldiers. From the outcry, one might think that the mistreatment of the Qur'an never took place. The "liberal media" had become the problem rather than the interrogation practices in Guantánamo and other U.S. detention centers.

Newsweek's well-publicized mistake obscured the public's ability to recognize that U.S. interrogators did in fact often abuse Islam's holy book in front of detainees. One national security expert offered the following description of operating procedures: "Contrary to White House spin, the allegations of religious desecration at Guantánamo . . . are common among ex-prisoners and have been widely reported outside the United States. Several former detainees at the Guantánamo and Bagram airbase prisons have reported instances of their handlers sitting or standing on the Koran, throwing or kicking it in the toilets, and urinating on it."[18] A CBS story on President Bush's failure to complete his Vietnam-era military responsibilities followed a similar pattern: *60 Minutes* ran a technically flawed report that reached the correct conclusion, that Bush did not meet the time requirement as a pilot in the reserve. Four producers resigned and the resulting brouhaha distracted attention from the fact that the president of the United States had really been absent without leave from his prescribed military duties.

But coverage of events is shaped by those in power even without explicit forms of control. Most stories are developed in response to events initiated by administration officials such as speeches, interviews, background conversations, photo opportunities. Reporting is thus "indexed" so that it becomes largely a reaction to "information" provided by government sources. The Bush administration established a reputation of being extraordinarily well disciplined when it came to choosing the message that it wanted to feature, thereby establishing "a commanding auditory environment" that sets the parameters of what becomes the news. Dan Bartlett, the White House communications director, held a daily morning meeting to determine the message of the day and to make sure that the rest of the government agencies would stay on track with that message. A Pentagon public relations official later said in an interview: "We want to make sure everybody's working off the same page of music, as far as what the sort of breaking stories are. It's a kind of an information-sharing thing that allows people to touch base with each other every day. We want to make sure that everybody is in step with one another in terms of what they're trying to get done in the world of communications. If nothing else it's a mnemonic of what all everybody's doing today. There's also a certain amount of, 'Here's a story that seems troublesome. Here's how we plan to handle it. What do you guys think?'"

Through the Office of Global Communication, this message was also coordinated with Alastair Campbell, then Bartlett's counterpart in the UK. Throughout 2003, Bartlett and Karl Rove cochaired a twice-weekly "message meeting" to review Bush's schedule and determine what they planned to say in the opportunities that lay ahead. The success of the public relations staff in determining the focus of the news was reflected in one study that found that of the 414 stories on Iraq broadcast on NBC, ABC, and CBS from September 2002 until the following February, all but 34 originated at the White House, State Department, or Pentagon.[19] Indexing may also make it difficult for reporters to raise issues that are not being discussed by officials. For example, very few prewar stories explored questions of what "postwar" Iraq might look like. Officials didn't talk about it, so reporters didn't write about it. Since stories were constructed around government sources, the dominant frame became "liberation" rather than "occupation."[20] And yet it has been the aftermath of the declaration of "victory" that has proved to be the most troubling.

Newspaper readers tend to be better informed than people who rely on other sources of information, yet the Newspaper Association of America has found circulation dropping significantly, especially after September 11. Daily circulation figures for the six months ending in March 2005 fell by 1.9 percent and Sunday circulation by 2.5 percent. Sunday circulation fell by 2 percent at the *Boston Globe*, 4.7 percent at the *Chicago Tribune*, and 7.9 percent at the *Los Angeles Times*. Even the *Washington Post* reported a 5.2 percent decline over the previous two years.[21] There are several reasons for declining readership, including the rise of cable outlets, Internet news sites, "blogging," and the dramatic increase in giveaway dailies.[22]

Letter writing to newspaper editors also tends to be a forum favored by Type I opposition while many radio talk shows are largely conservative. A sampling of ten papers of various sizes and locations conducted by the *Columbia Journalism Review* found at least twice as many antiwar as pro-war letter writers.[23] Individuals who called, e-mailed, or wrote their congressional representative also tended to be more anti- than pro-war. In September 2002, the national news radio show *Democracy Now!* conducted an informal survey of Republican and Democratic senators and found consistently strong opposition to going to war with Iraq. Even the staff of Senator Jesse Helms (D-N.C.) reported a majority against the war resolution.[24] Similarly, Representative Robert Filner (D-Calif.) told a meeting of the Peace and Justice Studies Association at Georgetown University, "I know of no congressman whose calls are running less than ten-to-one in opposition to the resolution [on the forthcoming war with Iraq]."[25]

More of the public has turned toward television, which has changed in many ways since Vietnam. Technology has enabled the dissemination of footage more quickly, easily, and cheaply. Sound, lighting, and editing have all gone through major transformations. Some of these changes have made it possible to better manage the space between the audience and war so that many viewers think and feel that they are close to a "real" battlefield. Coverage of Vietnam now appears clumsy: heavy cameras and dependence on exposed film, which had to be transported to the relatively few places where permanent satellite hookups had been installed. A relatively quick transmission between Vietnam and a network facility in New York City still took more than twenty-four hours. Now battlefield images, even at night, can be brought to viewers in real time. The new tools include lightweight cameras, digitized video, specialized thermal cameras, and robotic cameras, all with transmitters for immediate interface with satellites and network studios. Technology has brought virtual graphics of the battlefield, split screens, news crawlers, stock quotations, and station logos. Some of this information could be organized and presented to provide a stronger sense of the history behind military intervention and thus be of enormous benefit to the viewer. Instead, audiences for Iraq war coverage saw "up close and personal" encounters with individual soldiers, technical razzle-dazzle, waving flags on the bottom of the screen, and mandatory flag pins on news anchors' lapels.

Production values have been introduced that are more consistent with entertainment than with in-depth news coverage. The proliferation of young news executives who started their careers in other divisions of television and public relations has contributed to the blurring of the boundary between news and entertainment. The management of war's public face extends to the recent development of "reality television" programs, such as *Profiles from the Front Line,* that focus on the daily life of ordinary soldiers. More-traditional executives at ABC's news division complained that it was inappropriate for entertainment producers to make a documentary series on such a crucial subject but were rebuffed by the network's holding company, Walt Disney Productions. Other examples of "militainment" include *American Fighter Pilot* and *Military Diaries,* the latter produced for music channel VH1 and focusing on the musical tastes of the soldiers on the front line. Producer RJ Cutler handed out eighty digital cameras to military personnel who interviewed each other and recorded their own preferences. "Anytime you can put a human face on a soldier or a sailor or a marine," Cutler said, "I guess that is to the benefit of the Department of Defense."[26]

Some correspondents are well informed and would prefer more in-depth features. But they may be shunted to the sidelines by the emphasis on attention-grabbing immediacy. The result is a sometimes appalling lack of expertise. Michael Massing gives an example following a visit to the Coalition Media Center in Qatar:

> A correspondent for the *Los Angeles Times* told me of a gung-ho colleague who, embedded with a Marine unit that was racing toward Baghdad, excitedly declared over the phone, "We're about to cross the Ganges!" When told that he must mean the Tigris, he said "Yeah, one of those biblical rivers or other." When I mentioned to a reporter for *USA Today* how hard it seemed to cover the Middle East without much experience in the region, she was dismissive. "You can read one book, like *God Has Ninety-Nine Names,* and figure out what's going on here," she said, referring to the 1996 book by Judith Miller. "You can talk to any cabdriver and he'll tell you everything you need to know." As it happens, most of the cabdrivers in Doha are from India and Pakistan.[27]

The media's recent presentation of war also includes careful attention to background music. Even before the 2003 war in Iraq began, Fox News put together a CD called *Liberation Iraq Music* for its anticipated coverage. Fox News manager Richard O'Brien said, "I put in more tom-tom drums because they had more urgency. I wanted it to sound like, I don't want to say war drums, but ... "[28] Bob Israel, who created most of the music on ABC News including that for *ABC World News Tonight with Peter Jennings,* noted that the business of making sound tracks for war "sounds a little crass, but that's what you have to do in this business to be prepared." One commentator noted that CBS introduced "Dan Rather to an aggressive drumbeat with a reverberating bass guitar. The music on cable news channels had all the tone of crisis. On MSNBC, nerve-wracking strings, drums, and tolling bells ushered in war updates every fifteen minutes. CNN's theme was nearly identical to MSNBC's minus the bells."[29]

Other changes include the emergence of all-news cable stations that have cut into the ratings of the three major networks. During the Vietnam War, approximately 60 percent of the country watched the evening news on CBS, NBC, or ABC. By the 1990–1991 Gulf War, that number had been cut in half. Over the next decade, ratings were cut in half again so that the total audience for the three former giants is now only between 11 and 16 percent of the total audience.[30] In 1991, the public listed newspapers as the most frequently cited source of information about public affairs (slightly over 40 percent). By the start of military action in Afghanistan in the fall of 2001, cable TV news was the source most often mentioned (over 50 percent). The Internet has often been mentioned as a possible substitute source of information, but according to a survey conducted by the Pew Research Center, of those with Web access, 87 percent still received most of their news about the war from television.[31]

Cable news stations rely on crises to attract viewers, improve ratings, and raise advertising revenues. In this regard, war is the best crisis of all. Before September 11, 2001, the combined audience for CNN, Fox News Channel, and MSNBC averaged less than 0.4 percent of American adults, or about 800,000 people. For the rest of September, the viewing audience more than tripled, to 2.7 million, and then gradually declined. Yet in March 2002, the audience for these outlets remained over 1.5 million, more than twice the level prior to the attacks. This figure may seem small but the number of people who at some point during a day tune in to cable news has grown exponentially. Those who watched at least fifteen minutes of programming at one point during November 2001 totaled 93.4 million for CNN and 58.5 million for Fox (together, 75 percent of American adults).[32] (Fox first passed CNN in early 2002 and now usually has a larger audience share.)

At the immediate outbreak of war, networks and cable stations often provide constant coverage with no commercials, and they may experience initial losses. In 1991, NBC lost between $3.5 million and $4 million for each of the first three nights of the Gulf War. Advertising losses for the three networks came to $25 million a day compared to the $3 million a day they spent on reporting the war.[33] For the start of the 2003 war with Iraq, CNN budgeted $25 million to $30 million; its estimated cost of covering the conflict was $1 million a day. These expenses are not as large as they seem since newsrooms do not have to cover other stories, and the shows preempted by the war can be shown later, thus lowering future production costs. Costs for covering the war represent a tiny fraction of the revenue of the large companies that now own the networks. For example, the entire cost of NBC News is less than one-half of 1 percent of the $132 billion in annual sales of its owner, General Electric. Furthermore, substantial war coverage can help a company turn a profit. CNN was able to use the reputation it gained during the Gulf War to move its news operation into the black.

The move from newspapers to television and, within television, from the more traditional news divisions of the original three networks to less informative cable, has not nurtured the critical faculties of the American public. News programming on CNN, Fox, and MSNBC is often structured around a small number of "headline" stories and interviews rather than "hard" reporting. For example, in 2001 less than one-third of the public knew that the Republican Party had a majority in the House of Representatives, and less than 20 percent stated correctly that the federal government was running a deficit for the year. Yet that November, 90 percent knew that inhaled anthrax was more dangerous and more difficult to treat medically than cutaneous anthrax.[34]

The particular way that television chooses "guests" and "experts" also limits the range of views that the public is able to consider. One media advocacy group studied the background of experts who appeared on network newscasts during the two weeks surrounding Secretary of State Colin Powell's February 5, 2003, presentation at the United Nations and found that more than two-thirds were from the United States. Of these, 75 percent were either current or former government or military officials. Within this group, only one (Senator Edward Kennedy [D-Mass.]) expressed strong skepticism about the forthcoming war in Iraq. Typically, social movement opposition was marginalized in these telecasts with only one U.S. source coming from an antiwar organization (Physicians for Social Responsibility). Overall, only 17 percent of the total sources, both U.S. and non-U.S., took positions that were skeptical or critical toward Washington's policies.

Another survey of guests who appeared on six networks during the three weeks after the war started found that "nearly two-thirds of all sources, 64 percent, were pro-war, while 72 percent of U.S. guests favored the war. Antiwar voices were 10 percent of all sources, but just 6 percent of non-Iraqi sources and only 3 percent of U.S. sources. Thus viewers were more than six times as likely to see a pro-war source as one who was anti-war; counting only U.S. guests, the ratio increases to 25 to 1."[35]

Another example of marginalization of explicitly antiwar voices was provided by the *New York Times,* which consistently downplayed the size of large demonstrations before and during the war in Iraq. For example, the *Times* initially reported that "thousands" attended the October 26, 2002, march on Washington. The paper stated that the turnout was well below organizers' expectations. But the *Times* never spoke to the organizers about their expectations. The police estimated the actual turnout at one hundred thousand while the organizers placed it at two hundred thousand. In a rare about-face, made in response to a flood of e-mails and telephone calls, the *Times* published on October 30 a second and much more favorable article, which included the higher estimates of those attending the rally.[36]

Finally, the Bush administration took a more direct approach by trying to incorporate many media functions within its own ranks. One facet of this effort was an attempt to sell a more favorable image of the United States to the Middle East. After 9/11, the Office of Global Communications was established, in part to disseminate favorable information to Arabic-speaking audiences. The office funded radio stations, videos for television, and three hundred thousand copies of a pamphlet, eventually published in ten languages, titled *Muslim Life in America.* The first cover showed a picture of Muslim children happily playing on a swing set. Plans were announced for a Middle East Television Network, which planned to utilize the "production values of American news" to dispel misinformation about the United States. *Hi* magazine, subsidized by the State Department and selling across the Middle East for $2 an issue, focused on the similarities between American and Middle Eastern cultures with articles targeted to eighteen- to thirty-five-year-olds. Advertising executive Charlotte Beers was brought to the State Department and tried to promote U.S. policy as a positive "brand" but ended up leaving office after seventeen months when her efforts prompted as much ridicule as progress.[37] Surveys found that the department's $15 million public relations campaign about Muslims in the United States had failed to change Arab opinion significantly. In 2005, Karen Hughes, a communications expert in Bush's White House, was appointed to a new position in public diplomacy, but her "charm offensive" in the Muslim world was marred by a series of missteps and false statements. Favorability ratings of the United States in the region generally dropped into the single digits after the start of the Iraq war. In yet another overture, an Office of Strategic Influence was created within the Pentagon, which, according to the *New York Times,* was "developing plans to provide news items, possibly even false ones, to foreign media organizations" in an effort "to influence public sentiment and policy makers in both friendly and unfriendly countries."[38] Following a wave of negative reaction, the Office of Strategic Influence was soon officially closed. Yet the policy of creating an "in-house" media apparatus continued.

In 2005, it was revealed that a hitherto unknown public relations company called the Lincoln Group had a $6 million contract with the Pentagon to do public relations work in Iraq and to plant stories in that country's media that showed the U.S. effort in a favorable light. Under the program sympathetic Iraqi journalists were paid to write articles and then newspapers were paid to publish those articles. U.S. officials defended the "function of buying advertising and opinion/editorial space" as "customary in Iraq." Besides, they said, the stories "told the truth."[39] Others, including the chairman of the Senate Armed Services Committee, expressed concern that the arrangement might contradict professional journalistic norms at the very time that the State Department said that one of its goals in Iraq was to promote independent media. The work of the Lincoln Group also included a multimillion-dollar campaign to influence Sunni voters before the October 2005 national referendum.[40] The Rendon Group, yet another public relations firm, received more than $100 million in contracts from the Defense Department and has been involved on many fronts, including the creation of the Iraqi National Congress, preparation of stories of grateful Kuwaitis mailing twenty thousand valentines to American troops during the 1991 Gulf crisis, and the passing of "evidence" to Judith Miller of the *New York Times* and others to promote the case for Iraq's possession of weapons of mass destruction. After Secretary of Defense Donald Rumsfeld authorized the Pentagon to engage in "military deception," or planting false stories on the Internet, president John Rendon called himself an "information warrior and a perception manager."[41]

Embedded Reporting

Taken together, changes in the media industry and the attitude of the U.S. government toward it have weakened the quality of democracy. Even journalists who view their job as subjecting government officials to critical review must swim against the economic, political, and technical currents that prevail in the industry. Nonetheless, the possibility that the media can play an important role in undermining public support for conditional war continues to exist. The communication of war damages carries the potential to turn war into "another Vietnam" in which neither the media nor the public remain supportive. Embedded reporting became another way of covering war without showing the costs that could deepen opposition.

During the first stages of the war in Afghanistan, the Pentagon organized the press into a small number of tightly controlled press pools. There were few firsthand reports from the principal combat areas and the main news of the operation came from Secretary of Defense Donald Rumsfeld and U.S. Central Command (CENTCOM) commander Tommy Franks rather than from journalists themselves. Reporters often had a difficult time confirming or investigating specific statements offered by U.S. officials about controversial incidents such as the mistaken strikes by U.S. aircraft against Special Forces, Afghan allies, and civilians. The behavior of the Northern Alliance and other fighting units whose leaders had been bribed or otherwise induced to fight for the U.S. were also difficult to monitor, particularly when they, like the Taliban, were also accused of significant human rights abuses. Mainstream journalists largely played along. CNN, for example, required its anchors to add to any story on civilian casualties in Afghanistan that the U.S. bombings were in response to September 11, 2001. Executive Walter Isaacson told his staff that it was "perverse to focus too much on the casualties or hardship in Afghanistan."[42] The press also complied with government requests not to run an interview with Taliban leader Mullah Mohammad Omar or taped messages from Osama bin Laden. In Afghanistan, as in previous military operations in the Persian Gulf, Grenada, and Panama, the Pentagon tried to control the movement and vision of journalists as completely as possible.

But the structure of war reporting changed significantly during Operation Iraqi Freedom, where the Bush administration followed a far more sophisticated strategy. More than six hundred journalists were embedded in particular military units, and as long as they followed the rules, journalists could file reports on the war from a vantage point very close to those doing the actual fighting.[43] Assisted by lightweight, flexible technology that permitted the real-time transmittal of video and sound, embedded reporters provided footage that was extensively aired by television networks during the war. Afterward, both the media and the Department of Defense expressed pleasure at the arrangement. Reporters liked the access to the front lines and the feeling of being able to offer firsthand reporting. Many felt that their live reports were an effective way of preventing government censorship. Government officials discovered that they could enjoy more sympathetic reporting from those who thought they were independent than from those who thought they were being controlled. Embedded reporters offered a particular kind of credibility that government officials were not able to provide themselves. Postwar reports indicated that the placement of journalists among troops might become official Pentagon policy for future combat operations.[44]

Why did the Bush administration and the Pentagon like embedded reporting so much? First, they thought that journalists would be able to make a better case for their policies than they could make themselves. As stated by Victoria Clarke, assistant secretary of defense for public affairs, shortly after President Bush announced that the mission in Iraq had been accomplished:

> I knew with great certainty if we went to war, the Iraqi regime would be doing some terrible things and would be incredibly masterful with the lies and the deception. And I could stand up there at that podium and Secretary Rumsfeld could stand up there and say very truthfully the Iraqi regime is putting its soldiers in civilian clothing so they can ambush our soldiers. Some people would believe us and some people wouldn't. But we had hundreds and hundreds of credible, independent journalists saying the Iraqi regime is putting their soldiers in civilian clothing.[45]

The Pentagon also thought that journalists were in a good position to praise the military's preparation and effectiveness. As one official later commented in an interview: "We know something that reporters who haven't steeped themselves in matters military don't know. We know what these kids are like. We know what their training is like. We know what their equipment is like. We know what their motivation is like and we know what kind of leadership they're getting. And as far as we're concerned it's, frankly, very creditable."

Journalists and the military often bonded in ways that made it more difficult for reporters to file critical reports. As one Pentagon official with years of public relations experience explained in an interview: "The more we know about an organization, and the more we know about the people in it, the less inclined we are to make broad generalizations. And the more inclined we are to accept the organization and the people in it as fellow human creatures." Overcoming an initial period of distance and then becoming accepted helped reporters feel that they had become members of the team, in a sense co-opting them. For example, CNN reporter Bob Franklin said that in some units embeds were initially transported on what the troops called "clown carts." Franklin then went on to say: "They would assign these young marines who would come on, and it would take about five minutes to pollute their minds. They would go from sitting there at attention to realizing that we couldn't be all that bad because we had an MP3 player going loudly and the music would be blaring as we were going down the highway. Our biggest problem was explaining to these young people who the Righteous Brothers were."[46] As another Pentagon official later explained: "I would be disingenuous if I didn't say that the embedded journalist is very likely to develop relationships with the folks in the unit and that is going to have an effect on the editorial orientation of that reporter." He went on to note in an interview:

> Occasionally, somebody attacks them and the reporter finds himself in a position where these nine people that he's working with must respond correctly and quickly with discipline in order that his life will continue. And they do and he says, "Boy, I'm glad these guys are trained, equipped, motivated, and led the way they are because that just saved my skin." It's also, of course, more difficult to be objective about the moral equivalency of the enemy and your own folks if the enemy is the guy who's shooting at you and your folks are the guys who are trying to stop them from doing that. That's just human nature.

Many embedded reporters became accepted members of a "band of brothers." As one later explained:

> The military people got to see firsthand that we weren't just a bunch of "lazy pencil necks," to use the expression, who would sit at our desks in Washington drinking coffee and reporting ignorantly. One of my proudest moments came when this Marine colonel, a John Wayne type if there ever was one, came up to this riffraff group of reporters, all dirty, none of us had bathed, we were all eating MREs [Meals Ready to Eat], all that type of thing. And he said, "You guys are like the Marines. You'll do whatever it takes to get the job done. Whatever it takes, no excuses." That was a high compliment.[47]

Journalists became completely dependent on the military for food, transportation, and a place to sleep. They were also aware that they needed the soldiers' protection if they came under fire. The two photos on the following page contain examples of the proximity of news correspondents to combat soldiers. Objectivity and critical distance are hard to come by under these circumstances, and it is understandable that reporters would try to present soldiers in the best possible light. Pictures and stories of troops providing food, medical aid, and other forms of assistance to Iraqi civilians, and even to wounded Iraqi soldiers, came easily and without the more heavy-handed official briefings at the Coalition Media Center. Embedded reporters wanted their troops to succeed. They wanted to be part of a team that was liberating Iraq.

Fox News reporter Geraldo Rivera reports from Iraq, demonstrating the opportunity to enhance celebrity status through embedded reporting (http://mac.com/mkoldys/iblog).

An embedded photojournalist gets up close and personal with a soldier in the midst of an operation (Thorne Anderson/Corbis).

Embedded reporting was also an effective way to provide a connection between soldiers and people back home. A Pentagon official later explained this personal aspect of embedded reporting in an interview: "We wanted to change the face of the war from two people standing at a podium talking about the war to the sergeant, the NCO, and the junior officer. We wanted to actually bring people up to the front, because that is where their sons and daughters were. And no one can be against their sons and daughters. You can be against the war but regardless of how you felt about the war, you had to be for the troops. So changing the face of war was very beneficial for us." The proximity of journalists to the troops helped to humanize the military and build support. A postwar panel assessing media coverage of the war provides a further example:

Mr. Nessen [Moderator]: Now you have a lot of the Knight Ridder newspapers in cities and towns with military bases.

Mr. Walcott [Washington Bureau Chief, Knight Ridder Newspapers]: Yes.

Mr. Nessen: And the families are among your readers. Did that affect your coverage at all?

Mr. Walcott: Enormously. Here in Washington, I think we tend to talk about war as if it's another policy issue. And that's not the way it looks if you live in Columbus, Georgia, or if you live outside Fort Campbell, Kentucky.

Mr. Nessen: You have papers in those cities?

Mr. Walcott: We do. War is what your Dad or your Mom or your son or your daughter or your brother or your sister is off doing and why they're not home. And one of the reasons we had so many embeds was to perform the function which other papers don't necessarily have, and that is, being the hometown paper, telling the folks back in Columbus what the 3rd Brigade or the 3rd Infantry Division is doing.

We had a young reporter from the little newspaper we own in Biloxi, Mississippi, with a marine amphibian assault unit, and he became a local celebrity because he became the main line of communication between those reservists—most of whom seem to work at Wal-Mart. Every story that came through mentioned ...
[Laughter]
... Lance Corporal So-and-so from the Wal-Mart. The Wal-Mart must have been empty in Biloxi.

Mr. Nessen: They have a lot of employees. Obviously.

Mr. Walcott: It's a big store. But that was a function that we took very, very seriously.[48]

Finally, collateral damage, or the unintended killing of civilians, was, for the new wave of Pentagon media managers, actually handled more easily when reporters were on the scene. As one experienced official later noted:

> The troops are going to make mistakes. They're going to go out there and do things which are wrong, which they regret. But there's two things going here: number one, when they do that with a reporter around, the reporter will instantly give a hopefully objective, but certainly a third party account of what happened. That means there will be no additional dimension to the story, such as how we [government representatives] tried not to let this mistake get into the public arena.
>
> The second thing is that the reporter, with any luck, will give some insights into the reasons why the mistake happened in the first place, which are almost always favorable to us because our guys don't mistakes on purpose.

Another Pentagon official showed the same confidence in the inclination of the media to manage and minimize the costs of war that they encounter:

> JOSEPH: And you weren't worried about a possible downside to embedding? I have an example here of an Australian television team who filed a report of a jumpy American military unit that killed civilians by accident.
>
> OFFICIAL: They made a mistake. And I think we should not be threatened by our mistakes because war is not a clean thing.
>
> JOSEPH: But embedded reporting, potentially, could highlight those mistakes.
>
> OFFICIAL: But that's OK. They're going to be highlighted anyway so why not have our side of the story told first because then it's out there. There's no room for people to turn it into more or less than it is. War is going to have a dark side to it, and we need to get that out there publicly.
>
> JOSEPH: But yet the war is, I would say, fairly sanitized in its presentation, despite embedded reporting.
>
> OFFICIAL: It is, but it's not by our sanitation. It's by the media choosing what they report or not. We put no restrictions on them other than they do not give away classified material.

An example of the contrast between official and embedded reporting came during the march toward Baghdad when U.S. soldiers accidentally killed women and children in a van after the vehicle approached a checkpoint and failed to stop. The CENTCOM briefing in Doha described the incident as a "by the textbook" procedure in which sentries fired shots, first in warning, then into the van's engine, and finally into the passenger compartment itself. CENTCOM said that seven were killed. But the embedded reporter, William Branigan of the *Washington Post*, described much more chaotic circumstances in which the soldiers failed to follow procedures and then blew people away as the van approached the checkpoint. The unit commander was quoted as shouting at his troops, "You just [expletive] killed a family because you didn't fire a warning shot soon enough!" Branigan also reported that ten, rather than seven, civilians died, including five young children.[49]

Now the administration might have preferred the CENTCOM version of the events. A report of alert sentries who unfortunately kill a few civilians who they, with good reason, think might be a threat is certainly a more favorable account than a story that describes sentries who are asleep at the wheel and who make a mistake that ends up killing more than a few civilians in an accident that could have been avoided. But the frustrated appeals of the commander also carry the strong message that the military is not in fact targeting civilians and troops are even anguished when an accident does happen. And if accidents will happen, better the story is told in a way that frees the military from the judgment that it carried out the act deliberately. Increasingly, the Pentagon recognizes that embedded reporters have a credibility that CENTCOM briefers often lack.

A senior officer in the Pentagon provided the following rationale of how embedded reporting helps take the edge off the military's mistakes:

OFFICIAL: With embedding there is no possibility for turning a situation into a disinformation or propaganda point of view. Let me give you an example. In Afghanistan, we took armed troops in the villages to conduct raids without an independent observer or reporter. We'd go in. We'd do it right. We'd get done what we needed to get done, and we'd pull out. Well, guess what? We ceded the information battlefield to the enemy. Because reporters would come in the village 24 hours later, and the disinformation guy or the Taliban guy would walk people around and tell stories of how the Americans abused this or that person, and how they didn't follow the rules, and how they shot people under the beds.

JOSEPH: And so if you were to do it again, you would have had embedded reporters in Afghanistan?

OFFICIAL: Clearly would have. Every time I saw a situation where we were accused of one of those situations, I sent that article to the chairman [of the Joint Chiefs of Staff]. And then I'd go in and I'd say, See, if we would have just had reporters with those guys, we wouldn't be putting up with this shit. Because it distracts you. The best way to counter disinformation is an honest, independent report from your side of the line first. Because the media see your perspective. Even when you make a mistake, for example, shooting the vehicle and killing the women and children, guess what? They report it. The bad news is out there. But they also talk about the rationale you went through to fire on that vehicle, why you made the decisions you made, and how bad you felt when you found out.

Embedded reporters did capture some significant problems. For example, on April 18, 2003, journalists with an ABC affiliate in Minneapolis–St. Paul, located with the army's 101st Airborne Division, entered a bunker and videotaped hundreds of barrels containing 377 tons of extremely powerful explosives known as HMX, RDX, and PETN. The cache, located inside the Qaeda weapons facility and bearing seals that resembled those used by the International Atomic Energy Agency during its prewar inspection of Iraq's weapons program, subsequently went missing even though the area was under U.S. control. Presumably, the material was used by insurgents to make the deadly improvised explosive devices, or IEDs, that were eventually used against coalition forces. Embedded reporters could document that the military had the dangerous material in its own hands and yet the explosives somehow ended up controlled by the insurgency. A series of embarrassing questions for Bush administration officials followed.[50] Yet very few critical descriptions emerged during the March–April 2003 march that culminated in Saddam's overthrow. Despite the presence of embeds on the battlefield, remarkably few pictures of actual casualties were shown to U.S. audiences. On the day that U.S. troops entered Baghdad, CENTCOM claimed that between two thousand and three thousand Iraqi troops died, yet there was little coverage on television or in the newspapers. MSNBC put its live feed on five-second delay so that the more "disturbing" images could be edited out. That day, the only casualty shown on CNN was an Iraqi soldier who had been wounded and left on the side of the road. Audiences back in the States could view a CNN security officer and then a U.S. Army medic administering aid to the unfortunate man. The dead and larger-scale chaos could not be seen.

Public relations experts in the Department of Defense were pleased by how the destruction that dominated battlefield images in Vietnam had been replaced with a new set of dazzling visuals that conveyed technical prowess and success. Live-action pictures substituted for background reports or for stories about what happened to the people on the receiving end of these weapons. These visuals helped to create a sense of awe, tension, and excitement while obscuring what might actually be happening on the battlefield. Competency and efficiency trumped mayhem. Viewers could "see" the battlefield through green night scopes and handheld video cameras. And because many in the audience had been "prepared" by hours of viewing similar production values on reality TV, what they saw on the battlefield looked all the more real. The fact that the images were sometimes jumpy, or that the voice and visuals were occasionally out of sync, only contributed to their power.

Embedded reporting carries the advantages of immediacy but also the limitations of a narrow, or what was often called "a soda straw," angle of vision. In theory, the Coalition Media Center in Doha could have provided journalists a better opportunity to develop a comprehensive picture, and many reporters chose to be there in the expectation that the daily CENTCOM briefings would enable them to develop a broader perspective about the war's strategy and effectiveness. In this belief, they were sorely mistaken. Little information of value was disseminated from that source. The thousands of journalists who eventually gathered there were subject to a news blackout for the first two days of the war and thereafter to limited information that rarely departed from a closely controlled script. Michael Wolff of *New York* magazine later reflected on the limited perspective of reporters in the media center: "The only window that you had into actually what was going on in the war were the set of television monitors in front of the coffee bars. You could lean against the coffee bar and look up at the monitors and see at least what Fox was telling you was going on in the war." George Curry, another reporter, noted that the military representatives were speaking beyond the journalists to the public audience back in the United States: "What's going on is you're not even getting basic information that you need. They're not talking to us, they're talking to the audience beyond us and we're just conduits. The audience is in TV land, and we're in Never, Never Land."[51]

The Pentagon realized that the CENTCOM briefing stage did not offer the best vantage point for reporting on the war. One official later acknowledged that "the criticism of the journalists, that there wasn't enough information coming out of Qatar, is exactly right on." The Department of Defense actually preferred that war "news" come from embedded reporters. The purpose of Doha was different. The Coalition Media Center was used for what is euphemistically called "information operations," or attempting to influence the perceptions of the opposing forces. A Pentagon official confirmed this strategy:

JOSEPH: Could I ask you for an example of information operations?

OFFICIAL: Information operations is where you try and influence the

enemy to do something, or you try and present a different picture to
the enemy. Qatar was trying to present a message of hopelessness
to the enemy.

JOSEPH: So would the reports, on the first day of the war, that Saddam's
governing structure is in disarray be an example of information operations?

OFFICIAL: Right. That was a good message for them to get.

JOSEPH: Governmental disarray in Baghdad might have been true, or it
might not have been true. But you wanted Baghdad people who were
watching our television to receive that message no matter what?

OFFICIAL: That's right.

Or, as another reporter stationed in Qatar later observed: "If word
comes out of CENTCOM that there is an uprising against Saddam's
regime, they are certainly thinking, planning, hoping that the information will be picked up on and the local people will build on
that and that the idea will become a reality even if it never existed
in the first place."[52]

Media Coverage after "Mission Accomplished"

What are the implications of this discussion of the media for the
overall argument that Americans are becoming more peaceful? The
Bush administration managed the public directly through its own
rhetoric as well as through its virtuosity with the media to create
support for war in Iraq. Did the media present any counterpressures,
particularly after the early optimism of the war started to fade?

Despite many limitations, information began to be framed in a
more critical manner after the initial drive to Baghdad and as the
costs of the occupation began to rise over the summer of 2003.
Individual reporters, such as Anthony Shadid of the *Washington
Post*, filed vivid, firsthand accounts of the casualties of the war.
Newsweek's exposé "How Dick Cheney Sold the War: Why He Fell
for Bad Intelligence and Pitched It to the President" earned the
wrath of the White House.[53] Major newspapers and journals began
to publish articles about the prewar failures of the intelligence
community—and of the tendency of journalists to accept the unsubstantiated claims made by the administration's leading officials.
Judith Miller's reporting, particularly its overreliance on Ahmed
Chalabi and the Iraqi National Congress as sources, was subjected
to particularly close review.[54] Some press journalists tried to focus
on the consequences of the occupation for Iraqi citizens. Unlike

Vietnam, they were determined to put a human face on the people living in danger. Even the significance of embedded reporting began to change. When President Bush claimed in December 2005 that Iraqi forces were much improved and that a recent assault "was primarily led by Iraqi security forces," a reporter from *Time* was on the scene to declare the account "completely wrong."[55]

As the security situation deteriorated, just being a reporter in Iraq became more dangerous. In fall 2004, *Wall Street Journal* correspondent Farnaz Fassihi described her bleak working conditions and inability to move throughout the country in an e-mail that was widely circulated. Many reporters took great risks trying to bring news to the American public. Between March 2003 and the beginning of 2006, sixty-one journalists and another twenty-three media support staff, mostly Iraqis, died in the country.[56] (In Vietnam, over the twenty-year period between 1955 and 1975, sixty-one journalists died.)[57] Some journalists were abducted and killed by insurgent factions. Others were killed by U.S. forces. Reuters global managing editor David Schlesinger described "a long parade of disturbing incidents whereby professional journalists have been killed, wrongfully detained, and/or illegally abused by U.S. forces in Iraq."[58] And at the 2005 Davos, Switzerland, World Economic Forum summit, CNN president Eason Jordan also claimed that the U.S. military was deliberately targeting reporters critical of the war. (Jordan resigned after a vociferous campaign from conservative bloggers moved from the Internet to cable television.) Earlier, in Afghanistan, officials at a U.S. Marine base prevented the media, who were already on the scene, from reporting on a "friendly fire" incident that accidentally killed U.S. soldiers and Afghan allies. Similarly, a *Washington Post* reporter claimed that U.S. troops threatened to shoot him if he continued to investigate an incident in which civilians had been killed in the war in Afghanistan.[59]

Meanwhile, other forms of media nurtured opposition to the war. *Frontline's* October 2003 documentary, *Truth, War, and Consequences*, provided a damning account of the Bush administration's use of evidence. In addition to Michael Moore's *Fahrenheit 9/11*, Robert Greenwald's *Uncovered*, promoted by MoveOn.org, was screened throughout the country.[60] Some of these examples fell outside mainstream media and yet attracted large audiences. Indeed one key aspect of the period's Type I opposition is increased media activism not only through Internet sources but also in gatherings such as the "Free Press and Media Activism" conference held in Madison, Wisconsin, which drew two thousand people.

Growing criticisms seemed to be building toward another "Cronkite moment" in which the media, accurately reflecting on-the-ground pessimism, would conclude that the war could not be won. But the press and television pulled their punches even as prewar claims made by Bush administration officials began to unravel. Most mainstream media gave only back-page and temporary coverage to the "Downing Street Memo" that appeared in British newspapers during Prime Minister Tony Blair's 2005 reelection campaign. The memo indicated that in July 2002, nine months before the start of the Iraq war, "intelligence and facts were being fixed around policy" and that war was "inevitable." For peace activists, the document was the smoking gun that definitively exposed the chicanery of the Bush administration, and they tried to call as much attention as possible to the evidence that a decision to go to war had been made before the UN inspection and political process were completed. They tried to make "Downing Street" to Iraq as the "Pentagon Papers" were to Vietnam. A special Internet site was established, and Type I opposition worked with sympathetic members of Congress to hold hearings on the hyping of intelligence. But a story that carried at least as much potential for political scandal as did Watergate was virtually ignored by much of the press.[61]

Nonetheless, public skepticism continued to grow. A November 2005 poll found 43 percent of respondents believing that the White House lied about Iraq's WMD programs.[62] The previous month, at least 250,000 gathered in Washington, D.C., for an antiwar rally, thus matching the size of the Vietnam-era national demonstrations. But increased opposition within the public did not yet translate into political traction. Pennsylvania congressional representative and former marine John Murtha called for withdrawal from Iraq but most of the media continued to consider the proposal "unrealistic."

For all its favorable treatment, the Bush administration tended to have a hostile attitude toward most mainstream media, especially after the initial enthusiasm for embedded reporting started to subside. Bush himself began to call the media "a filter" that stood between his own preferred message and what the public was actually receiving. My own impression from the series of interviews that I conducted in the Pentagon is that the public relations experts there regarded the press as more enemy than friend. In their view, any pessimistic story threatened to evoke Vietnam, "quagmire," and loss of public support. An interview with a Pentagon public relations expert provides an example:

> Last night driving home I heard an NPR report and I thought I was going to run off the highway. The words that were used: "abysmal," "chaos in Baghdad," "the citizens of Iraq don't want us there." Bad news hurts us strategically. Spot reporting of bad news can be necessary but when the whole story is that it's a morass, we should pull out, it was

a mistake to go in, and our reason for going to war was wrong—what enemy in a million years would not want to hear that?

Media Coverage and Fallujah

As the Iraqi security situation continued to deteriorate and it became very dangerous for journalists to venture outside their hotels, all types of reporting—embedded or otherwise—became severely limited. U.S. audiences were able to learn very little from Western media about Fallujah, a city where Iraqi insurgents continued to maintain control long after Baghdad fell. In early 2004, U.S. forces could not enter the city without facing a strong counterattack. But in April, after four Blackwater security contractors were killed, burned, and finally hung from a bridge, military authorities decided to invade the city. In preparation, U.S. aircraft bombed various targets in the Fallujah. Al-Jazeera, the only remaining news outlet, described the destruction of mosques and hospitals and documented numerous civilian deaths—some from American snipers. On April 11, *USA Today* reported that doctors had been gathering data and names from health clinics and the main hospital. Based on newspaper accounts and hospital records, the Internet site Iraqbodycount.org estimated that six hundred civilians were killed by the preliminary attacks. International reports described the conversion of the soccer stadium into a cemetery because there was no longer enough space in the city's graveyards.[63] Photographs and video of hundreds of civilians being buried in the stadium could be seen throughout the world—except in the mainstream media of the United States.

This information did reach antiwar activist circles and political magazines but with very few exceptions received little attention from the mainstream media. Military strategists continued to vacillate over the decision to go ahead with entry into the city. On the one hand, seizing the city with acceptable U.S. and civilian casualties seemed difficult if not impossible. Moreover, an invasion of the city would certainly inspire clerics in the rest of Iraq, who were already using the news coming out of Fallujah to encourage further opposition to the occupation. On the other hand, stopping the ground operation before it even started would send a message of weakness. Military authorities tried to negotiate a solution and, at one moment in this process, Brigadier General Mark Kimmitt, the deputy director of U.S. military operations in Iraq, claimed that a unilateral U.S. ceasefire was in effect. At that moment al-Jazeera cut away to live images of U.S. fighter jets attacking different neighborhoods in the city. Some footage showed women and children killed by the missiles.[64] Kimmitt later called the network's coverage a "series of lies," and when he was questioned persistently about the live images, his answer was "Change the channel. Change the channel to a legitimate, authoritative, honest news station."[65] But later the military commander said that he was not arguing that the pictures had been faked. The problem, he said, was that al-Jazeera "looked at things differently." Meanwhile, executives at the Arab channel claimed that U.S. forces had fired on a reporting team in Fallujah.[66]

In Vietnam, during the Tet Offensive, a U.S. military officer defended the bombing of a city held by revolutionary forces by arguing that it had become necessary to "destroy the town in order to save it." The comment was heard by a reporter, published, and repeated over and over again in subsequent press accounts. The Orwellian phrase seemed to capture the futility of the military effort. How could the United States ever hope to win if it had to destroy exactly what it was trying to save? Now it looked like history was repeating itself. Would the United States also destroy Fallujah in an effort to save it?

The short-term answer was no. The marines backed off Fallujah, in large measure because of the anticipated public reaction to expected casualties to both U.S. forces and Iraqi civilians. (The *New York Times* later referred to the "disastrous assault on Fallujah that was called off when unconfirmed [*sic!*] reports of large civilian casualties drove the political cost too high.") Destroying a town and killing many of its civilian inhabitants would exceed acceptable limits of conditional war. The Western media were not inside the city. There was no contemporary equivalent of Morley Safer, the CBS correspondent who captured the destruction of the Vietnamese hamlet of Cam Ne. But al-Jazeera was present as were a few independent reporters, and in a world of global communication integration, the story of "destroying a town" would have been told even if its point of origin was perceived as hostile to the United States. The invasion of the city would have been a living room war. The Pentagon negotiated a temporary accommodation that left the insurgency in control of the city. For the moment, it was not possible to "destroy a town in order to save it." In November, in an illustration of the limitations of the constraints offered by Type II opposition, the marines did invade Fallujah. In an effort to lower collateral damage, civilians were ordered to clear the town prior to the attack. The soldiers did not completely destroy the town, although they certainly damaged a good part of it. The significance of the high-profile, prolonged street fighting, largely exceptional in the broader context of U.S. military conduct in Iraq, is examined in chapter 8, "Managing Casualties." The specter of another Vietnam had to be avoided.

Chapter 5

Managing Photographs

A full-size reproduction of Pablo Picasso's famous reaction to the bombing of Guernica hangs near the entrance to the UN Security Council. The detailed canvas, which portrays women, children, and animals screaming in terror during a Spanish civil war assault, is one of the few, globally recognized, antiwar icons produced during the twentieth century, and its position fronting the deliberations of a world body dedicated to preserving peace seems appropriate.[1] During the 2003 UN debate that preceded the war on Iraq, and in compliance with a request from Washington, a large blue curtain was placed over *Guernica*. Evidently, the State Department found the painting too disconcerting a background for press briefings from U.S. ambassador to the UN John Negroponte or Secretary of State Colin Powell. Horses writhing in pain, broken human beings, buildings in shambles, and crying birds were too jarring a background for explanations of why war was necessary.

The decision to hide Picasso's work raises a series of questions: What role do visuals play in the tension between war management and war opposition? Do explicit, graphic images have a specific, predictable impact? Will images showing the violent consequences of war for soldiers and civilians make the public less likely to accept official justifications for war? And what types of photographs have the American people actually been able to see in conditional war, and are these different in any way from those published during mobilized war?

The earliest wartime photography dates from the Crimean War. The typical picture of the period shows uniformed officers, carefully posed, at rest or standing around a table at some distance from the scene of battle. Exposure times at this initial stage of the technology were on the order of twenty seconds and the development of handheld cameras was still several decades in the future. Photographers were limited in their movements, and capturing events on the battlefield itself was impossible. The U.S. Civil War, occurring some fifteen years later, supplied the first pictures of war dead. Some were quite explicit and clearly conveyed the horror of the battlefield. Their appearance also prompted the argument that presenting more graphic images of the battlefield to the public might not always be a good idea. Consider a *New York Times* editorial on a series of Civil War photographs shown at Mathew Brady's Manhattan gallery in October 1862, a month after the battle of Antietam:

> Mr. Brady has done something to bring home to us the terrible reality and earnestness of war. If he has not brought bodies and laid them in our dooryards and along the streets, he has done something very like it.... These pictures have a terrible distinctness. By the aid of the magnifying-glass, the very features of the slain may be distinguished. We would scarce choose to be in the gallery, when one of the women bending over them should recognize a husband, a son, or a brother in the still, lifeless lines of bodies that lie ready for the gaping trenches.[2]

Thus, as soon as technology emerged, a tension was created between two contending perspectives on photography and war. The first reflected the ability to present battlefield catastrophes in a "true light." Photographs offered a seemingly straightforward reality, an opportunity to present the horrors of war and thereby encourage public opposition. On the other hand, harsh pictures of the battlefield produced simultaneous recoil that prompted some cultural agents to argue that the public needed to be protected from powerful, rude, or subversive images. The reality of war was in "poor taste." Photographs could bring the war experience closer to the public. But photographs might themselves be considered a type of assault. Guidelines had to be established.

Graphic Pictures and Mobilized War

In *Regarding the Pain of Others*, the late Susan Sontag argues that photographs encourage more in-depth contemplation than the fleeting, transitory, and impatient medium of television. Television producers think that their audiences are always on the verge of changing channels, and they shape their product so that it is immediately interesting. The emphasis is not on depth or detail but on maintaining perpetual fascination. The medium cannot afford to be demanding because the viewer always has another option. Television stays superficial and invites indifference.[3]

But photography offers an invitation to explore more deeply. What are the motivations of the characters in the picture? What are the consequences of the actions that are portrayed? What was happening immediately before the picture was snapped? What is missing, what essential parts of the story did the camera fail to capture? Wartime photographs offer their own special questions. Who are the victims and the perpetrators? Who deserves compassion and who should be brought to justice? Who is responsible for the deaths? Are there any heroes?

Many photographers have tried to answer these questions by taking pictures that display war "realistically." For them, explicit photography served as a constraint against war. After World War I, the German photographer Ernst Friedrich published *War Against War!* a collection of almost two hundred photographs that conveyed the full gamut of wartime horrors and that he hoped would have a significant impact on public opinion. The volume was eventually published in more than a dozen languages. Perhaps the most famous combat photo ever taken, Robert Capa's grainy shot of a Republican soldier during the Spanish civil war, was taken at the precise moment of death and shows the victim falling backward, arms outstretched, losing his rifle, all forward momentum checked.[4] Pictures of the Holocaust continue to shock, as does the visual record of the atomic bombing of Hiroshima and Nagasaki. The Vietnam War provided its own examples, including Huynh Cong Ut's picture of terrified children running down a road, screaming in agony from napalm burns delivered by a U.S. jet.[5] The record also includes Eddie Adams's stark photo capturing the moment when South Vietnam's General Nguyen Ngoc Loan fires a bullet into the brain of a National Liberation Front suspect in the middle of a Saigon street, and Robert Haeberle's documentation of hundreds of women and children lying dead in shallow canals, killed by American soldiers in My Lai. Their photographs have been used time and again by activists trying to deepen Type I explicit opposition to war.

Photography can also underscore the bravery, sacrifice, patriotism, and friendship that sometimes accompany combat. World War II was the source of the "multicultural platoon," an enduring concept of a small group of culturally disparate men who overcome their differences and in the process express the underlying strength of what it means to be an American. The war also supplied many pictures of "buddy posing," another principal theme of wartime photography, which stressed the intimacy of the relationship between comrades in arms. Joe Rosenthal's famous photograph of six marines raising the flag on Mount Suribachi on the island of Iwo Jima managed to combine both buddy posing and the multicultural platoon. Another common theme was embodied in the gaunt soldier staring off into the far distance in what became known as the "thousand-mile stare."

Nonetheless, many photojournalists saw the ultimate goal of their work as providing a powerful counterweight to governmental preferences to present only a sanitized version of events. Consider the following comment by Don McCullin, one of the most famous wartime photographers:

> War's not glamorous. It's total madness, it's evil, and it's a crime.... The only positive thing about photographing war is turning it into a negative. You show the negativity of dying children. What contribution can a dying child make to a political situation? War murders the innocent; they're the last people to be told when war's coming. Who are the refugees on the road? It's always the peasants. We need to be informed about war.[6]

Perhaps it comes as no surprise that McCullin was denied permission by the British government to go to the Falklands to take photographs of the war with Argentina. Still, war can be so damaging that sometimes no method of framing photographs seems to work. Photojournalist Laurent Van der Stockt said of Chechnya: "The country's totally shattered, both physically and psychologically. Everything is destroyed. You can't even communicate it through pictures."[7]

Explicit pictures do not automatically create opposition to war but on balance lend weight in that direction. In most circumstances, governments recognize this potential and many have followed a policy of censorship. They try to control the flow of images coming out of the conflict. The terrifying pictures of trench warfare in World War I did not appear until after the war was over. In World War II, photographs of dead U.S. servicemen could not be found until twenty-one months after Pearl Harbor. At that point, the national leaders decided that they wanted the public to know that the war would be long and costly. Policy changed and combat photography that embraced sacrifice became more prominent.[8] The contemporary reader will find *Life* magazine almost pornographic in its reflection

Life *magazine, February 1, 1943.*

of the horror. The photo here, which appeared in February 1943, provides one example. The original caption reads, "Japanese soldier's skull is propped on a burned-out Jap tank by U.S. troops. Fire destroyed the rest of the corpse." A similar picture, even of a leading al Qaeda terrorist or one of the Ba'ath regime leaders targeted in the set of "playing cards" prepared by the Pentagon, could not be shown today. The Pentagon had to think twice before distributing photographs of the carefully prepared bodies of Saddam's two sons after they were killed by U.S. forces in a raid.

During World War II, photographs of dead American soldiers were never gruesome. The cost was communicated but within a particular set of rules. A typical shot would be of bodies, faces averted, sprawled on a Pacific island beach or trapped against invasion defenses placed by the Germans. Photos of mutilated bodies were not published, nor were pictures showing American corpses being handled as if they were inanimate objects. Nonetheless, dead American soldiers were shown to the American public. The scale and frenzy of the war came through even though censors withheld photographs of gaping wounds or of situations where captors had abused American POWs. Heroic images still predominated over those that showed casualties, but the fact that death could be seen and felt signified a certain confidence that the public would accept powerful visual reminders of sacrifice in a war of significant scale and mobilization.

Showing the human costs of war has become much more problematic in conditional war. As with mobilized war, the first preference of government officials is to try to control images. In 1991, Operation Desert Storm continued the post-Vietnam Pentagon practice of organizing journalists into pools with restricted access to the battlefield. Few combat pictures of the Gulf War ever reached the public except for footage of "smart" bombs that appeared to destroy their targets with devastating accuracy. These pictures were misleading. Only 6 percent of the munitions used in the Gulf War were precision guided and many of the touted weapons, such as the Patriot batteries used to defend against Scud missile attacks, were not nearly as effective as originally claimed. Despite the presence of CNN, pictures that conveyed the impact of bombing attacks on the city of Baghdad, or on the civilian infrastructure, were largely unavailable. What the public did see was a sanitized version of the battlefield coupled with an avalanche of photographs of soldiers preparing for battle or at rest. These more casual pictures embodied the multicultural-platoon and buddy themes of earlier wars although without the feeling of imminent combat. The public could sympathize with the soldiers and appreciate the considerable disruption that the deployment to the Gulf had created in their personal lives. And it was impossible to ignore the potential of being placed in harm's way. But these were not pictures of a battlefield; with few exceptions, death, on either side, was not placed before the public.

Public sensitivities became apparent during the one moment where a visible battlefield event eclipsed the boundaries of conditional war. Toward the end of the conflict, Iraqis fleeing Kuwait in a military convoy became bogged down and trapped by U.S. airpower. Pilots later called the attacks near Mutlah Gap a "turkey shoot"; others compared it to strafing Daytona Beach during spring break. The public vision of this situation was restricted to aerial photographs of bombed, wrecked, and charred vehicles strewn along the highway. Nonetheless, the transmittal of these pictures to the public may have forced the United States to stop the war and avoid any attempt to overthrow Saddam himself. As Colin Powell, then chair of the Joint Chiefs of Staff, later noted:

> Saddam had ordered his forces to withdraw from Kuwait. The last major escape route, a four-lane highway leading out of Kuwait City toward the Iraqi city of Basrah, had turned into a shooting gallery for our fliers. The road was choked with fleeing soldiers and littered with the charred hulks of nearly fifteen hundred military and civilian vehicles. Reporters began referring to this road as the "Highway of Death."
>
> I would have to give the President and the Secretary [of Defense Dick Cheney] a recommendation soon as to when to stop, I told Norm [Schwarzkopf, the commander of U.S. military forces in the field]. The coverage, I added, was starting to make it look as if we were engaged in slaughter for slaughter's sake.[9]

And stop they did. As a British correspondent who interviewed key members of the first Bush administration noted: "President Bush saw TV pictures of the apparent carnage after allied warplanes attacking retreating Iraqis in the Mutla Gap on the road north from Kuwait City to Iraq.... Those pictures did play a major part in Bush's decision to halt the ground war at a moment which coincided conveniently with 100 hours of battle. It was not the *horror* of the pictures that swayed the President, but the realization that the war was effectively over and TV should not be allowed to show needless further casualties."[10]

Photographs showing the human cost of the incident were not published until after the war. One exception, a particularly gruesome picture of an incinerated Iraqi soldier trapped in the passenger seat of his jeep, was at the time carried only in England's *Sunday Observer.* The next photo is in many ways similar to that of the Japanese skull featured in *Life* in World War II. But publishing it in a newspaper in 1991 would have violated the prohibition against showing explicit war costs that is part of conditional war. A U.S. antiwar agitprop group called Refuse and Resist carried out

The burned remains of an Iraqi soldier are propped up in his charred vehicle, attacked during a retreat from Kuwait during the Persian Gulf War (Kenneth Jarecke/Colorific).

a protest against the media's refusal to publish similar pictures by projecting the image of the Iraqi against the side of UN headquarters and the walls of the ABC, CBS, and NBC buildings in New York.[11] The picture is undeniably awful. But is it more so than that of the Japanese soldier published in the pages of America's leading weekly fifty years before? Why did one gruesome portrayal of the enemy appear and not the other?

Photographs and Antiwar Opposition

Graphic pictures do not automatically become constraints on war. And effective war constraints are not always graphic. Photographs that encourage effective war opposition combine subject matter, historical circumstances, and sense of audience in a way that concretizes the human loss and encourages compassion for the victim. Respect for the perspective that the viewer brings is also important and underscores the limitations of any approach that seeks a direct, unmediated connection between image and understood message.

The simple grouping of graduation yearbook pictures of young people who have been killed is extremely sad, especially when considered against the background of an unsuccessful military effort. The June 27, 1969, issue of *Life* contained page after page of snapshots of Americans who had been killed during one week of fighting in Vietnam—217 in all. No Vietnamese were included; to include them probably would have required the entire issue. Nonetheless, the effect was devastating.

A similar point can be made in connection with the Khmer Rouge, an extremist political group that seized power in Cambodia as the war in Indochina ended in 1975. The Khmer Rouge tortured prisoners in a Phnom Penh detention center called Tuol Sleng. Just before executing their victims, they took a photograph. After the Vietnamese invaded Cambodia and ended the barbaric rule of the Khmer Rouge, Tuol Sleng was turned into a museum. Visitors can now see these pictures, which have been pasted together into a chilling montage. The victims are in repose; none are being actively tortured at the moment. Yet the view of the sea of faces, each waiting for a lonely death, is more moving than the collection of torture implements in the adjacent rooms. The visitor's reaction is amplified further still with the discovery that Tuol Sleng was originally a secondary school.

Pictures of those who perished in the September 11 attacks were featured in the series "Portraits in Grief," which appeared in the *New York Times*. Photographs were coupled with synopses of the lives, activities, friends, and family members of the victims. As the director of the New York Historical Society, Kenneth Jackson, said about the series: "The peculiar genius of it was to put a human face on numbers that are unimaginable to most of us.... As you read those individual portraits about love affairs or kissing children goodbye or coaching soccer and buying a dream house ... it's so obvious that every one of them was a person who deserved to live a full and successful and happy life. You see what was lost."[12]

An unrelenting barrage of graphic images is unlikely to be an effective antiwar visual strategy. A method is required that helps select pictures that communicate the pain and loss of war and yet does not overwhelm the viewer. Several years ago, I served as the curator of an exhibition of the atomic bombings of Hiroshima and Nagasaki in the Aidekman Art Gallery of Tufts University. The planning committee grappled with the issue of how to depict the victims of the bombings and how to strike a balance between the political and the human side of the tragedy. Including numerous explicit photographs and videos ran the risk of simply devastating the visitor, and we declined an offer from Japan to display a "wall" of pictures of the civilian victims of the bombing. Yet it would have been untruthful to present an exhibition that ignored the impact of nuclear weapons on the human body. After much discussion, we ended up with a single picture showing the shadow of a vaporized body, a series of photographs that displayed keloids and other forms of radiation scarring, and a short video that showed the physical and human destruction of Hiroshima.[13]

As the date approached for the opening of the exhibition, we invited middle and high schools in the area to visit. Despite our deliberate choice to present only a minimal amount of explicit material, more than half of the middle schools that had expressed initial interest in viewing the exhibition decided that they would not come. Typically, advance teams of teachers would review the material and decide that it was too powerful for sixth, seventh, and eighth graders. They did not want to run the risk of their students becoming upset. On the other hand, high school teachers generally felt that their students could "handle" the exhibition. A boundary line of what was considered acceptable for students to see ran between the two educational levels. Yet in Japan, as any visitor to the A-bomb museums in Hiroshima or Nagasaki will attest, young children in the primary grades see far more explicit material than that included in the Tufts exhibition. Considerations of what viewers "can handle" and where the boundaries marking "good taste" are located will always be present. But pictures that attempt to say something about war cannot fully strip away the pain that is inflicted on human beings without becoming a lie.

Another example of how photographs can be used to support active peace work is provided by Mary Wareham, a senior advocate at Human Rights Watch (HRW) and global research coordinator for the International Campaign to Ban Landmines (ICBL). Among her responsibilities, Wareham selects the photographs for HRW publications that are used to strengthen the 1997 Ottawa Treaty, which bans the production and deployment of antipersonnel land mines. Her work is to draw attention to the victims of war and political violence. But the importance of context remains, particularly in preserving respect for the victim and conveying the message that there is a social movement that is trying to do something about the problem of antipersonnel land mines. Wareham tries to use pictures to deepen self-conscious Type I opposition to war.[14]

> JOSEPH: You are the editor responsible for choosing photographs for publications by the International Campaign to Ban Landmines, such as your annual *Landmine Monitor Report*. What strategy do you follow for making the selection?

WAREHAM: During the early stages of our campaign [1992–1996], the photographs we used included more hardheaded looks such as an injured person lying in a hospital bed. We still run those types of photos because it is important to show that land mines are still claiming casualties. But we also want pictures from places where most people do not really think there is a land mines problem. For example, Burma is now believed to have more victims every year than Cambodia.

JOSEPH: Are there any particular guidelines that you use?

WAREHAM: I receive photographs from all over the world and some are really stunning. But if I don't know who this kid standing on a crutch is, or where they live, or in what context they were injured, I usually don't run the photo.

JOSEPH: So you want to make sure that there's a certain respect that is communicated?

WAREHAM: That's right. On the latest cover of the *Landmines Monitor* report I put a picture of a girl named Kiran Dip, who lost her foot when she followed her goats into a minefield laid by the Indian army. I thought, "Wow, this is quite compelling." She obviously has quite a horrific injury. It's a pretty stark image. But she is not lying on the hospital bed with a bloody stump. She is sitting there with a crutch looking directly at the camera with an expression like, "OK, look what's happened to me. I have to deal with it. What's next?" She's a woman, she's a civilian, she's a youth, so its represents the future.

JOSEPH: So how did this happen to her?

WAREHAM: When you think about land mines, you usually think about countries like Angola, Afghanistan, and Cambodia. You don't think about the escalation between Pakistan and India in December 2001. Yet all of a sudden the India army is laying millions of mines along its border and saying that it is doing so according to international rules. They claimed that they were marking, mapping, fencing, and informing the local population. But it is questionable whether these precautions really happened. In the case of this girl, the army came to her village on the border, planted a few minefields, and put up some barbed wire, but they didn't provide any information about the need for locals to stay away from the area. So when her goats went in, she followed and got blown up.

JOSEPH: What will happen to the girl?

WAREHAM: We'd like to bring her to a diplomatic meeting in Bangkok and say, "This is what India is doing to its own people with land mines that it manufactures itself. This girl represents dozens of communities and countless numbers of people who have been killed or maimed in mine incidents over the last two years. Your government hasn't banned antipersonnel mines, but 150 other governments have. We deplore any land mine, no matter who is using the weapon. It is unacceptable. What are you going to do about it?" But because she is only thirteen

On August 14, 2002, twelve-year-old Kiran Dip was grazing her family's goats near her home village of Karanpur in Rajasthan province, India. Her goats passed under a fence and, unaware that it was a minefield, she followed them and subsequently lost her right foot in the explosion. The antipersonnel mine was one of millions laid by the Indian Army in late 2001 along its 1,800–kilometer-long border with Pakistan (Suresh Dhingra, Suresh Studio, Sri Ganganagar, Rajasthan, December 20, 2002; Human Rights Watch).

or fourteen years old and has probably never traveled outside of her village we're not going to do that. She would have to be accompanied and would be thrown into a major diplomatic event with hundreds of people and it would be just too much.

The land mine survivors who do participate in international meetings are usually briefed before they leave their country. They are informed about what to expect and sometimes what not to expect. For example they should not expect to be taken to the States and fitted with a new $20,000 leg, which might break when they go home and where there would be little ability to fix it. We see if there is a way for them to contribute to the process and for them to learn so they can perhaps follow up once they return home and become part of the leadership in this movement to eradicate land mines. Survivors have to be carefully chosen if they are going to represent us.

We have to do this so we are not accused of failing the survivor. We also have to present it in a way that encourages the media to become part of the effort to resolve the problem.

JOSEPH: The process of taking photos of land mine survivors and presenting them to the public is more complicated than it first appears. Anything else to add?

WAREHAM: It might be interesting to consider what we don't show. You will not see pictures of diplomatic meetings or press conferences. You will not see people holding land mines, because in the field that's a big mistake. If you are doing an educational campaign, you cannot, under any circumstances, have a person standing out there holding a mine. We also tend to avoid running many pictures of actual land mines because there is no context. But we sometimes do use photos of mines manufactured by governments we are lobbying to join the 1997 Mine Ban Treaty such as China, Russia, and the United States.

Photographs and Humanitarian Intervention

Photographs have also played an important role in furthering peace-making efforts and supporting humanitarian intervention. Public support for these missions forms one part of the overall argument that Americans are becoming more peaceful. One difficulty in tracing this support is that "peacekeeping," especially as conducted by the U.S. military, can also seem like war, and the humanitarian dimension becomes lost in the midst of military conduct that continues to rely on deadly force. Some humanitarian missions will look peaceful; others will involve armed conflict and be subject to the understandings of conditional war.

Beginning in late 1992, pictures of starving children in Somalia and other countries in East Africa shocked Western publics and helped reverse the Bush administration's initial reluctance to support a program of food assistance. One picture published at the time shows a thin child, head out of proportion to an emaciated body, with flies covering his face. The child is huddled in a bare field while in the near background a large vulture waits patiently. Television provided similar images of distress and did so repeatedly. On the Thanksgiving broadcast of the *CBS Evening News,* Connie Chung told the nationwide audience that on "a day when Americans are filling up on a holiday feast, one million people are in danger of starving to death half a world away."[15] An estimated 240,000 Somalis died before the rest of the world started to pay attention to the problem. As a Department of Defense official in the Clinton administration noted in an interview:

> These pictures [of the famine in Somalia] were affecting policy in the sense that it helped set our conception of who constitutes our neighbors, what responsibilities we had to people outside our own society, and therefore how our national interests were evolving as our world becomes smaller and we receive more information. The media made certain things unavoidable and in that way pressured decision makers to confront issues they would otherwise avoid.

Somalia became the place where the public decided that it was impossible to turn their backs to the suffering. Before leaving office, President George H. W. Bush sent 28,000 troops to help feed the vulnerable civilian population. Photographs did not by themselves force the Bush administration to change its policy, but they interacted with other political motivations such as the possibility that humanitarian measures in Somalia would relieve growing pressure for a more difficult intervention in Bosnia.[16]

The synergy between images of humanitarian emergencies and the public's desire to have the government help relieve the suffering is certainly erratic. The media's inconsistency is often driven by commercial and competitive motivations. Television jumped on the Somalia story partly because of the timing of the operation, which came immediately after the November 1992 presidential elections and the resulting opportunity—and need—for the media to focus on a new issue. Journalists came in droves and the public could witness rather bizarre footage of camouflaged, heavily armed U.S. Marines and Navy Seals arriving on a beach on the outskirts of Mogadishu that had already been secured by television crews and reporters earlier in the day. Over seventy-five journalists, their cables and klieg lights strewn across the sand, met the troops as they waded ashore. CNN received many telephone calls complaining that the

This award-winning photograph of a starving child was published in the New York Times *(March 23, 1993). The photographer later committed suicide (Kevin Carter/Corbis Sygma).*

network's coverage put the lives of U.S. troops in danger. Yet it was the Pentagon and the State Department that encouraged the media to film the military's arrival. The *New York Times* pointed out, "All week the Pentagon had encouraged press coverage of the marine landing. Reporters were told when the landing would take place, and some network correspondents were quietly advised exactly where the marines would arrive so that they could set up their cameras."[17] The day before the landing, the schedule for live coverage was carried in *USA Today.*

Meanwhile, other crises went unrecorded. As ABC's Ted Koppel later noted: "*Nightline* went to cover Somalia and I was there and that meant bringing along our huge electronic tail. Now what are the chances of *Nightline* doing a story while we're in Somalia on Rwanda, or Latin America, or anywhere else? Slim or none."[18] There was a virtual absence of images from early 1990 conflicts in Algeria, Sudan, Kashmir, Angola, Liberia, Peru, East Timor, Tajikistan, Afghanistan, and the Tuaregs of the Sahara. The BBC's George Alaagiah reported massacres in Burundi in October 1993 that were taking place on a significantly larger scale than in Bosnia, but repeated images were not shown to either the British or American publics and no diplomatic response was forthcoming.

With the Clinton administration, the focus of the humanitarian mission in Somalia changed. Ranger and Delta Force troops expanded the mission by attempting to capture Somali warlord General Mohammed Farah Aidid. These efforts culminated in the October 1993 debacle in which two Black Hawk helicopters were shot down, eighteen soldiers died, and at least seventy-four were wounded. Pictures of a dead U.S. soldier being dragged through the streets of Mogadishu also made the front page of many U.S. newspapers. President Bill Clinton later called it the "worst day of my life." Congress exerted great pressure for withdrawal from Somalia and Clinton did little to resist except for extending the timetable for the troops' removal. Public support for military involvement in Somalia was based on the premise that it was a humanitarian mission. And while a politically neutral intervention does not exist, the new policy relied on elite, aggressive troops whose conduct toward the local population was often rude and racist. It was a very different type of external impact than the delivery and distribution of supplies, which might have affected the relationships among the tribal elders that governed Somalia. The humanitarian mission had been transformed into something that evoked Vietnam, although on a smaller scale. Despite the Black Hawk incident, there is evidence that a bare majority of the public was still willing to remain in Somalia.[19] But the inability of the Clinton administration to provide steady leadership and a strategy that promised success eventually frittered away what was left of public support.

The impact of photography is not always immediate. In Bosnia, it took more than three years of pictures to have the region finally embraced as part of Europe. With this development came the obligation to provide more protection against ethnic cleansing. Ron Aviv, a photographer for *Newsweek*, later wrote about his own work in the region:

> It was incredibly frustrating. Over and over again, the same pictures were being published, with absolutely no reaction. But the solution was not to stop; the solution was to keep doing it, to build on the existing evidence, and to make sure that eventually people were going to be held responsible for what was happening. Anger and frustration became the impetus to keep going. In 1994, I was photographing the same poor refugee women I photographed in 1991. It was a different woman in a different part of the country, but it was the same exact picture. And the people from whom you were working would say, "Yes, it's the same picture. That's why we're really bored with it and why we don't want to publish it." But the whole point was that it was the same picture.[20]

One reporter in Bosnia at the time said, "This will be recorded as the first genocide in history where journalists were reporting it as it was actually happening, and governments didn't stop it."[21] Yet the images did have an impact, not an automatic "CNN effect" where pictures determine policy, but an influence nonetheless. Images may not be deterministic but they are often agenda setting. They can force an administration to consider new options based on the need to reduce the appearance of innocent victims in the media. By 1994, a complex interaction had been established among photographs, public compassion, a fear that NATO would become only a "paper organization" if it continued its policy of no response, and administration officials who were finally willing to push for change in policy. For the Clinton administration, Secretary of State Madeleine Albright and national security adviser Tony Lake took the lead for stronger intervention in Bosnia against congressional and military opposition.[22]

Pictures of suffering that appear—repeatedly—on the front pages of the newspaper contribute strongly to the felt need to respond. An administration may not want to intervene in a humanitarian crisis and may try to manage the news so that the victims no longer are visible. Certainly, the victims of the 1994 genocide in Rwanda did not appear before the public while the atrocities were carried out. Pictures of the genocide could have been used by Clinton to build an argument that it was necessary to respond. But we now know that members of the U.S. government were under orders to avoid even the use of the word "genocide" when discussing Rwanda and no significant effort was made to save those who being massacred.

In Haiti, another humanitarian crisis emerged when a junta led by Lieutenant General Raoul Cedras overthrew the elected government of Jean-Bertrand Aristide and forced him into exile in the United States. The situation worsened, and many pro-democracy supporters of Aristide were killed or maimed in machete attacks carried out by thugs connected to the Cedras regime. The violence prompted many to try to flee to the United States on homemade boats. Some refugees drowned and corpses began to wash against the coastlines of Florida. Photographs of these victims did appear in U.S. newspapers. As one former Pentagon official in the Clinton administration later noted in an interview: "Haiti wasn't only about pictures, but actual human beings washing up on our own shores. That's about as direct an example of a humanitarian crisis affecting your society as you are likely to find."

After a series of negotiations failed to remove Cedras from power, a small but committed group of activists pushed both the Congressional Black Caucus and the White House to use military force to bring Aristide back to office. As the same official noted: "The administration wanted to manage the problem and avoid intervention. But we couldn't get these pictures off the front pages without the military getting in on the ground." Clinton was finally convinced that there was no alternative but to prepare for military intervention and Cedras, despite a negotiated agreement with a U.S. diplomatic team composed of Jimmy Carter, Colin Powell, and Sam Nunn, did not leave Haiti until the planes carrying U.S. troops were in the air. In a later interview a highly placed official in the White House addressed the balance between national and humanitarian interests in the public explanation of why intervention was necessary:

> I remember arguing that we would have to make both arguments but more on the national security side of it. It was in the national interest to expand democracy and stop refugees before they reached our shores. But Clinton said, "No, no. We need to tell the story first in humanitarian terms, Haitian faces covered with machete cuts, how awful the human rights situation is, because that is what will bring the American public along." And that is the way we did it and he was right. It did bring the public along.

In Kosovo, pictures of refugees fleeing Serb "ethnic cleansing" were actually welcomed by the Clinton administration and used to bolster support for NATO intervention. By 1999, Slobodan Milosevic's actions had created not only a humanitarian crisis but also a challenge to the credibility of NATO. A failure to respond would have produced still more unease, certainly among Europeans, but also in the United States regarding the institution that was supposed to provide for collective security.[23] Unlike in Rwanda, the administration this time highlighted human rights violations because it wanted to intervene. Visuals helped bridge the government's concern with security and the public's concern with humanitarianism to build support for military force.

Operation Allied Force, the bombing program against Serbia, became an almost perfect example of a conditional war. To keep domestic costs low, Clinton's speech on the eve of the campaign removed any mention of the possible use of U.S. ground troops. (Most of his military commanders thought that this was strategically foolish but the decision did have the advantage of avoiding significant casualties to U.S. personnel.) NATO and U.S. commander General Wesley Clark spent more time negotiating the rules for engagement between the United States and its European allies than with the supervision of military operations.[24] NATO bombed Serbia but conducted extensive

debates, even while the planes were in the air, about the legality of
strikes against particular targets and the risks of collateral damage.
Despite these concerns, mistakes were made that resulted in the
deaths of innocent Serbs and the bombing of the Chinese Embassy
in Belgrade. Clark had difficult relationships with Hugh Shelton, the
chair of the Joint Chiefs of Staff, and William Cohen, the secretary of
defense, both of whom were extremely cautious in their views. Clark
favored more aggressive actions against Milosevic and was not shy
about using the media to generate more support for his own agenda.
One of his proposals, the deployment of Apache helicopters, was
viewed by many as a "Trojan horse" for the commitment of ground
troops. Clark's comments at one press conference were construed
to mean that the bombing campaign alone was not having much
effect on Milosevic's ability to send troops into Kosovo. The White
House was greatly concerned about this "Vietnam theme"—Rolling
Thunder, the bombing campaign against Hanoi, had failed to stop
the flow of North Vietnamese troops into South Vietnam. Clark also
implied a need to reverse Clinton's original decision to fight without
ground troops. Clark's memoirs include the following description of
the phone call he then received from General Shelton:

> "Wes, at the White House meeting today there was a lot of discussion
> about your press conference," Shelton began. "The Secretary of De-
> fense [William Cohen] asked me to give you some verbatim guidance,
> so here it is: 'Get your f—g face off the TV. No more briefings, period.
> That's it.' I just wanted to give it to you like he said it. Do you have
> any questions?"[25]

Optimistically, photojournalism and televised coverage of famine
and other examples of humanitarian emergency have prompted
sympathy and generosity, and contributed to pressures leading to a
government response. The presence of striking visuals is not by itself
a sufficient explanation. Images need to be combined by authoritative
reporters into a coherent narrative that is repeated and reinforced
over time. Where this has taken place, the media have served as a
type of "electronic bridge" linking the relatively affluent West with
the desperately poor and suffering. As Martin Shaw has observed:
"The same media that figure in one context as entertainment com-
modities and vehicles for corporate profit, appear in another as
instruments of state policy, and in yet another as representatives
of an emergent global-democratic civil society."[26] Pictures carry the
potential to elicit public compassion and possibly serve as a site of
moral responsibility where the barriers of ethnicity, religion, and
physical space are becoming less significant. It is not normal for

human beings to die while others sit around doing nothing to help. But they must be visible. Where they are, and when there is a program that promises success, the sympathy that Americans show is part of the process of becoming more peaceful.

Of course, it is more complicated. The public may also exhibit "compassion fatigue." And visuals may bring not only empathy but also a more twisted form of voyeurism in which suffering serves only to titillate the sensibilities of those who are already secure. Images can also serve as a pseudoreality in which contemplating the pain becomes a substitute for doing and acting. These reactions may be particularly strong where the public feels that a good-faith effort has been made and yet the suffering and violence continue. Other influences on the public's political support for humanitarian measures include the credibility of the sitting president, the capacity to intervene in a way that realistically makes a difference, and whether there are sympathetic local figures who can be considered allies. Haiti's deposed president, Jean-Bertrand Aristide, was largely although not universally supported, which made it easier to gain public support for his return. In contrast, the only public figure to gain even nominal recognition in the devastating conflicts in Sierra Leone and Liberia was the emphatically antihero warlord Charles Taylor, which contributed still more to the pressures against a more active policy.

Most government officials do not see a base of support among the public that could be used to sustain a policy of humanitarian intervention. A typical point of view was expressed by a Clinton national security council staffer who said in an interview:

> Humanitarian issues may work for the public for a very short time but it is impossible to sustain military intervention on moral grounds alone. When committing troops to potential combat, humanitarian goals alone are not enough. My relatively realpolitik view is that purely altruistic reasons are never enough to sustain a policy. There may be situations where the right moral actions and the right humanitarian actions also serve to support U.S. interests but to make it sustainable you have to be able to articulate the important U.S. interests beyond human rights.

Neither political party nor any prominent political figure in the United States has ever tried to establish a clear, consistent link between national interest and global human security for the American public. Until such a connection is made, the public will usually respond sympathetically to pictures of suffering but political will to support a strategy that effectively protects the lives and human rights of others will vary in different contexts. Images that highlight victims are not a substitute for a strategy that can effectively help victims. Washington has shown little interest in developing such a strategy, either on its own or through the United Nations. Even without a commitment to humanitarian intervention, the repeated exposure of the public to pictures that convey the pain of others can force an administration to change policy in an effort to move those pictures off the front page. The public's nascent support for humanitarian intervention can sometimes be managed so that little to nothing is done. At other times, the demand cannot be met without military operations that may not look much different from war. The resulting confluence of humanitarian missions and the constraints of conditional war is one reason why opinion polls may sometimes show only lukewarm support for a policy of offering aid.

Photographs and the War in Iraq

One important pathway followed by Americans as they become more peaceful is Type II opposition, or sensitivity to war costs. Explicit, visual reminders of war damages will reduce support for military force and thus serve as an effective constraint. But pictures that reinforce more heroic narratives of combat are also present and can become a crucial dimension of war management. To measure what the public was actually seeing about Operation Iraqi Freedom, I reviewed the 465 photographs that appeared on the *Boston Globe*'s front page and in a special section titled "War in Iraq" between March 20 and April 17, 2003. On the typical day, the *Globe* carried 2 or 3 pictures on the front page and another 15 to 20 in the special section. The entire back page of this section was devoted to photographs. The photographs were chosen from a daily pool of 2,500 to 3,000 available to the *Globe* through various news services.

My review classifies photos into four main subject categories: the Iraqis, the United States, soldiers, and public reaction. Each category is further subdivided into particular themes such as destruction or looting in Iraq, soldiers giving aid, soldiers preparing for battle, U.S. officials, or reactions to Operation Iraqi Freedom in Europe or elsewhere in the Middle East (see table 5.1 for detailed categories and distribution results).

One of the most important findings is that of the 465 pictures, only 12 were of U.S. soldiers who had been killed in the conflict. Of these, all but 1 was similar to a wallet-sized snapshot, taken in the United States, with the soldier usually in formal uniform. Only an additional 7 photos were of U.S. wounded. All of these followed a

Table 5.1 *Boston Globe* Photographs by Subject/Theme

Phase I: March 20–April 17, 2003   Phase II: April 1–May 17, 2004[1]

	PHASE I		PHASE II	
	# of Photos	% of Total	# of Photos	% of Total
IRAQ				
Images of Saddam Hussein[2]	14	3	0	0
Destruction/looting	52	11	4	2
Civilians	35	8	18	9
Soldiers	15	3	0	0
Wounded or dead	14	3	3	1
Grieving	7	2	1	1
Kurds	21	5	0	0
Subtotal	158	34	26	13
UNITED STATES				
Washington, D.C., officials	22	5	31	15
United Nations	5	1	1	1
Misc. officials	8	2	12	6
Family of combat dead or POWs	3	1	6	3
Subtotal	38	8	50	25
SOLDIERS				
Preparation and rest	66	14	16	8
Shooting	29	6	13	6
Giving aid	40	9	1	1
Liberators	43	9	0	0
Capturing Iraqi POWs	23	5	3	1
Wounded	7	2	5	3
POW/MIA	8	2	7	4
Dead[3]	12	3	13	6
Subtotal	228	49	58	29
PROTEST				
United States	12	3	3	1
Europe	6	1	5	3
Middle East "street"[4]	23	5	0	0
Subtotal	41	9	8	4
Total	465	100		
Insurgency			39	20
Abu Ghraib			16	8
Returning home			3	1
Total			200	100

[1]Maps and graphics excluded; some percentages rounded.
[2]Pictures of toppled Saddam statues classified as "liberators."
[3]All but one picture of dead U.S. soldiers were wallet-sized snapshots taken in the U.S.
[4]Further subdivided into "angry" (57 percent) and "measured" (43 percent).

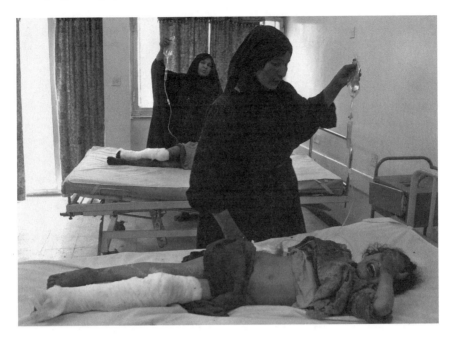

Iraqi children injured during U.S.-led air attacks on Baghdad are treated in a hospital (Samir Mezban/AP Photo).

convention in which the injured soldier—face, body, and nature of wound obscured—is carried on a stretcher by his (or her) comrades. Eight pictures were of U.S. POWs or MIAs. There were also very few pictures of Iraqi dead or wounded (14, or a total of 3 percent). Seven pictures showed Iraqi civilians grieving.

Only 3 photos showed a person who had been, or was currently, suffering physical pain. A moving photo of a wounded Iraqi girl in a Baghdad hospital is one of these exceptions. Despite the limited number of such pictures, some readers called the newspaper to complain about what they felt were some overly graphic presentations of war. "Please, please, it's so awful as it is, this war, please don't print photos like that," said one in response to a large color photo of a dead Iraqi soldier sprawled in front of a destroyed car. Another reader worried that children would see the picture and added, "This is something I would expect of the *Herald* or a tabloid—it is beneath the *Globe*."[27]

In contrast, almost 10 percent of the pictures were of the U.S. military dispensing aid. Another 10 percent showed U.S. troops in the role of liberator. The next photo, showing a combat engineer

An Army combat engineer shares food with a captured Iraqi soldier on the banks of the Euphrates River during the march to Baghdad (Reuters/Corbis).

sharing food with captured Iraqi soldiers, typifies this theme. There were more than five times as many pictures of soldiers giving aid or liberating Iraqis as there were of Iraqis who had been killed or wounded (83 to 14). Five percent of the photographs were of Kurds, often portrayed in the heroic mode of scanning the horizon with a pair of binoculars. Antiwar protest in the United States was reflected in only 3 percent of the photos. Of these, 75 percent appeared in the first four days of the war. Thereafter, pictures of the U.S. antiwar movement almost entirely disappeared from the newspaper.

To find out more about the process by which particular photographs appeared in the paper, I interviewed Paula Nelson, the deputy director of photography for the *Boston Globe* and the person most responsible for managing the selection process. I was particularly interested in learning about the paper's policy on graphic photographs and in reviewing the more controversial decisions that Nelson and the *Globe* had to make.

JOSEPH: Beyond the rule that prohibits running photos where the dead can be identified, were the pictures that you received from news sources screened in any way?

NELSON: Not to my knowledge. There were controversial cases, such as where Reuters decided to digitally blur faces when issues came up about the Geneva Convention and the treatment of prisoners. They would send them out on the wire and include an editor's note in the caption saying, We blurred the face. Then it was left up to the individual news publication to decide what to do.

I know there was a picture from the *Dallas Morning News* that caused some controversy. These guys had been taken prisoner and were in their underwear and had both hands tied behind their back with plastic handcuffs.

JOSEPH: These were Iraqi POWs?

NELSON: That's right. They were in a ditch. I think the [*New York*] *Times* used that picture and I think there was some involvement with the State Department whether or not the picture should have been transmitted.

JOSEPH: Because the U.S. might have been in violation of the Geneva Convention?

NELSON: Right. We had it in our section for about five seconds and then [laughter] we pulled it.

JOSEPH: Can you give any other examples of pictures that were controversial?

NELSON: We had many discussions about appropriateness and what we would do if Americans were taken prisoner—would we put that picture out there? Also, body photos, dead soldiers, especially identifiable dead soldiers, children and how they were pictured. There was one picture of a soldier carrying a kid who had just a little shirt on, no panties but nothing was showing. I wanted to run it but one of the editors said that it compromised the child. I didn't really agree with that because it was a two-year-old and all you could see was a little bum. But I don't get to make the top calls.

We did have discussions over bodies: When is it too gruesome? Is it going to be in color or black and white? We did have case-by-case decision making but we also tried to develop guidelines. Is it too bloody? If it's too bloody, it's not going to be on the front page. But perhaps it might be okay in black and white? Is the dead person identifiable? Again back to the question if that was a dead American lying there that his mom could identify. Dead Iraqis were less of an issue in these particular discussions because obviously the chances of someone in Iraq picking up the *Boston Globe* and seeing a relative is remote.

We did have an amazing photo that took a great deal of discussion on the day that Baghdad fell. I thought it really took us back to World War II. These soldiers were inside this building. It was bombed out with broken bricks and plaster and all that, and there is a body covered with dust on the ground. The soldiers are standing there and their faces are really intense and they have the whole gear, all the armor and guns. It was just a really compelling photo and I wanted to run it in black and white. One of the top editors decided not to run it because he said it was too graphic. I strongly disagreed because I didn't think it was too graphic and I thought it was handled very well by the photographer. I don't think the person was identifiable. I thought that the content value of that photo far outweighed anything else. I thought it was very important to run something like that on that particular day because we had dedicated so much to the fall of Baghdad. There were celebrating people and celebrating soldiers. I wanted to remember that there is still is a war and people were dying still and would continue to die for weeks to come. I thought that balance was really important.

JOSEPH: I'd like to come back to that but while we are on the topic, can you give me any other examples of editorial disagreement?

NELSON: There was a photo of a car that was bombed and some charred bodies. It was a really strong photo and I wanted to use it. To compromise on that one, we cropped it in a way that took some bodies out but left some in. It was a good compromise because we still got the message across of war and how awful it is but not so much as to shock people. I think if you go too far, people don't look at it. What you want is for people to look at it and to study it and to say this is an awful thing. You want them to get the message of the photo but you don't want to make it so gruesome that they no longer pay attention and go right over it.

In my opinion, Paula Nelson carried out her work with competence, intelligence, and sensitivity. She also seemed skeptical about many aspects of the war. And yet the *Globe* published so few pictures that focused on the human cost. The net result of the photo-selection process was a fairly clean view of the war, even as Nelson thought of her work as contributing to just the opposite message. I asked her about this directly:

JOSEPH: I have the impression listening to you that you would have preferred to see more pictures that could give readers a deeper sense of the nature of war.

NELSON: It was really a struggle. I didn't want to, using someone else's words, "sanitize too much," because there are many people just sitting over here saying we are doing really well. They don't think about the other aspects. They don't think about the innocent people who were next to the building that was bombed in the belief that Saddam was there. I didn't want people to forget about how the war was affecting regular people. I remember paging through the system and finding a picture of this little Iraqi girl. She was in this neighborhood, there was a big tank in the background and big tears coming down her face. Later on that day I found a picture of a soldier who was on the phone with his wife. They had been married three months before and he is crying too. I put those two together for a reason. Pictures together can say things that they can't by themselves.

But you have to be careful. Once there were Iraqi reports of five hundred civilians killed in this bombing. But the photographers that were in Baghdad showed the same three injured kids for two days. So you start to think, "Okay, where are all those people that are injured? Why aren't they in hospitals? Are they exaggerating the casualties?" You don't know. I would ask myself questions while paging through the pictures. "Isn't this the same kid that showed up yesterday without an arm? So where are all those other people that were supposed to be injured?" You try to be really conscious of balancing the visuals just as you would the words. I was always trying to make sure that we showed grieving family, injured civilians, Iraqi soldiers, and American soldiers.

JOSEPH: But if you look at a small number of dead and the conventions in which they are actually shown, especially in comparison to the number of pictures that embody what I call the "liberator theme," there is a very big difference. The pictures of those grieving in Baghdad are very powerful but also very small in number.

NELSON: You know, there is an argument that the American press doesn't show those pictures because they have ulterior motives. But there is also an argument that the American press doesn't show that kind of stuff under any circumstances because its audience is not able to handle it. So papers also make decisions based on their readership.

One photograph that appeared in the *Globe* caused more controversy than all the rest put together. It shows a group of soldiers celebrating in one of Saddam's presidential palaces in Baghdad. One sits in a chair smoking a cigarette while his comrades gather around basking in the glow of victory. They are smiling in satisfaction amid the debris. A caption says that the troops "rifled through the files" and took "souvenirs."[28]

Dozens of readers called or emailed their thoughts to the *Globe* ombudsman. "The image of the U.S. is tarnished enough without broadcasting what looks like a post-battle frat party," wrote one reader arguing that the photograph should not have been published. "All that is missing is a keg of beer on the marble top table," the reader added.[29] Another felt that the "the *Globe* chose to put people who are risking their lives for their country in a very bad light. Everyone was talking about the photo. It looks bad. People change how they talk about the *Globe*." Yet another reader thought that the image "helps fuel the hatred and irrational anger" at the United States and that "that makes more 9/11s."

Paula Nelson said later about the reactions to the photograph, "That's what they [the soldiers] did. We didn't make them sit in chairs. It just shows you the incredible power of photography and how much people can read into something. Here are American

*U.S. Army Staff Sergeant Chad Touchette relaxes with comrades in
a presidential palace in Baghdad (John Moore/AP Photo).*

soldiers sitting in his place of power, his palace, and are just there
smoking a cigarette. It was amazing what people saw in that photo."
The strong reactions to the picture illustrate the sensitivity of the
public to behavior that seems to transgress the boundaries of conditional war. For the public, it is not normal for their troops to act
like conquistadors.

U.S. military operations did not appear nearly so successful during subsequent phases of the war in Iraq. The "insurgency" grew
and casualties began to climb. A year later, Washington was still
fighting a war that appeared inconclusive and yet carried steadily
increasing human, political, and economic costs. In one particularly
difficult period, four civilian contractors were abducted and killed.
Photographs of their burned bodies hanging from a Fallujah bridge
appeared in many newspapers. The Abu Ghraib scandal broke and
photographs of U.S. soldiers abusing and torturing Iraqi prisoners
appeared in many major news outlets. For an increasing number
of observers, poor preparations for the occupation, continued fighting, and other self-defeating aspects of the situation brought back
memories of Vietnam. Public approval of the war in Iraq dropped
significantly. What did the public see of the new circumstances? Did
the *Globe*'s selection of photographs change in any way?

To answer this question, the two hundred photographs that appeared in the *Boston Globe* in "Phase II," from April 1 to May 17, 2004, were compared with those published a year earlier (see Phase II column in table 5.1).[30] The main difference is in the number of pictures that conveyed "giving aid" and "liberator" themes, each of which dropped dramatically in 2004. These comprised almost 20 percent of the photographs during Phase I but only one picture of U.S. soldiers giving aid appeared in Phase II. None fell into the liberator category. In addition, there were significantly fewer pictures of Iraq during the second period and more emphasis on various government officials in Washington, D.C., in part because these officials chose or were asked to defend the war in press conferences or in congressional testimony that was covered by the press. The proportion of photographs of the wounded and dead increased slightly but the photos did not change significantly in style or convention. Eight graphic pictures that communicated the pain of war, most of the killing of the civilian contractors, were chosen by the *Globe*, but in general more explicit images continued to be avoided.

Did the *Boston Globe*'s selection of photographs differ from that in other newspapers? To answer this question, a comparison was made with the *London Times* and the *New York Post* for each of the two time periods.[31] During 2003, the *Times* printed almost twice as many photos as the *Globe* and tended to show more of the "home front." The paper would often print a short anecdotal story and picture about the girl-friend, wife, or mother of a British soldier in Iraq. On the other hand, less than 1 percent of their photos focused on grieving Iraqi civilians, approximately one-quarter of what the *Globe* published. As could be expected, the percentage of Europe/Asia reaction photos was six times greater in the *Times* than in the Boston paper. Both papers devoted 3 percent of their photos to public reactions in the United States. The *Times* also made a more concerted effort to show the costs of war. While only 7 percent of the *Globe* photos focused on wounded, POW/MIA, and dead soldiers, 16 percent of the photos in the *Times* fell into these categories. Three percent of the *Globe* photos were of the dead; 10 percent fit this category in the *Times*. Another contrast came in the giving-aid and liberator themes, which figured so prominently in the *Globe*. Only twenty-one such pictures were published in the *Times*, approximately one-seventh the proportion found in the U.S. newspaper.

As in the *Globe*, Phase II saw a marked decrease in the *Times* in the total number of photos of the Iraq war. Several prominent stories competed for space, including an alleged affair by soccer star David Beckham, the entry of several Eastern European countries into the European Union, and the quality of the British school system. In contrast with the *Globe*, which published relatively few pictures of the Abu Ghraib scandal, the *Times* printed many photos showing the humiliation of prisoners carried out by U.S. prison guards. Photos of alleged prisoner abuse carried out by UK soldiers appeared in a British tabloid at this time and were reprinted virtually daily in the *Times* until it was determined that this set of photos was faked. While the potential British abuse scandal was brewing, articles about the destructive emotions soldiers face when they have seen their comrades killed were run alongside the abuse photos. Once the British abuse photos were shown to be false, these articles were no longer run and Abu Ghraib was suddenly described as "America's Shame."

The *New York Post* also published numerous photographs during both phases under review. Compared with the *Globe,* the paper chose more pictures of soldiers in preparation and rest and in active engagement such as shooting or patrolling. The *Post* had three times as many pictures of soldiers in action as did the *Globe.* On the other hand, there were no pictures of grieving Iraqis, many fewer pictures of Kurds, and roughly half the number of pictures of Iraqi civilians. Similarly, the *Post* did not include many pictures of the reactions to the war from people throughout the Middle East. The *Post* seemed especially interested in focusing the reader's eye on Americans in Iraq rather than on Iraqis in Iraq or on how other people throughout the world might be reacting to what was going on in Iraq. During Phase II, a period of heightened political turmoil in Iraq, the *Post* published only one-ninth the number of photos of Iraqi civilians included in the *Globe.*

The New York tabloid also included fewer pictures on the liberator and giving-aid themes that played such a dominant role in the *Globe*'s coverage during Phase I. In 2004, neither paper published many photographs along these lines. There were more than twice as many pictures of dead and missing soldiers in the paper, many from the New York area (which may reflect that the status of the *Post* as more of a "local" paper than the *Globe*). The *Post*'s photographs followed the conditional war convention of avoiding the body in pain. The only exception to this pattern was the string of pictures of dead or missing U.S. contractors from April 2004, although here too the paper tended to use photos of the individuals and their family members back in the United States rather than bodies.

Photographs, Bodies, and Conditional War

The first impulse of an administration at war, be it mobilized or conditional, is to attempt to control the flow of information, including visuals, that reaches the public. The State Department asked the UN to cover the reproduction of *Guernica* hanging outside the Security Council. The Pentagon banned pictures of dead soldiers returning through its Dover airfield, and there have been remarkably few photographs of the thousands of wounded at Walter Reed and other military hospitals. Despite claims of more open access, the military continued to push journalists away from stories that conveyed the cost of war. Photojournalists have had their film seized and destroyed by the military and even had warning shots fired over their heads as they attempted to cover controversial incidents, such as the downing of helicopters by hostile fire. In November 2003, representatives of thirty media organizations sent a joint letter to the Pentagon complaining that they had "documented numerous examples of U.S. troops physically harassing journalists and, in some cases, confiscating or ruining equipment, digital camera disks, and videotapes."[32] Images that conveyed stalemate, or simply chaos, pointed toward the uncertainties of the Vietnam War story. Even in a situation where the war against terrorism has been defended as a fight for the U.S. way of life, many barriers to the presentation of more-candid photographs remained intact. War managers still want to direct the public gaze so that only certain themes can be seen.

Bodies—be they American, Afghan, British, or Iraqi—have largely disappeared from public view. The main reason is that the visibility of the killed and injured demands a moral accounting. The public could see bodies from World War II battlefields because Washington was confident that U.S. citizens would think that the killing, while certainly sad, was also necessary in the context of a just fight against fascism. Government officials no longer think that the public will come to the same conclusion. Instead, they limit the possibilities of seeing the explicit evidence of war and hamper their ability to make their own moral judgment that takes this loss into consideration. As one social commentator has observed, the preference of war managers is for "a system of representation which marginalizes the presence of the body in war, fetishizes machines, and personalizes international conflicts while depersonalizing the people who die in them."[33]

A democratic public sphere contains controversy. Pictures that convey the real pain of war do not carry an automatic antiwar message and their presentation will always be to some degree managed, even by activist organizations, intellectuals, and publicists explicitly opposed to war. Even some war supporters favor a more visible method of communicating the war's costs. Some military families simply want a more honest approach. But "truth telling" about war requires a confrontation with its consequences. And Washington and the press are often reluctant to present photographs that detail the human costs. This inclination is not absolute, and the careful reader of the nation's newspapers will be able to see some indicators of battle. To some degree, newspapers also differ from each other in their selection of photographs. Press photography is far from being a conspiracy, especially when one considers the many photographers who have risked their lives to communicate the tragedy of war and the decisions of editors to bring their work to a large audience. But most who manage the flow of visuals from the battlefield share a desire to "protect" the public from the rudeness of killing. News executives and editors also share a sense of what constitutes good taste when presenting the tragedies of combat. It is also very difficult for them to present a consistent set of images, running day to day and week to week, that run counter to government policy. And it is the repetitive reframing of the story rather than the occasional appearance of a countermessage that has the most public influence. To some degree, the disinclination to consider what happens to human bodies in war also exists at the popular level. Many people do become upset when they see violence. But should they be protected from this emotion? There is also evidence that much of the public would prefer to make up their minds in a visual context that includes the tangible costs of war. But government officials do not want this process to take place because the public is likely to conclude that it is not photographs of the war but war itself that is in poor taste.

Chapter 6

Managing Gender

Americans are becoming more peaceful due to explicit opposition to war and increased reluctance to accept the visible costs of war. In the movement from mobilized to conditional war, the very social organization of war is also changing. The two processes, consciousness on the one hand and structural relationships on the other, are interrelated. Different kinds of connections between preparation for war and society are being challenged by war opposition and are becoming structurally less important.

What about the specific connection between gender and conditional war? A generation of feminist scholars has established the axiom that "gender is everywhere," an insight that is especially apt for the relationship between society and war. Shared understandings of "masculine" and "feminine" have influenced the war-making process. In turn, the experiences of war have helped shape our concepts of gender. These crucial interactions still exist—it would be extremely difficult to argue that gender has been "demobilized" from war. But during the movement from mobilized to conditional war, the links between war preparation and gender preparation have become more varied, complex, and contradictory. These conflicting pressures are restructuring the previous, relatively straightforward evocation of masculinity in support of the war effort. The result is that new types of suspended judgment now lie between the public and support of conditional war.

For most of U.S. history, the warrior role reaffirmed traditional understandings of gender. Soldiers were "real men": strong, brave, and in control of emotions that could interfere with their ability to fight. Women were noncombatants who either needed the protection of male soldiers or provided support to their husbands, sons, or brothers as they went off to battle. But this dichotomy has been recently challenged on many levels, most of all by the many more women who now serve in the military and have sought greater equality within it. If women can fully participate in health care delivery, the legal profession, teaching, and policing, why should they not be able to do so as soldiers? But their visibility within the armed forces, and their new exposure to harm, raises a fundamental question: Is it more difficult to go to war when the casualties will include not only men but also Mom, sister, daughter, or the girl next door?

This chapter begins with World War II, a conflict that clearly reinforced a strong sense of masculinity among soldiers. The transformation of young boys to strong men capable of withstanding the rigors of combat was presented as one of the keys to victory—and to the recovery of the nation from the collective weaknesses of the Depression. The war instilled a strong sense of national purpose and in the process helped restore American masculinity. But not all the men who fought could withstand "combat fatigue," a psychological syndrome now called post–traumatic stress disorder (PTSD). Indeed, the medical profession began to expect that those facing sustained combat would become psychologically damaged. But the fighting soldiers were male, and combat fatigue was a problem faced almost entirely by men.[1] The chapter ends with a summary of the early studies of the psychological costs of the war in Iraq, where one in six soldiers returning to the United States reported signs of psychological trauma. Unlike World War II, those returning also included a significant number of women with PTSD.

Between the PTSD bookends, many other issues are explored. These include the use of women as victims to obtain war support and the persistence of sexual harassment and other forms of violence against women within the armed forces and service academies. Traditional methods of legitimating war have not been fully displaced. On the mythic frontier, strong men rescued females in distress. The enormous publicity surrounding the effort to "save Private Jessica Lynch" cast a more favorable light on the U.S. military effort during a particularly difficult moment in the war in Iraq. Much of the public felt better about Operation Iraqi Freedom because it seemed that a young, white, vulnerable, pretty woman had been saved from dark, evil, mysterious strangers by honorable, virtuous men. But one year later another, very different, woman became the face of the infamous Abu Ghraib scandal. Pictures of Lynndie England leading shackled Iraqi prisoners around on a leash, or giving the thumbs up sign while standing next to naked detainees, shocked the public. Gender-laced honor had been replaced with gender-stained shame.

The chapter also reviews the critical debate over the opening of combat roles for women. As of February 2006, forty-eight female service members had died in Iraq, thirty-four as the result of hostile fire. Another six military women have been killed in Afghanistan.[2] Many more have been wounded. This loss has been the source of both pain and pride. Many of my own students, including those exhibiting strong Type I opposition to war, also strongly believe in the right and ability of women to serve in whatever military capacity they choose. This leads to another question: how does the process by which Americans are becoming more peaceful intersect with the process of becoming more gender equal?

World War II, Masculinity, and PTSD

In his *End of Victory Culture*, Tom Engelhardt argues that World War II was the high-water mark for an American war narrative that embraced the frontier and carried several important messages. First, westward expansion was about freedom, not empire. Occupying the territory held by "inferior" native peoples was a means for progress and resurrected the underlying truth that the mission of the "first new nation" was sacred. Second, frontier war consisted of a series of defensive skirmishes rather than conquest. Violence was forced upon white Americans. There was no choice: either you pulled the trigger against the native onslaught or you died. Infrequent setbacks, such as Custer's last stand, served only as brief preludes to an eventual victory that cast a satisfying and purifying glow on the entire country. Third, pioneer women were especially vulnerable to capture. Once abducted, their treatment by the "savages" would be unspeakably brutal, so men had to protect their women at all costs.

World War II reprised this frontier mythology. The United States recovered from a sneak attack at Pearl Harbor, and the eventual victory in the Pacific brought progress for all—even those who had been defeated. The war had been forced on a reluctant America by an untrustworthy enemy. As with Indians, the stories told about the fighting focused upon savages who seemed to hold no regard for human life. Dozens of movies were made showing Japanese soldiers charging foxholes until there were literally no more to send. As with the western continental frontier, the Others were made evil and expendable. The faceless enemy died at a distance but American deaths were more intimate. While painful, World War II was also a satisfying story because it confirmed U.S. strengths: perseverance, scientific supremacy, and freedom. The sacrifice helped make the world a better place.

World War II also helped rescue masculinity from the discouraging depths of the Depression. The 1930s helped trigger an acute crisis in masculinity in which men no longer seemed to be in charge of their own fate. In *Puzzled America,* Sherwood Anderson appealed to his readers for sympathy for the now vulnerable male: "The moral fiber of the American man, through being without a job, losing sense of being some part of the moving world of activity, so essential to an American man's sense of his manhood—the loss of this essential something in the jobless can never be measured in dollars."[3] World War II helped repair this social wound. Advertisements and public service announcements sought to establish the idea of a stronger, more determined male, one who worked hard and was now under self-control. The war provided the means for men to venture into the unknown, undergo a trial, and prove their self-worth. But first they had to rid themselves of any weaknesses.

The medical profession, particularly psychiatrists, began to play a larger role in the screening and selection of military recruits. Christina Jarvis's study of masculinity and the war notes that "the military's classification and control of male bodies during World War II had profound effects on both individual servicemen and American culture. Three particular procedures reveal the remarkable ways that military management of male bodies operated: initial medical inspections, physical training programs, and screenings for venereal disease and potential homosexuality."[4] Many civilian and military leaders were concerned that American males had become too "soft." Psychiatrists commonly blamed "overprotective, rejecting, withdrawn, aggressive, coddling, pushy, 'nervous,' uninformed and/or divorced mothers for this disturbing social trend."[5] In particular, the country's leaders worried that too many men of the Depression generation would break down in the midst of combat. In the view of the Freudianism that then held sway, many males shared a childhood-induced predisposition to stop functioning under enemy fire. At first, the military attempted to screen recruits so that only those who could withstand the rigors of fighting would be inducted into the armed forces. The favorable indicators included participation in team sports, aggressiveness, and overt sexuality. Young men who had played cowboys and Indians as kids, became quarterbacks in high school, and dated girls seemed to be the best. (In contrast, women applying to join the auxiliary corps were asked questions such as "Do you feel faint when you see a mouse?" or "Do you run when you see a bug or a snake?")[6] Proper screening would enable the government to separate the fighters from the weak-kneed malcontents. As late as January 1943 a *Time* article could claim that "when a man has a mental crackup in battle, his local draft board may be to blame."[7]

But as the war went on and the fighting intensified, it became increasingly clear that "combat psychoneurosis" was a problem for virtually all soldiers, including those who conformed most closely to the characteristics of "real men." Everyone seemed vulnerable to breakdown. More astute medical personnel began to recognize a particular clustering of symptoms. Joshua Goldstein notes that "studies of Allied troops in the 1944 Normandy campaign showed that after one or two weeks of becoming battle-wise a soldier's period of maximum efficiency lasts only about a month."[8] Afterward a period of exhaustion sets in, followed by "a highly reactive stage," then apathy and a vegetative condition. A 1943 medical report from the Pacific stated that after six months, many troops in the tropics were of no further use in the fighting. The majority shared "a marked loss of weight, decrease in physical stamina, lethargy, a 'lackadaisical' attitude, and suspended compliance to orders." Another memo agreed, stating that "at this time personnel endurance is waning, alertness nil ... [and that] twenty months served without furlough in tropical bush country speaks for itself."[9]

In May 1943, *Time* ran a story titled "Guadalcanal Neurosis," which quoted Lieutenant Commander Rogers Smith, a leading military psychiatrist who had discovered a "group neurosis that had not been seen before." Smith noted that the "500 neurotic Marines" suffering from this disorder were not weaklings who had somehow made it through initial screening. Instead, they were strong, "steady men" who had proved themselves in battle. Far from being of dubious quality, they were the proverbial high school quarterbacks who were outwardly confident and went out with girls. "Never before in history," wrote Smith, "have such a group of healthy, toughened, well-trained men been subjected to such conditions." The symptoms included "headaches, sensitivity to loud or sudden noises, periods of amnesia, feelings of panic, tense muscles, tremors, and hands that shook when they tried to do anything."[10] The men were short-tempered and hyperaggressive.

Initially, the U.S. public was spared from pictures and other evidence of the viciousness of the fighting. But this cover became more difficult to preserve as the war progressed. Letters from the front and returning soldiers told stories of arduous, prolonged combat and pervasive combat fatigue. As some became increasingly suspicious of overly optimistic news, the government changed direction and approved press stories about the difficult fighting in the Pacific. In an April 1943 memorandum from the Office of Chief of Staff, General

George Marshall informed leading military officers that victory would be achieved, not quickly, but only after "a long and bloody haul."[11] Preparing the home front for the additional sacrifice included both more graphic representation of the violence and renewed emphasis on the personal traits of strength and masculinity that would pull everyone through.

A full-page *Life* photograph that showed three Americans killed on a New Guinea beach was accompanied by a story that linked masculinity and the forthcoming victory in the Pacific: "From this picture, we can still see, in every line of action, why it is that American boys win. We can still sense the high optimism of men who have never known oppression—who, however scared, have never had to base their decisions on fear. We are still aware of the relaxed self-confidence with which the leading boys ran into the sudden burst of fire—almost like a halfback carrying the ball down a football field."[12]

A series of public service announcements aimed at securing resolve on the home front also invoked reassuring masculinity. One of the most famous, titled "The Kid in Upper 4," first appeared in the *New York Herald Tribune* on November 22, 1942, after the country had been at war for nearly a year. The advertisement, which has been called the most effective in U.S. history, focuses on a boy about to be shipped overseas.[13] He looks very young and worried as he lies on his upper bunk on a railway car. The text reads:

> Tonight, he knows, he is leaving behind a lot of little things—and big ones.
>
> The taste of hamburgers and pop ... the feel of driving a roadster over a six-lane highway ... a dog named Shucks, or Spot, or Barnacle Bill.
>
> The pretty girl who writes so often ... that gray-haired man, so proud and awkward at the station ... the mother who knit the socks he'll wear soon.
>
> Tonight he's thinking them over.
>
> There's a lump in his throat. And maybe—a tear fills his eye. *It doesn't matter, Kid.* Nobody will see ... it's too dark.

War is about to transform this boy, despite his fears, into a man. The kid represents hope, the future, and everything that is good about the nation. His soon-to-be-realized contributions are contrasted with the "gray-haired man," presumably the Depression-era father who couldn't hold a steady job. The kid has strengths that he is just beginning to realize and his contributions to the war will be welcomed by others. The advertisement continues:

But people all over the world are waiting, praying for him to come.
And he will come, this kid in upper 4.
With new hope, peace and freedom for a tired, bleeding world.

The connections among sacrifice, masculinity, and mobilization of
the public behind the war effort are contained in another public

BY HIS DEEDS . . . MEASURE YOURS

JOHN FALTER

The civilian war organization needs your help. The Government has formed Citizens Service Corps as part of local Defense Councils.

If such a group is at work in your community, cooperate with it to the limit of your ability. If none exists, help to organize one.

A free booklet telling you what to do and how to do it will be sent to you at no charge if you will write to this magazine.

This is your war. Help win it. Choose what you will do — now!

EVERY CIVILIAN A FIGHTER

Life *magazine, March 15, 1943.*

service announcement, this titled "By His Deed . . . Measure Yours," which was published in *Life* a few months later.[14] This extraordinary advertisement shows a young, dead combat soldier with a barbed-wire crown around his head. He is lying in a crucified position. The text reads: "It is not pleasant to have your peaceful life upset by wartime needs and restrictions and activities . . . It is not pleasant to die, either . . . Between you who live at home and the men who die at the front there is a direct connection . . . By your actions, definitely, a certain number of these men will die or they will come through alive." The announcement, which was contributed by the Magazine Publishers of America, concludes with an appeal in the "name of God and your fellow man" to support the newly formed Citizen Service Corps, which served under local Defense Councils.

To contemporary sensibilities, the proximity to death is rude and jarring. But a certain level of confidence lay behind the decisions to place these images before the American public. National leaders and the public shared an understanding that the war would bring unfortunate but also necessary death. The sacrifice required was fully legitimate. The war effort mobilized society and shaped many of its core structures, including gender roles. Masculinity became defined in the context of the war effort, and the war effort helped rescue men from their weak Depression-era status. At the same time, an appreciation that war could also lead to combat fatigue began to spread. This consequence of violence could affect soldiers no matter how traditionally masculine. There were limits to masculine strength. But it would take another war—Vietnam—and another political generation for this awareness to become broadly accepted by the medical establishment and the general population.

Another important gender-related point about World War II concerns the large number of women who moved into the defense industry or into other necessary jobs vacated by men off doing the fighting. Most of the population supported this development. One of the earliest Gallup polls found approximately 80 percent of the country agreeing with the argument that the army should be able to draft women aged twenty-one to thirty-five for nonfighting jobs rather than drafting married men with families for the same work. More than half favored giving local draft boards the right to draft single women for noncombat jobs with the armed forces.[15] The new opportunity to participate in the public arena did not relieve women of their more traditional responsibilities and many went home to a "double shift" of housework and parenting.[16]

Women in the Military, Women in Combat

Since World War II, more women have moved into occupations as
diverse as the law, the academy, business, and public safety. Women
are now one-half of the entrants to medical school and hold more
than half of the university and college faculty positions in the hu-
manities. This movement toward formal equality also includes the
armed forces: 15 percent of members of the military services are
now women, up from only 2 percent when the all-volunteer military
was established in 1973. There are now more than 210,000 women
in uniform. One consequence is that the military has taken steps to
become more "family friendly." There are now approximately 850,000
military families with more than 1.3 million children, and more than
60 percent of service members are married. In a large number of
couples both members serve in the armed forces, and there has
even been a recent increase in the number of military wives with
civilian husbands. Military policies and programs have an important
effect on family life and the commitment of the soldier to the service.
Military sociologists argue that the perception that unit leaders are
genuinely concerned with their families has a positive influence on
retention rates, morale, and "affective commitment" to the army.[17]
The military provides child care, relocation assistance, and financial services, as well as counseling services aimed at reducing the
considerable stress produced by overseas deployment.[18]

On the other hand, going to war is not particularly healthy for
family life. The divorce rate for active-duty soldiers deployed in Afghanistan and Iraq more than tripled for officers between 2000 and
2004 and went up 53 percent for enlisted personnel. "If the numbers
are right," said one expert, "then we have more to worry about than
just fighting a war. We're trying to fight a war with families that are
struggling, and that's a real challenge."[19] The U.S. Army has initiated "marriage enlistment" seminars and vouchers for romantic
getaways, but divorce continues to be a relatively hidden but real
cost of war.

But the implications of more women in the military extend far
beyond family issues. With this increased presence has come an
important debate on whether women should be able serve in combat
roles. The Pentagon viewed the 1991 Gulf War as a largely successful test of the contributions that women could make to a military
force deployed overseas. Afterward, a Presidential Commission on
the Assignment of Women in the Armed Forces conducted hearings that led to revised regulations. After 1994, women could fly
combat aircraft and serve on surface-combat ships. Women have in
fact been increasingly integrated into more dangerous positions in

the military and they are now eligible for more than 90 percent of military career roles. But they are still excluded from "direct" and "near" combat roles, submarines, and the Special Forces. During the war in Iraq, President Bush reiterated the formal ban on several occasions, especially when his conservative base expressed alarm that women were being pressed into de facto combat roles.

Those favoring exclusion from combat argue that women lack the upper-body strength and other physical and emotional attributes necessary to become effective fighters. They also fear that the close proximity of men and women in combat situations will encourage immature behavior that undermines unit discipline, and "fraternization" that compromises morale, particularly in closely confined quarters such as naval ships. Critics of full equality claim that pregnancies will inevitably result and undercut expensive training and the readiness of fighting units. During 1991 Operation Desert Storm, the press started to call the USS *Acadia* the "Love Boat" after it became known that 10 percent of the women, thirty-six in all, became pregnant while deployed in the Persian Gulf. A more contemporary and particularly well-publicized example involved a mud-wrestling party among military police at army-run Camp Bucca in Iraq; a female soldier was later demoted for "indecent exposure."[20] No male was punished for participating but pictures of the well-endowed soldier were featured in newspapers throughout the country. Yet another argument in favor of the ban concerns the perceived vulnerability of women in combat and the prospect that male soldiers would be more concerned with protecting their female counterparts than fighting the enemy. Finally, some hawks feared that it would be more difficult for a president to order a sexually integrated combat force into battle.

Those arguing that women should be able to serve in combat positions offered a different perspective. Recent changes in technology have reduced the importance of physical strength for many types of soldiering. This argument has worked particularly well for helicopter pilots, a classification in which women have become more numerous. With proper training many women can achieve the necessary strength and in some areas such as endurance may even have better physical capacities than men. At any rate, meeting a specific standard, such as lifting a particular weight or running a mile in a certain time, should be the selection mechanism rather than the sex of the person trying to meet the test. Meanwhile, violence and sexual harassment continue to afflict the military and will not change significantly until women are accepted as fundamental equals. In the military, "equal" means the right to enter combat. Moreover, modern warfare has already blurred the distinction between combat and noncombat roles. Artillery or rocket attacks and improvised explosive devices leave radar operators, cooks, mechanics, and military police vulnerable. If they serve in a combat zone, women are in harm's way. Those advocating the removal of the combat ban also note that the movement for greater equality also met resistance in civilian life where alleged physical limitations were often cited as a reason to limit women's access to work that had been reserved primarily for men. Eventually, women proved that they could perform at the same level of competency. Given the opportunity, the same should prove true for the military as well.[21]

No matter the outcome of the debate, the on-the-ground reality of Afghanistan and Iraq found military women closer to combat. Women were placed in newly created "forward support companies," which provided food, maintenance, and other services to combat units, in part because of the shortage of male soldiers. A May 2004 army briefing found that all-male forward support companies would create a "potential long-term challenge to Army; pool of male recruits too small to sustain force."[22] In a policy called "collocation," female soldiers patrolled with combat units and had special responsibility for searching female civilians. The military defended this practice as culturally necessary given the sensitive issue of male soldiers touching Muslim women. The policies of intermingling mixed-sex forward support companies and including selected women in combat battalions added another chapter to the debate over combat roles. Social conservatives argued that the ban had been violated and Bush restated his opposition to the prohibition. The army's largest professional organization contributed $20,000 to the Center for Military Readiness, whose leader, Elaine Donnelly, maintained that there "is no excuse for forcing unprepared female soldiers to face the physical demands of violent close combat and a higher risk of capture.... Combat commanders will have to cope with significant personnel losses, distractions, and social turmoil. Predictable problems include far higher rates of medical leave and evacuations, primarily due to pregnancy. Making the mix even more volatile will be sexual attractions, personal misconduct, and accusations."[23]

Yet the military needed female soldiers. Supporters of full equity pointed out that the battle lines, particularly in Iraq, had merged and that every unit, whether "front-line" or in "the rear" was targeted. Ending the combat ban would only acknowledge reality. "It doesn't seem to be a big deal," said retired navy captain Lory Manning. "We could not do what needs to be done over there without women."[24] Air force brigadier general Wilma Vaught (ret.) noted, "With each conflict, women are used more than in the previous conflict. In Vietnam, we were restricted on where we could go, we didn't go out on convoys.

More than ever before, the military is accepting that women are there to do a job. If the job takes them in harm's way, well, that's the way it is."[25] In fact, *not* recognizing the de facto combat role of women could also be a danger. In June 2005, three male and three female marines were killed when a cargo truck used to transport the women back to their base camp was rammed by a car driven by a suicide bomber. The women, a twenty-year-old who had enlisted to support her mother, a twenty-one-year-old former cheerleader, and a forty-three-year-old single mother on her second tour, had been assigned to duty at a Fallujah checkpoint. But the ban required that they be billeted separately from the men in their unit, hence the daily, and eventually deadly, transport in a predictable convoy that was relatively easy to target.[26] Basing the women along with the men would have provided not only better security but also explicit acknowledgment of their forward deployment. As more women became involved in direct combat, several received the Bronze Star with the combat V for valor under fire. The public recognizes that it has become more common for women to serve in the armed forces; but it is not yet clear whether it has become publicly acceptable for women to engage in combat.

The Amazons of Dahomey

Historically, warfare has tended to be the exclusive preserve of men. Women have been known to fight but usually against outsiders and only episodically. Israeli women fought in the late 1940s in underground units that conducted terrorist actions against the British. (Women are still required to serve in the Israeli armed forces but the widespread notion that they serve as combat equals is a misperception.) Vietnamese, Chinese, Yugoslav, and Soviet women also fought at various times but only in the special circumstances of a desperate fight against invaders. Women have also served in several national liberation movements, including those in Cuba, Mozambique, Algeria, and El Salvador. They also fought during the Mau Mau rebellion in Kenya. But only in Dahomey on the west coast of Africa (present-day Benin) did women become a professional and permanent fighting force: during the second half of the nineteenth century, there was a female army numbering between four thousand and six thousand. This unique situation can be used to reflect on the current circumstances of women in the U.S. military, particularly on the question of whether they will be accepted in combat roles by the rest of the public.

The so-called Amazons of Dahomey trained long hours and with considerable discipline. They became an elite force that was strong, fast, and skilled in the use of many weapons. Smooth-bore, muzzle-loaded flintlock muskets were their favorite weapons, and they proved themselves able to load and fire more quickly than their male counterparts. The female soldiers also used machetes, which a French trader noted they "wield[ed] with much skill and with which they lop[ped] off a limb or a head with a single blow as if it were an ordinary cane of bamboo."[27] They also used round-headed clubs as battle axes and occasionally carried giant straight-edged razors weighing more than twenty pounds, which when fully extended may have been as long as four or five feet. Some warriors filed and hardened their fingernails for use as weapons. Training included barefoot sprints over the eight-foot thornbushes that served as defensive perimeters for the typical village. As a French lieutenant reported to a foreign legionnaire, "I don't know who taught them military tactics, the handling of arms and shooting, but that one certainly didn't steal his money."[28]

The female soldiers were trained initially as palace guards and were considered more loyal and trustworthy than the men, whom Dahomey kings did not permit to enter their palaces after nightfall. But war was also an annual affair largely to capture slaves from surrounding territories. Some Dahomey men were also killed in these conflicts or were captured themselves and shipped to the New World. This led to a shortage of men and additional need for women warriors.

The women developed strong bonds and were recognized and accepted as elite soldiers. They were recruited, trained, and barracked apart from men and were led by women officers. Dance, song, and instrumental music built esprit de corps. Training included the classic emphasis on desensitization. They engaged in fierce competition against male soldiers, and the women frequently came out on top. They wore standardized uniforms, took blood oaths, and rejected many of the traditional earmarks of feminine beauty. Prizes and privileges, including promotions, slaves, alcohol, and tobacco, were distributed to those who performed well and honor came to those who succeeded on the battlefield. Not infrequently, women commanded men on the battlefield.

In considering the contemporary significance of the Dahomey female warriors, one key point stands out: those who went to war saw themselves, and were seen by the rest of society, as men. The illustration shows a Dahomean warrior dressed in male attire and carrying a battle trophy. Sexual intercourse with men was prohibited, and death was the stated penalty for breaking the code.[29]

Songs and battle cries reinforced this identity. One chant went, "As the blacksmith takes an iron bar and by fire changes its fashion so have we changed our nature. We are no longer women, we are men."[30] Another called:

> We are men, not women ...
> Whatever town we attack
> We must conquer,
> Or bury ourselves in its ruins.

And another:

> Let us march in a virile manner,
> Let us march boldly, like men.

A Dahomean warrior as drawn by an English visitor, 1850 (Forbes 1851, plate 2, Smithsonian Institution Libraries).

Uniforms were designed to conceal feminine attributes from enemy warriors, and the women learned to walk with a masculine gait. Thomas Birch Freeman, an Anglo-African missionary, once witnessed a brigade of several hundred warriors who "were dressed so much like men, that a stranger would not have supposed that they were women." They wore "a loose shirt without sleeves, which comes nearly down to their knees, and is fastened round the waist by their cartouch-belt."[31] The distinction between the sexes was blurred in other ways. Both male and female warriors shaved their heads, leaving only a thin crest of hair running along the top of their skulls. Civilians also thought along similar lines about gender. A warrior named Tata Ajache disemboweled an enemy farmer with her hoe and was greeted upon her return home by the shouts, "You are a man!"

In the early 1890s, an appalling number of the women warriors were killed in a series of battles against better-armed French colonialists seeking to extend their control over the region. The women's bravery was no match for the machine guns, modern rifles, and bayonets that extended the lethal reach of the legionnaires. The all-female cadre of fighters was decimated.

Masculinity and the Warrior Role

Dahomey remains the only known example of a standing, professional, exclusively female fighting force. The training, bonding, and fighting central to the women's transformation to warriors was simultaneously a transformation of gender. What does this signify for the current position of women in the U.S. military?

Dahomey warriors served in a caste that stood apart from male fighters and from the rest of society. But the creation of an all-female fighting force appears inconceivable in the United States. Women will continue to serve in an integrated force. Some will want to serve in combat roles but many others will not. Furthermore, it is extremely unlikely that women as a whole will adopt rigid gender codes of masculinity. A few might wish to become warriors in the same sense as the most masculine member of the Special Forces, but most come to the armed forces with very different motivations for their service. For them, the military is an opportunity to learn a skill, travel, or acquire financial credits for college. Some are also escaping from difficult or boring circumstances at home. The opportunity to kill other people in combat is not particularly high on their agenda. Yet the military has become increasingly dependent on women to meet its "manpower" needs, and the line between combat and noncombat is increasingly difficult to define. The result is a paradoxical situation that must be managed by female soldiers and by the public. A renegotiation is required as women move closer to occupations in the armed forces that were exclusively reserved for men. Becoming a warrior means acquiring strength and endurance and a specific set of skills with a rifle or other weapons. It also requires traits that are not classically feminine.

In the film *GI Jane*, Lieutenant Jordan O'Neil, played by Demi Moore, is finally accepted as a full fledged SEAL (a member of the navy's special operations unit) but only after shaving all her hair and adopting the dress and speech codes of the men in her unit. She meets the training standards required of the men, not the "adjusted" level established for women. The Demi Moore character also confronts a deeply entrenched masculine culture, which she eventually manages to overcome only by adopting it as her own. In the climatic scene where she is finally accepted as an equal by her comrades, Lieutenant O'Neil endures an ugly sequence of violence meted out by one of her officers in a SERE (survival, evasion, resistance, and escape) training exercise. The officer ties her hands behind her back and pushes her head repeatedly into a bucket of water until she nearly drowns. She is unable to defend herself but stoically endures the abuse in a way that gains the admiration of her fellow male "prisoners." Her tormentor / training officer is so unfair that the others in the exercise signal their disapproval by turning their backs in disgust. "Men," says the officer, as he punches the tied-up Demi Moore to the ground yet again, "I'm trying to save your lives and hers too. She is a liability." "Master Chief," she yells back after spitting the blood out of her mouth, "Master Chief, you can suck my dick." Her fellow prisoners go wild with approval. Though the Demi Moore character is heterosexual in every other context, her triumph in becoming a SEAL comes only via complete gender transformation.

Gender identity and the warrior role remain problematic for those in the military. One study found a majority of women in the armed forces believing that there were "penalties for being perceived as either 'too masculine' (60 percent) or 'too feminine' (64 percent), while about half (49 percent) felt that there were penalties for perceived excesses in both directions."[32] Two-thirds of women answered affirmatively the question of whether they were penalized when they were perceived as being "too feminine." As a female drill instructor in the Marines states, "The qualities and traits that we demand and are supposed to be training in our recruits are the same traits that make us look homosexual." Women can try to protect themselves against this charge by presenting themselves with classic feminine traits. But this strategy works against their acceptance in combat roles. Women who are not aggressive enough may receive poor evaluations and be regarded as unfit to serve in leadership positions. As a lesbian captain in the air force states, "If you are too feminine, then you are not strong enough to command respect and lead men into battle, but if you're strong and aggressive you're not being a woman. It's like a double standard." The unorthodox gender role of warrior poses a distinct personal challenge to individual women and creates cultural conflict for the rest of society.

A majority of the public appears to accept women, not only in the military as a whole, but also in positions that could put them in harm's way.[33] The conditional phrase "appears to accept" is used because the *combat presence* of women during the wars in Afghanistan and Iraq is still being established. Shortly before the initiation of military force in Afghanistan, the *New York Times* ran a front-page photograph of a husband and wife about to leave their two small children in the States as they deployed to Afghanistan. On the verge of war with Iraq, *Time* magazine placed a female helicopter pilot on

Sergeant Keith Kravitz and Specialist Jaimie Strathmeyer leave their two children as they prepare to depart for duty (Timothy Shaffer).

its front cover with the following title: "When Mom Goes to War: This helicopter pilot and her husband are now based in Kuwait leaving behind their 14–year-old daughter. A Family Tale." The decision by *Time*'s editors seems to indicate greater public acceptance of this new role for women soldiers.

Time *magazine, March 24, 2003.*

Modest support among the public for women's right to serve in combat was found in a survey conducted by the Triangle Institute for Security Studies in 1998–1999. The survey compared three groups: military officers; a range of civilian leaders including clergy, politicians, labor leaders, scholars, writers, and journalists; and members of the general public chosen at random. When asked, "Do you think women should be *allowed* to serve in all combat jobs?" (emphasis in original), 53.1 percent of the general public and 57.5 percent of the civilian elite answered yes. But only 37.6 percent of the military elite replied in the affirmative, largely because they feared a negative impact on group cohesion and morale. Only slightly more than 10 percent of both the civilian and military elite thought that women should be *required* to serve in all combat roles.[34]

The Triangle Institute survey found an even larger gap between civilians and the military on the military rights of homosexuals, another topic that challenges the link between the warrior role and masculinity. When asked "Do you think gay men and lesbians should be allowed to serve openly in the military?" majorities of both the general public and the civilian elite answered yes, but only 18.1 percent of the military elite agreed.[35] Similarly, two-thirds of the military stated that they would be equally confident with either a male or a female commander, but only 20 percent said they would be equally confident with a straight or a gay commander. In fact, the military elite stated that they were more likely than the civilian elite to be comfortable with a female commander.[36] Since the first year of the Clinton administration, the military has in theory followed a policy of "don't ask, don't tell," but more than ten thousand people have been discharged since the inception of the policy. A report by the Government Accountability Office found several key military occupations weakened because gays had been forced out of the service due to their sexual orientation; for example, more than three hundred language specialists have been dismissed.[37] A recent report prepared by the University of California Blue Ribbon Commission puts the cost of discharging gays at $363.8 million over ten years.[38] As with women, formal recognition on the part of the military of the right of gays to fight raises troubling issues for the warrior role. At issue is not the actual ability of women or gays to serve alongside men in combat, but whether their presence will interfere with the cultural props that connect masculinity and fighting with relative approval.

For all their differences, World War II and the wars fought by the Dahomey kingdom shared a straightforward connection to gender: the mobilization of masculinity was a central part of the preparation of warriors. During the transition to conditional war, gender has certainly not disappeared. But an ongoing renegotiation of what is "acceptable" for women in the military is creating a more complex and contradictory context for public approval of the use of force. There are more women in the military, and both leaders and the public are grappling with the increased possibility—and ongoing reality—that they will be harmed. The struggle for equity is taking place on many fronts and it is difficult to see how changes that recognize the full contributions of women can be halted. At the same time, continued and even fierce resistance can also be expected. Social conservatives and many in the military will object in principle. For everybody, militarized feminist equality, or ending the formal ban, collides with the continued masculinity of the war- rior role. Cultural and perceptual complications follow the explicit right of women to kill or be killed. The question remains open: Is the public ready to have their daughters, wives, and mothers, as a matter of policy, placed in harm's way? Will women be free, as a matter of policy, to use deadly force? Meanwhile, many women will have to confront sexual violence, not from the enemy but from within the military itself.

Violence against Women in the Military

The continued presence of violence against women within the armed forces forms yet another dimension of gender. Since the 1991 Tail- hook scandal, in which more than eighty women reported being as- saulted by drunken male pilots at a navy convention in Las Vegas, the military has been forced to defend itself against the charge that the institution is not a safe place for women. The 1990s saw a series of well-publicized reviews of army and navy personnel accused of mistreating women. In 1995, the General Accounting Office warned that women at the military academies faced widespread problems, with more than 70 percent of the female cadets reporting that they had been the victims of harassment. A survey of female U.S. Air Force cadets conducted by the Defense Department found 18.8 percent reporting that that they had been the victims of at least one incident of sexual assault or attempted sexual assault, while 7.4 percent said they were the victim of rape or attempted rape.[39] More than 80 percent of these victims had not reported the incident for fear that the authorities would either ignore the problem or take steps that would hurt the careers of the complainants. A report from the congressionally appointed Panel to Review Sexual Misconduct Allegations at the U.S. Air Force Academy noted "a deep chasm in leadership," which has made resolution of the ongoing problem much more difficult.[40] From 1996 to 2002 the Air Force Academy hotline logged ninety-six reports of sexual assault, which resulted in the expulsion of just eight men.[41] The first comprehensive survey of sexual misconduct at the naval, air force, and army academies found more than half the women reporting some form of sexual harassment, and one in seven indicating that they had experienced at least one incident of sexual assault.[42]

A full accounting of the costs of U.S. intervention in Afghanistan and Iraq must include the many disturbing examples of violence against women. One of the most dramatic examples occurred in Fort Bragg, North Carolina, where the partners of four military men were killed in 2002. Three of the cases involved soldiers from special operations forces who had recently returned from Afghanistan. Two of the men later committed suicide.[43] The series of murders raised important questions about the impact of the military and the spillover influence of war on those who fight it—or who are near those who fight it. Many also questioned the depth of commitment of the institutional structure of the armed forces to solve the recurring problem.[44] In the Central Command, which includes Kuwait, Afghanistan, and Iraq, there were at least 112 reports of sexual misconduct during the eighteen months ending in February 2004.[45] The Miles Foundation reported receiving 350 reports of sexual assaults from CENTCOM by January 2006.[46] In the Pacific, at least 92 accusations of rape involving air force personnel were recorded between 2001 and 2003. As in the case of the Air Force Academy, the report to the commander of Pacific Air Forces found serious flaws in the handling of sexual assault claims, a failure to provide assistance to the victims, and questionable commitment to prosecute those responsible.[47]

In Senate hearings the Pentagon's top military leaders were questioned about their ability to protect servicewomen from sexual assaults by their fellow soldiers. One female officer who had been attacked in Iraq testified that she ended up trusting the Iraqi who sympathized with her plight more than the American military personnel with whom she worked on her base.[48] Complaints included the absence of emergency care and rape kits, incomplete investigations, and negative reactions from other military personnel after women came forward with their charges. The experience of former army captain Jennifer Machmer typifies the pattern of nonresponse. Machmer told the Congressional Caucus for Women's Issues that she had been raped in Kuwait in 2003 and reported the incident "within a half-hour." According to one news account:

> Military authorities questioned whether Machmer's assault should be considered a rape, she was not provided any immediate counseling

and she had to continue working in the same location as her assail-ant. Machmer says she was eventually given a medical discharge, against her wishes, for suffering from post–traumatic stress disorder. In April, she told the PBS program *News Hour* that the soldier who raped her in Kuwait was still in the Army. "He is now serving at Fort Knox, Kentucky, finishing out his career, while I'm here being raped out of my career."[49]

Most military men do not assault women and some military authorities are genuinely concerned with the treatment of female service personnel. In some circumstances, improvements have been made. But the overall record remains a disturbing feature of gender and the military.

Using Women to Legitimate War

While it is difficult to gauge with precision, public awareness has grown of the plight of women in Bosnia, Rwanda, Kosovo, Sudan, and Haiti. In Rwanda, at least 250,000 women were raped during the 1994 genocide and more than 20,000 Muslim women were raped during so-called ethnic cleansing campaigns in Bosnia.[50] The sym-pathies of the world and the U.S. public have slowly inched toward the need to provide protection during these emergencies. On an institutional level, this awareness is also reflected in the decision of the international tribunals for Rwanda and the former Yugoslavia to include rape as a war crime. But sympathy for women has also been exploited to support other agendas, most notably in Afghanistan where the Bush administration claimed that intervention against the Taliban would both eliminate a terror threat and promote the liberation of women. The cynical side is revealed most clearly in the administration's failure to criticize continued shortcomings in the treatment of women after the fall of the Taliban, or in Iraq after the downfall of Saddam. The selective and political use of women as victims should not interfere with the recognition that at least some of the public is becoming more responsive when women are threat-ened on a massive scale. Both sides of the issue, the use of gender in war management and increased awareness of the vulnerability of women as part of the process in which Americans are becoming more peaceful, are reflected in a November 2001 survey that found 85 percent of U.S. women aware of the difficult situation of Afghan women during the Taliban's rule. A majority believed that the United States and other countries creating a new government should insist that Afghan women be included in the negotiations.[51]

In Afghanistan, the Pentagon intervened to respond to terrorism and to overthrow the Taliban government because it harbored the al Qaeda terrorist network. An additional benefit, claimed several members of the administration, would be the removal of an obstacle to the advancement of women in the country. The Taliban's fundamentalist interpretation of *sharia*, or Islamic law, banned women's education and activism, and even the possibility of their playing a significant role in most aspects of public life. More-private forms of social control included rape and domestic violence. Few in the Bush administration had paid attention to this situation until planning for Operation Enduring Freedom reached an urgent stage. In November, however, Laura Bush suddenly became interested in the status of Afghan women. Andrea Ball, her chief of staff, called twelve Afghan women who were visiting Washington for a leadership workshop and invited them to the White House to meet the president's wife and tour the premises. Melanne Verveer, chair of the Vital Voices Global Leadership Institute, which hosted the visit, said, "There is no doubt in my mind that the first lady is sincere, thoughtful, cares deeply about advocating for women's rights in Afghanistan, and wants to make a contribution."[52] "The plight of women and children in Afghanistan," the first lady later said in a radio address, "is a matter of deliberate human cruelty, carried out by those who seek to intimidate and control." These words produced considerable surprise among representatives of other women's organizations who until then had failed to appreciate the depth of Laura Bush's commitment to women's rights. Her husband also invoked the plight of women to justify his policies. "The last time we met in this chamber," Bush said in his State of the Union address following the fall of the Taliban, "the mothers and daughters of Afghanistan were captives in their own homes, forbidden from working or going to school. Today women are free, and are part of Afghanistan's new government." Bush then paused to introduce Dr. Sima Samar, the new minister of women's affairs.

Two years later, in a speech at the close of International Women's Week, Bush again invoked women and children to defend his policies in Afghanistan and Iraq: "More than 50 million men, women, and children have been liberated from two of the most brutal tyrannies on earth—50 million people are free. And for 25 million women and girls, liberation has a special significance. Some of these girls are attending school for the first time. Some of the women are preparing to vote in free elections for the very first time."[53] Yet, even as Bush spoke, the Karzai government was unable to exert much control beyond the capital city of Kabul. Some of the girls who finally had an opportunity to attend school faced new threats from assailants who burned classrooms and threatened teachers where they attended school. Shah Agha, a water and power department worker whose daughter attended a village school in Zahidabad, said, "We were very happy when this school opened, but one morning we went to pray and we found it was all burned. Unless the government brings us more security, we cannot let our daughters go back there."[54] Despite the determination of many parents and teachers to provide new opportunities, neither Laura Bush nor the rest of the Bush administration found it necessary to call attention to the continued danger for girls seeking greater equality in the post-Taliban period. In 2004, Amnesty International documented a case of a sixteen-year-old girl who had been sentenced to prison for more than two years for running away from the eighty-five-year-old husband whom she had been forced to marry when she was nine. During the same year, there were only twenty-seven female judges out of a total of 2,006. And an international aid worker told Amnesty that during the Taliban era, "if a woman went to market and showed an inch of flesh she would have been flogged—now she's raped."[55]

Meanwhile, Samar, the new minister for women's affairs whom Bush highlighted in his national speech, was forced from the Karzai government by fundamentalist forces only six months after becoming the deputy prime minister. Fearing for her life, she was forced to hire two bodyguards and travel in a blacked-out van. Bush did not call attention to her alarming situation. Nor did he respond to a call later issued by Samar and Louise Arbour, UN high commissioner for human rights, for a commitment to bring war criminals to justice after a long period of human rights abuses. Many of those who would have faced prosecution were now officials in Karzai's government. The human rights report included the results of a survey finding strong popular support among Afghans for investigating what happened in the past and establishing accountability, but there was little interest in Washington or official Kabul for such a thorough examination for fear that it would undermine political stability.[56]

In March 2005, Laura Bush traveled to Afghanistan, where she spent a total of six hours meeting with women training to become teachers. She also thanked U.S. troops for overthrowing the Taliban leaders who had kept girls from attending school. Unfortunately, the security situation did not permit a longer visit. On that very day, the United Nations revised its earlier estimate of the civilian death toll in the Darfur region of Sudan, now placing the number of dead at "somewhere around 300,000."[57] Women typically bear the brunt of civil wars, yet neither Laura Bush nor any other prominent figure in her husband's administration thought that it was important to call special attention to this humanitarian disaster. In December,

Ali Mohaqeq Nasab was temporarily imprisoned and faced execution after publishing several essays asserting that women should be given equal status to men in court.[58]

Nor did the Bush administration do much to highlight or respond to the new wave of kidnapping and rape that actually reduced the security for women in Iraq following the overthrow of Saddam. A December 2003 delegation of Washington representatives found a "brewing women's rights crisis" in the resolutions passed by the U.S.-backed Iraqi Governing Council. The IGC had decided to cancel laws aimed at protecting women and instead transferred this area of jurisdiction to Islamic law and to the interpretations of more socially conservative clerics. These steps were particularly ironic because in prewar Iraq women had gained more rights and professional status than in much of the rest of the Arab world. In the same month, a coalition of Iraqi women's groups, many of whom had originally supported Operation Iraqi Freedom, wrote to the U.S. Coalition Provisional Authority, noting that only three women sat on the twenty-five-person IGC, that no women governors had been appointed in any of the eighteen provinces, and that there was only one woman in charge in the country's twenty-five government ministries.[59] In some cases, U.S. authorities did try to advance the rights of some particular women. In one instance, they ordered a reelection in a neighborhood council when the leading women's candidate was not informed of the timing of the vote. And in 2005, the U.S. ambassador to Iraq tried to highlight the importance of equal rights for women in the development of the new constitution. But the impact of these efforts was undermined by the news that at least some of the U.S. soldiers who had tortured and humiliated male Iraqi prisoners at Abu Ghraib had also raped and sexually abused women in the prison. The internal Pentagon report by army major general Antonio Taguba acknowledges that soldiers videotaped and photographed naked female detainees and forced at gunpoint at least one Iraqi woman to show her breasts. But pictures of these acts were among the second wave of Abu Ghraib images, which were reviewed by top Pentagon officials and members of Congress but, as of January 2006, not yet made public. Iraqi women have also been detained and used as bargaining chips by U.S. troops seeking to put pressure on suspected insurgents.[60] One case involved a twenty-eight-year-old mother still nursing her six-month-old baby. In another, a U.S. officer urged a military police colonel to tack a note on the door of a suspected insurgent demanding that he "come get his wife" who was being taken away and held in detention.[61]

"Saving Jessica Lynch"

In the ongoing process of renegotiating gender during the transition from mobilized to conditional war, new questions have emerged that challenge the usual link between traditional concepts of gender roles and support for war. Yet the more conventional gender themes have not been completely displaced. The "rescue" of Private Jessica Lynch from a hospital in an early period of the war in Iraq shows how orthodox gender practices continue to serve as important legitimation mechanisms for conditional war.

Lynch and other members of the 507th maintenance unit were captured after their convoy made a series of wrong turns in Nasiriyah and was ambushed by an Iraqi force. The unit was staffed primarily by mechanics, cooks, and supply clerks and their exposure illustrates the difficulty of separating combat from noncombat roles. Lynch was injured during the fight, taken to a hospital, and then retrieved by a special operations team a week later. The team took a nightscope video and the jumpy, green-tinged footage was later incorporated by the Pentagon into a dramatic clip that was shown to the U.S. public and around the world. Military authorities presented the episode as the first successful rescue of a U.S. POW behind enemy lines since World War II. Lynch later received the Bronze Star, Purple Heart, and Prisoner of War medals.

The rescue, which occurred during a time when war news was not particularly good, captured the imagination of the media and the public. The leading assaults unit headed toward Baghdad had been bogged down by a strong sandstorm, supply lines appeared overextended, and possible street fighting in the Iraqi capital loomed ahead. Some in the media and even some retired military experts had begun to question the strategy followed by Secretary of Defense Donald Rumsfeld and central region commander General Tommy Franks. Comparisons to Vietnam had begun to proliferate and the words "stalemate" and "quagmire" were being used more often. The early emergence of comparisons with Vietnam, misleading in the immediate context of overthrowing Saddam but telling when measured against the long-term problems of the occupation, point to the fragility of public support for conditional war.

Following Lynch's evacuation to safety, the media described her original capture in breathtaking terms. The *Washington Post* reported that she had "fought fiercely and shot several enemy soldiers after Iraqi forces ambushed the Army's 507th Ordnance Maintenance Company, firing her weapon until she ran out of ammunition.... [Lynch] continued firing at the Iraqis even after she sustained multiple gunshot wounds and watched several soldiers in her unit die around her.... 'She was fighting to the death,' one U.S. official said. 'She did not want to be taken alive.'"[62] Some reports said that Lynch had also been stabbed. During that week, according to a report in the *Columbia Journalism Review,* Lynch drew 919 references in major newspapers, compared to 639 references for General Franks and 549 for Vice President Dick Cheney.[63] She was pictured often with an American flag in the background and described as small, petite, "weighing less than 100 pounds," "only 19 years old," "delicate," "pure," "waiflike," "vulnerable," and possessing a "childlike innocence." At the same time Lynch was also "God-fearing," "scrappy," and "spunky." She was a "country girl" who believed in "small town values." According to her father, Lynch had never even set foot in a shopping mall until she was a senior in high school. Her survival was credited by Governor Robert Wise to the effects of a rural West Virginia childhood. "People here rely on their own resources and strengths," Wise told newspapers.[64] Lynch had become an overnight hero complete with "America loves Jessica" T-shirts, mugs, fridge magnets, children's stickers, and a country song.

These gender-laden descriptions of Jessica Lynch serve as modern examples of the captivity narrative in American history. Stories of the capture and rescue of hostages have been told in novels, movies, and television, and fit the self-image of a people threatened from the outside but whose virtue and faith is affirmed by the ultimate safe return of one of their own.[65] The heartwarming story of Jessica Lynch can be compared to tales of frontier women such as Mary Rowlandson, a New England minister's wife who was captured in 1682 after a battle during King Phillip's War and endured subsequent fear and hunger. In a popular account published after she was freed, Rowlandson described her captors as "barbarous" and "Black creatures of the night." The Lynch saga even contains a "good Indian": Mohammed al-Rehaief, a local lawyer whose wife worked in the hospital, walked six miles across the desert to inform U.S. forces of Lynch's situation, subsequently going back and forth several times to provide words of assurance for Lynch and additional intelligence for Marines. This heartwarming sidebar reinforced the concept of anti-Saddam Iraqis primed to come to the assistance of Americans—especially Americans in trouble.[66]

The story of a young, injured, virginal damsel in distress who is rescued by strong, brave men twice her size is certainly appealing. It is also completely wrong. Lynch did not receive her wounds while fighting. In fact she and several others in her unit might not have even been able to fire their jammed M-16s. Instead, she was injured when her Humvee collided with another truck in the convoy. One of her doctors, Harith al-Houssona, later said: "I examine her, I see she has a broken arm and broken thigh with a dislocated ankle. Then we do another examination. There is no shooting, no bullet inside her body ... no stab wound, no other thing, merely RTA [road traffic accident]." Lynch's physician told of other efforts on her behalf: "We give her three bottles of blood ... two of them from medical staff ... because there is no blood at this time." Another doctor, Anmar Uday, considered "Jessica as one of our injured patients ... one of our Iraqi women injured in the war."[67] The two physicians said that no Iraqi troops had been in the hospital during the raid and that they had themselves been trying to release Lynch to U.S. Marines for several days. In fact, two days before the rescue mission, Harith attempted to deliver Jessica back to U.S. troops using an ambulance but was forced to return after Americans opened fire as the vehicle approached a checkpoint. The BBC later called the rescue story as presented by the Pentagon "one of the most stunning pieces of news management ever conceived."[68]

I had an opportunity to interview a Pentagon public relations manager about the Jessica Lynch operation:

JOSEPH: There were particular stories that emerged from the war that did not stand up to later scrutiny. An example was the Jessica Lynch story.

OFFICIAL: Yes, I was very involved in that.

JOSEPH: As I recall, the rescue mission came during a pause in the march toward Baghdad. Criticism began to emerge from retired military analysts, and the word "quagmire" was being used more often.

OFFICIAL: Right. They were saying that we had a bad plan, that we should have had more troops, that supply lines were overextended, etc.

JOSEPH: And that street fighting in Baghdad looms ahead.

OFFICIAL: Right, right. The red line, once we cross the red line, we're going to get slimed. So suddenly—boom—we rescue Jessica Lynch. The euphoria, on the uniform side, was incredible. The human reaction to rescuing one of our own. I had not seen her photograph until the evening before, while the rescue was going on. When I saw her picture, I thought: if we rescue this woman, America's response will be incredible. I mean, she was everybody's daughter. You didn't need to talk to her. It was all about pictures and television and front pages, and you looked at her, and she was America's daughter. Every single human being could relate to that woman, just by looking at her. The euphoria on the media was also amazing. The American press were excited, they were ecstatic. Rescuing her was a strategic event in the war.

JOSEPH: You used the word "strategic" in connection with her rescue. Could you tell me what you mean by that?

OFFICIAL: It kind of goes to the whole. The will of the country is extremely important, the will of the people. And where we were at that time in the war, if the mission had failed, it would have sent the country deeper into an "Oh, my gosh" attitude. Whether it was strategic from a strictly military perspective, that's for a guy who shoots guns to answer. From my perspective, as you said, people were saying that we're in a quagmire. For the mission to fail it would have caused the country to go "Oh, no, we are losing." We're a win/lose society. There are no ties. None of our sports games end in ties. So we win or we lose. When we pulled her out, and the country's reaction was what it was, it turned the tide.

The Pentagon used the Lynch rescue mission to reassure the public that its soldiers, specifically its white, pretty, female soldiers, were well protected. This message invoked a classic connection between gender and war, namely, that deadly force was necessary to provide security against "dark savages" who threatened our women. This message resonated with the media, the public, and the military itself.

The Lynch saga is also instructive for what was not said. The press might have paid more attention to her original plans to become a kindergarten teacher and her decision to enter the military because she couldn't afford college tuition. The press barely mentioned Jessica's fallen comrades—nine bodies were recovered during the same rescue mission. Lynch received far more attention than other women serving in the 507th including Specialist Shoshana Johnson, a Panamanian American single mother and cook, wounded and captured in the attack, who temporarily remained in Iraqi hands; and Specialist Lori Piestewa, a member of the Hopi nation, mother of two young children, and the first Native American woman to be killed while fighting for the U.S. military. Several days later, a *New York Newsday* story on "women at war" featured pictures of the three women but gave Lynch top billing. An accompanying article asked readers, "Why not write a note to welcome home Jessica Lynch who was rescued last week in a U.S. raid on an Iraqi hospital?" As an afterthought, the story added, "You can also write to the families of two other women from that same unit."

Nor did many members of the public know the story of another brave woman, Rachel Corrie, a student from Evergreen College in Olympia, Washington, and a member of International Solidarity Movement, which was monitoring the activities of the Israeli Defense Force in the Gaza Strip. On March 16, 2003, about two weeks before the Lynch rescue, Corrie attempted to block a military bulldozer from demolishing the homes and property of Palestinians in the Hi Salaam area of Rafah. She was run over and killed. Witnesses to the incident maintained that Corrie was deliberately attacked. The incident received attention on the back pages of some U.S. newspapers but efforts to force an investigation of the killing were unsuccessful. Rachel Corrie was honored by Palestinians, some even naming their newborn girls after her, and by peace movements throughout the world but was largely ignored by the mainstream press.

Jessica Lynch returned home to a reception that she richly deserved. Her town remodeled her house, a local car dealer contributed an SUV and a pickup truck, and the governor offered her a scholarship to any public college or university in the state. Lynch herself went out of her way to express her concern for all her comrades (she even helped to build a new house for Lori Piestewa's family) and to distance herself from the stories told in her name. "That wasn't me," she told the *Toronto Star* when asked about the Pentagon's version of her story. "I'm not about to take credit for something I didn't do.... I'm just a survivor."[69] ABC's Diane Sawyer asked if the military's account of the events bothered her, and Lynch replied, "Yeah, it does. It does that they used me as a way to symbolize all this stuff. Yeah, it's wrong."[70] What she remembered most about her time in Iraqi hands, Lynch later said, was the dedication of the medical staff of the hospital who took it upon themselves to obtain fresh orange juice for her each day she was in their charge.

Abu Ghraib

Photographs from Abu Ghraib prison showing U.S. soldiers abusing, torturing, and humiliating detainees have become one of the most important representations of the occupation of Iraq. Visual "proof" of the abuse coincided with declining support for the war because the behavior shown in the images is not supposed to occur in conditional war. Three pictures came to be most commonly associated with Abu Ghraib. One was of a black-hooded prisoner balanced on a wooden block with electric wires attached to various parts of his body. The other two showed the same female soldier. In the first, she stands alongside a line of naked Iraqi prisoners while grinning widely, cigarette jutting from the corner of her mouth, and proudly extending an upturned thumb. In the other, the soldier is seen "walking" a prisoner who has been forced to crawl along the floor like a dog. A leather leash is tied around his neck. The soldier's name is Lynndie England.

Abu Ghraib provoked a firestorm of critical questions: Why were the prisoners being treated in such a degrading manner? Who authorized this treatment? Did the problem lie with inadequate

Private First Class Lynndie England holds a leash attached to a naked prisoner at Abu Ghraib (http://theage.com/ftimages).

training, a failure of supervision, or with administration officials back in Washington? Why did the guards and interrogators take self-incriminating photographs?[71] Why was sexual humiliation of the prisoners such a dominant theme? And how could women allow themselves to participate in practices such as stacking naked prisoners on top of one another and forcing men to masturbate or engage in simulated oral sex?

U.S. women humiliated Arab men at Abu Ghraib. Pictures showing this treatment were distributed through Arab media and shown throughout the Muslim world. On one level, no reference to special cultural sensitivity is necessary to understand how Muslims felt. The same horrified response could be predicted regardless of nationality or religion. It is not difficult to imagine the outrage in the United States if Iraqi prison guards had treated American prisoners in the same manner. But beyond the indignation that anyone would feel lies an acute, specific, and unusual violation. White women dished out punishments that asserted their power while brown men were on the receiving end of behavior that signified their weakness, vulnerability, and effeminate status. Women were clothed and in control.

Men were naked, exposed, and powerless. The ultimate responsibility for the interrogation techniques used against detainees throughout the post–September 11 penal system lies with men working in Washington but at least some of the frontline agents in Iraq had an undeniably female cast.[72] The movement toward equal opportunity for women now seemed to include not only participation in combat but also violations of international law and the military's own code of conduct. As well as a militarized feminism, there would also appear to be an imperialized feminism.

Some women at Abu Ghraib found themselves in key positions by happenstance, as a result of a military occupation that became increasingly desperate for personnel no matter their sex or professional expertise. But the theme of sexual humiliation was certainly deliberate, as was the use of female guards and interrogators. The faux social science circulating within some circles in the Bush administration held that Muslim men were particularly vulnerable to invasions of their sexual privacy (and also particularly fearful of dogs) and would therefore be more likely to provide information to avoid shame and degradation. In Guantánamo Bay, a female interrogator attempted to break the will of Muslim prisoners by wearing a miniskirt and thong underwear. She engaged in sexual touching and smeared fake menstrual blood on the face of detainees in an effort to humiliate them and to make them talk.[73] In this respect, the use of women as guards may have been part of a deliberate strategy to send a gender-laced message of control to the Middle East as a whole. It is difficult to believe that the implications of placing women in charge of male prisoners were never considered by leading officials. "In our faith," said Sheik Muhammad Muhammad Ali, a leading Shiite scholar, "it is strictly forbidden to have women confront naked men." Anthony Sullivan of the Center for Middle Eastern and North African Studies at the University of Michigan echoes this point, stating that it is "grossly insulting to Muslims" to have women participate in the humiliation of prisoners. Sullivan further suggested that "this had to be a conscious policy to add the element of shame to the physical pain inflicted on Iraqis. To Muslim Arabs, it would have been inconceivable to be placed in that degree of vulnerability before a woman."[74]

What was the reaction to the presence of women abusers at Abu Ghraib? The tendency of social conservatives was to shove the evidence of dehumanization beneath the surface by blaming the low-level, poorly trained personnel themselves. Others dismissed it as relatively harmless fraternity stunt, or blamed the mere presence of women. Linda Chavez, president of the Center for Equal Opportunity, an organization that supports the combat ban, argued that mixed-sex units helped create "sexual tension" in the military and that the very presence of women in the police unit may have encouraged the abuse that took place.[75] Elaine Donnelly of the Center for Military Readiness said that the abuses are the consequences of the Pentagon's "social engineering" and the failure of Congress to recognize the warning signs that followed the movement of women into combat situations. For Rush Limbaugh, the guards humiliating Iraqis were just "having a good time" and the pictures looked like anything "you'd see Madonna or Britney Spears do onstage. . . . I mean, this is something that you can see onstage at Lincoln Center from an N.E.A. grant, maybe on 'Sex and the City.'"[76]

But for others, the actions of female abusers could not be dismissed so easily. A more complex accounting was necessary to grapple with such a jarring gender anomaly. Modifying the sexual identity of Lynndie England so that her female attributes were tucked beneath the surface was one possible strategy, although this task was complicated by the fact that she was pregnant. Zillah Eisenstein suggests that England and other women found in the forefront of prison abuse operated as "gender decoys" to create confusion by "participating in the very sexual humiliation that their gender is usually victim to. This gender swapping and switching leave masculinist/racialized gender in place. Just the sex has changed; the uniform remains the same. . . . Masculinist depravity can be adopted by males and/or females."[77] On the front stage, white women force Muslim men to strip naked and leashes are tied around the prisoners' necks. But on the back stage, the same women continue to be vulnerable to sexual abuse perpetrated by their own comrades. Women may look like they are increasingly in charge but they are actually being forced to assimilate to a hypermasculinized culture of power and control. Obviously, women were not automatically above the behavior exhibited at Abu Ghraib. Their biology did not make them always more caring or peaceful, and some succumbed to a culture of power that they did not create and were not in a position to change. Like so many others, female guards were corrupted by the extreme inequalities of power that existed at the prison.[78]

The concept that Lynndie England is a gender decoy who obscures the underlying connections among patriarchy, militarism, and abuse implies the management of perceptions so that England does not appear as *typically* female. War support depends on seeing Abu Ghraib and women's participation abuse as anomalies. For the public, England must undergo a "sex-change operation" so that she does not appear as a real woman. Joan McAlpine offers an example of this transformation of identity:

Look at the pathetic, pouchy-faced Lynndie England and contemplate the damage she has done. She has been likened to an androgynous elf, a girl whose femaleness is not immediately apparent—even while seven months pregnant. She's androgynous on the inside too. Lynndie behaved like one of the lads—except that she showed the lads how to use her femininity to torture Iraqi prisoners and provide the platoon a bit of a sexual kick as well. She probably watched the same home-made porn as they did. Why, she even starred in her own "gonzo flick," a DVD where luscious Lynndie engages in sexual acts with another soldier in front of the prisoners.[79]

Media comparisons found some similarities but focused more on the differences between England and the more typically feminine Jessica Lynch.[80] Both were small-town girls from West Virginia who joined the military to escape from the limitations of their immediate surroundings. Each grew up in a tight-knit family. Lynch entered the military after high school but actually wanted to teach kindergarten. England joined the Army Reserve after her junior year in high school and reportedly enjoyed chasing storms and wanted to be a meteorologist. But Lynch's appearance and vulnerability were used to build support for the war. England was different: short, dark haired, a smoker, already divorced, and now pregnant from an illicit affair with Corporal Charles Graner Jr., another soldier in her unit.

To better measure press treatment, an analysis was conducted of a selection of articles about Lynndie England and the Iraqi abuse scandal that appeared in major American newspapers in 2004.[81] Most describe England as she appears in the abuse photos: "grinning" or "with a cigarette at a jaunty angle in her mouth as she points to a naked prisoner masturbating before her." Many make specific mention of her masculine appearance, military fatigues, and "swagger." About two-thirds portray England as a perpetrator who was primarily to blame for the abusive treatment of Iraqi prisoners. Only 12 percent suggested that she might have been a victim of a flawed system that would send untrained, inexperienced soldiers to a foreign country to guard prisons. All maintained that she was responsible for the acts she committed. A large majority of the articles (84 percent) included the fact that England was pregnant. Most authors thought this status made her conduct even less acceptable because she was capable of simultaneously abusing Iraqi prisoners while consorting, against military law, with a fellow soldier in a combat zone. (An article on the birth of England's son was titled "Dog Leash Soldier Gives Birth.")[82] Her social background is also held against her. While relatively few articles (16 percent) mentioned that England was raised in a trailer park, those that did used this circumstance to explain her behavior at Abu Ghraib. According to one example, England represented the "depressingly limited cultural horizons of young, trailer-park America, the army's main recruiting ground."[83] Another argued that England was a "small town sadist" and, having grown up in "a trailer park in rural West Virginia," she could not possibly have been expected to know how to behave.[84] A comment by Colleen Kesner, a hometown acquaintance, was used to confirm this view: "A lot of people here think they ought to just blow up the whole of Iraq. To the country boys here, if you're a different nationality, a different race, you're sub-human. That's the way that girls like Lynndie are raised. . . . Tormenting Iraqis, in her mind, would be no different from shooting a turkey. Every season here you're hunting something. Over there, they're hunting Iraqis."[85] Few articles raised the possibility that the abuse was by design. England herself has stated that she was given orders to "soften up" prisoners and was praised for her work and told to keep it up.[86] England also said she took no joy from abusing prisoners because "it's another human being."[87] England later said that sometimes she felt "kind of weird" but "to us, we were doing our jobs, which meant we were doing what we were told."[88] But rather than follow the implications of these comments for the overall chain of command, it was easier for the press to blame an individual female soldier, who wasn't a real woman anyway. She became an almost impossible figure to embrace. As M. S. Embser-Herbert has observed: "If Pfc. Lynndie England had come home in a flag-draped coffin, killed by an Iraqi detainee, we would have been far less shocked than we are at the now-infamous image of this young woman holding a leash attached to a naked Iraqi prisoner. At least then she would have been something we're used to seeing—a woman as a victim."[89]

Post-Traumatic Stress Disorder

War kills and can leave soldiers with physical wounds. Another, less apparent but nonetheless acute burden of military conflict is psychological trauma, a factor that is present wherever warfare involves significant numbers.[90] In the case of Operation Iraqi Freedom, an early study published in the *New England Journal of Medicine* found approximately 16 percent of those returning from U.S. combat infantry units experiencing "major depression, generalized anxiety, and post–traumatic stress disorder."[91] Of these, only 23 to 40 percent had sought mental health care. Soldiers cited concerns about stigmatization from peers and commanding officers and fear of being perceived as weak. The study may have underestimated the severity of the mental strain because it was completed before the war entered its more difficult counterinsurgency phase and because the symptoms of combat-induced stress may not appear for months or even years after return. "The bad news is that the study underestimated the prevalence of what we are going to see down the road," said Dr. Matthew Friedman, professor of psychiatry and pharmacology at the Dartmouth Medical School and executive director of the Department of Veterans Affairs' National Center for Post–Traumatic Stress Disorder.[92] According to Captain Jennifer Berg, the chair of psychiatric services at the Naval Medical Center in San Diego, military psychiatrists expect that 20 percent of those coming back from Iraq will experience some form of trauma. Berg noted the impact of conditions that were increasingly compared to Vietnam: "In comparison with the combat phase, what we are now seeing are conditions of chronic stress which the troops are experiencing every day. It is a combination of danger, boredom and sleep deprivation, and the knowledge that they are a long way from home. In addition people are no longer sure when or what the end will be. No one knows when they will be going home. They are also working in an environment where the people they came to help are very hostile."[93] "These troops know no front line," added Alfonso Batres, a clinical psychologist in charge of readjustment counseling centers. "It's just like Vietnam. They have to be on guard with everyone; they're always facing an unknown. In some ways, fighting a conventional war is a lot easier on the psyche."[94] By mid-July 2005, there had been fifty-three suicides among those fighting in Iraq and another nine among those serving in Afghanistan.[95] These numbers understate the problem as most suicides occur after troops return home. An official report found the overall army suicide rate higher than it had been during and since the Vietnam War even though the usual pattern during wartime is for suicide rates to decline.[96]

Despite the recurring connection between combat and psychological distress throughout the history of modern war, two differences now stood out: first, women made up a greater proportion of the U.S. fighting force; and second, many of these women also suffered from the symptoms of psychological stress. Nurses and other women who served during the two world wars and in Vietnam experienced what was then called combat fatigue but the number involved was relatively small. Many more could now identify with Jenni McKinley, a twenty-seven-year-old career soldier with eight years in the army. "I didn't handle war the way I thought I was going to," she said upon her return to the United States from Iraq. "I thought I was going to do my job, be strong. But three days into it, I broke down crying.

The Scuds were flying. We were waking up to the sounds of explosions over our heads. It was terrifying."[97]

During World War II, soldiers going to war were expected to demonstrate their strength by remaining immune to combat-related stress. Unfortunately, that proved to be impossible. Despite overall success and strong support at home, many paid a heavy psychological price. Among the many costs associated with the Vietnam War was combat-induced stress. In fact, it was Vietnam that helped to public to see that that the psychological costs of combat are high no matter how strong or classically masculine the individual. Vietnam led to the official recognition of post–traumatic stress disorder in the *Diagnostic and Statistical Manual* used by the psychiatric profession and to the application of the term in a number of other settings involving exposure to violence including rape, battering, and child abuse.[98] Vietnam and the pervasiveness of PTSD have contributed to public sensitivities about the social and personal costs of violence regardless of gender and to the recognition that people in combat, or even near combat, remain vulnerable no matter how strong or well-prepared by socialization into the traditional male role.

By late 2004, print journalists and the media began to pay more attention to the issue of psychological damage among female veterans returning from Afghanistan and Iraq. A Defense Department health questionnaire administered to 60,000 servicewomen and 466,000 servicemen returning from Afghanistan and Iraq between June 2003 and March 2005 found 24 percent of the women and 18 percent of the men reporting that their health had worsened during their deployment. Yet, for both sexes, only 4 to 6 percent said they wanted help with "stress, emotional, alcohol, or family problems."[99] The Veterans Affairs Department launched a study of PTSD among female veterans. Preliminary indications from that study show that active duty and retired women suffer from PTSD at a rate roughly equal to that of men, although women may also suffer from more pronounced and debilitating forms of the disorder than men.[100] A book that became increasingly popular among military families bore the title *Why Is Mommy Like She Is? A Book for Kids about PTSD.*

What are the implications of this multilayered treatment of gender and war for the argument that Americans are becoming more peaceful? The social construction of gender and the social organization of war have always been linked, and the movement toward conditional war has not changed that sociological fact of life. But the links are now more numerous and run in different directions, making it more difficult to enlist gender to secure public support for war. War management via gender is still possible but it is also countered by gender-inspired war constraints. Indeed, the public relations approach of the Bush administration has been to invoke the frontier and other themes that sustain the heroic mode of strong men rescuing vulnerable women. Abuses suffered by women in civil wars have also been enlisted by administration officials to provide support for war, even as their true concern for the status of women has proved inconsistent at best. Washington is still a long way from developing a commitment to recognize and redress the abusive treatment of women within patriarchal institutions. This vulnerability extends to women within the armed forces, where sexual harassment and rape continue to afflict the service academies and personnel deployed at home and abroad.

The military now has many more female soldiers, and many of them are moving closer to combat, whether this development is officially recognized or not. A majority of the public seems to approve—or at least respect—militarized gender equality although public attitudes on this score have yet to be fully tested. Social conservatives, many of whom otherwise support war, will continue to resist opening combat positions to women. For doves and those who explicitly oppose war, full equality creates ambivalence: on the one hand, Type I opposition rejects policies that place individuals in harm's way regardless of their sex; on the other, most in this popular current are not willing to accept situations that assign second-class status to women. Personnel demands within the military and the broad movement toward social equity will continue to push women toward full combat roles. But there are many challenges. Clearly, many women are capable of performing well at whatever men do. But the warrior role remains masculine. It is not known if female combat soldiers can be accepted as women or if they will have to undergo a more complex process of gender transformation. Combat-induced PTSD used to be experienced almost entirely by men; is the popular culture prepared to have thousands of women so afflicted as well?

In mobilized war, traditional constructions of gender could be counted on to help produce war support. For conditional war, it is not possible to argue a simple-minded reversal in which contemporary understandings automatically lead to war opposition. What can be said is that the multiple crosscurrents surrounding gender outlined in this chapter contribute to the current tenuous relationship between the public and war.

Chapter 7

Managing Militarism

At a March 10, 2003, London concert, Natalie Maines, lead singer of the Dixie Chicks, signaled her opposition to the forthcoming war in Iraq by telling her audience, "Just so you know, we're ashamed that the president of the United States is from Texas." Back in the United States, Maines's comment was posted to a country-and-western Internet discussion group and then included in an Associated Press story. Then came a firestorm.[1] Many country-and-western fans called for a boycott of the Dixie Chicks, and within a few days a significant number of radio stations, especially those owned by Clear Channel, dropped the group from their playlists. Hostile talk show hosts and newspaper columnists joined the attack, referring to the group as the "Dixie Sluts" and "Saddam's Angels." Radio stations set out trash cans to collect returned CDs. In Louisiana, KRMD 101.1 FM organized "Dixie Chicks Destruction Day." One listener came in with his tractor to run over a pile of recordings. A mock CD cover from one Web site showed Saddam Hussein embracing Natalie Maines as the newly-formed "Dixie Duo." Flag-waving country star Toby Keith also projected a doctored image of Saddam and Maines during his national tour. The group's bus driver quit and Maines decided that it would be better to order twenty-four-hour security outside her home. Four days after her comment, Maines apologized for the tone of her remark (but not the content), saying that "whoever holds that office should be treated with the utmost respect."

184

The reaction to the Dixie Chicks' mild protest raises the question of cultural militarism in the United States and the degree to which patriotism, support for military values and for a president during a time of war, and more narrow concepts of what it means to be an American work against the tendency of Americans to become more peaceful.

Militarism links war preparation with the rest of society. In highly mobilized societies, cultural practices as diverse as entertainment, education, and children's play are connected to, and tend to support the normalization of, military force. Mobilized-war culture also makes it more difficult to offer resistance to war; opposition is seen as a sign of treason and those carrying out protests are regarded as the internal enemy. In the movement toward conditional war, cultural militarism has receded. The policy may involve military force but mobilization behind the war effort, such as targeting of entire nationalities or religions, is becoming more difficult. The public is still patriotic in ways that can be harnessed to support for war policies. But countercurrents, such as widespread opposition to the draft, are also significant. Americans may love their country but are less willing to send their sons and daughters to fight. Some continue to blame entire nationalities or religions for threats to their safety. Hate crimes, discrimination, and prejudice still characterize some parts of the population. But the enemy-making process has been complicated by significant support for religious and ethnic pluralism, which provides a barrier against deeper, more virulent forms of militarism. This chapter explores the tempering of some features of militarism in the United States, particularly regarding attitudes toward conscription and the treatment of Muslim Americans. Recent developments have established important bulwarks against full-fledged militarism and form part of the widening pool of Type II nonacceptance of the social practices that normally accompany war. This trend also presents opportunities for the development of more explicitly peaceful policies. But first, we return to the Dixie Chicks.

The Dixie Chicks Recover

With their music virtually absent from the April 2003 airwaves, weekly sales of the Dixie Chicks' latest album, *Home,* plummeted from 124,000 before Maines's critical remark to 33,000 several weeks after. Their two current singles, "Travelin' Soldier" and "Landslide," also fell from the top of the charts. Radio airplay data collected from *Radio and Records* and reproduced in figure 7.1 shows the dramatic

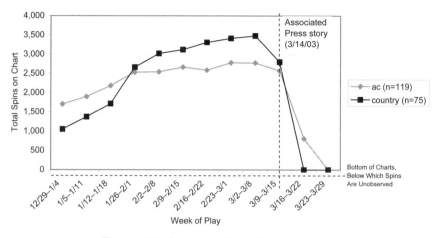

Figure 7.1 Trends in Dixie Chicks Airplay

Source: Gabriel Rossman, "Elites, Masses, and Media Blacklists: The Dixie Chicks Controversy," *Social Forces* 83 (Sep. 2004): 61–78.

decline in the number of Dixie Chicks "spins" on both adult contemporary and country stations. Clear Channel, which owned more than
1,200 radio stations in fifty states and commanded 20 percent of the
radio industry's $16 billion in revenue in 2001, played a key role in
the boycott.[2] After September 11, many Clear Channel stations had
banned John Lennon's "Imagine," Cat Stevens's "Peace Train," and
several other "suspect" songs from their playlists. Member stations
sponsored a "Rally for America" in Atlanta, Cincinnati, San Antonio,
Cleveland, and other cities. But how deeply rooted was the hostility
to the Chicks, particularly in a musical genre often associated with
patriotism and loyalty? Would their antiwar message mean that their
audience would desert them permanently? Would militarism claim
the Dixie Chicks as a victim?

Before the controversy the Dixie Chicks were credited with single-
handedly reviving country music. As Brian Philips, general manager
of cable channel CMT, offered, "The thought of country music ever
carrying on without them is just unthinkable."[3] The group had
recently won a Best Country Album Grammy and sold more than
25 million CDs. Now, relatively quickly the ban against their music
began to ease. Some DJs were never comfortable with keeping their
music off the air and two Colorado Springs KKCS employees were
suspended for getting a jump on the station's decision to start to
play the Dixie Chicks again. The station manager noted that out of
a couple of hundred listener calls, 75 percent favored a return of
the Dixie Chicks to the airwaves. A poll of the three thousand e-mail
members of Boston's WKLB showed roughly the same proportion

of listeners wanting to hear the group played on the station. But the Chicks also faced a national tour. Though the group had set a one-day concert record on March 1 with 867,000 tickets and $49 million in sales, questions remained about the success of the U.S. tour. Would each concert be greeted by pro-war rallies and a boycott? The Chicks offered a three-pronged response. They defended their right to make statements as part of the time-honored commitment to free speech. They clarified the distinction between their opposition to the war and their continued support for the troops. And they appeared naked save for a series of well-positioned mock tattoos, on the cover of *Entertainment Weekly*.

The Dixie Chicks stage a comeback (Entertainment Weekly), *May 2, 2003.*

The tour was a success. Maines did not duck what had come to be called "the incident." During each show, a photomontage of other examples of censorship was flashed on a screen as the Dixie Chicks played "Truth No. 2." The first concert was held in Greenville, South Carolina, and was attended by a sell-out crowd of fifteen thousand. The performers were prepared to face up to opposition and Maines invited those who wished to boo to do so, but the crowd cheered instead. Small protest rallies typically accompanied their appearances, but attendance during the tour was overwhelming and sales of *Home* rebounded nicely and eventually passed 5 million. The Dixie Chicks had recovered and once again found themselves at the center of country music.

The campaign supported by Clear Channel was over, and the public did not accept the organized effort to exclude the Dixie Chicks from the airwaves. On one level, the strategic reentry of the Dixie Chicks to acceptability shows the influence of conventional public relations and commercialism. Certainly, the *Entertainment Weekly* cover combines antiwar protest with a time-honored attention-grabbing ploy. The Dixie Chicks might have been making a comeback, but it was along a particular, well-trodden path. The group was well managed in this regard, perhaps because recent history has provided many examples of how other prominent Americans, including presidents, a Speaker of the House, and CEOs, have been able to fight their way back from the status of temporary moral outcast. On another level, the Chicks' reinstatement illustrates the relatively shallow nature of war mobilization. While some features of popular culture continue to provide war support, full-scale targeting of those opposed to war, practices that evoke the earlier period of McCarthyism, will be met with both Type I and Type II opposition. Attempts to mobilize popular culture in support of war will continue and may even find temporary success. But militarism will also be challenged by Type I opposition and by the more muted but still significant Type II opposition's reluctance to jump on a cultural bandwagon.

Patriotism and the Draft

Patriotism is a complex force with many meanings. "Love of country" is often seen as support for the military and loyalty to political leaders who formulate and carry out defense policy. Presidents can count on a "rally effect" in which their approval ratings improve dramatically following a military response to a crisis.[4] Every post–World War II president has been the beneficiary of such surges, including Jimmy Carter following the seizure of the American Embassy in Iran;

Gerald Ford after the capture of the *Mayaguez*, which occurred as the United States was leaving Indochina; and John F. Kennedy during the Cuban missile crisis. Following the September 11 attacks, George W. Bush received an unprecedented bounce of more than 30 points and a record 90 percent approval rating.[5]

For others, patriotism has different meanings including resistance to unnecessary war being carried out in their name. Post-9/11 Type I opposition has been notable in this regard, especially in comparison with the movement against the Vietnam War. The American flag can often be seen in demonstrations and rallies and provides a strong counterpoint to the symbols of the Vietnamese National Liberation Front, which was often displayed during the resistance to the Vietnam War. Those who challenge war and call attention to the multiple costs of armed conflict are now more likely to call themselves the "true patriots."

In either case, Americans consider themselves to be very patriotic. Seventy-two percent say that they are "very proud" of their nationality, a proportion that is significantly larger than in most of the countries in Europe.[6] A September 2002 poll found 91 percent of respondents "extremely" or "very" proud to be American. Only 2 percent said that were not at all proud.[7] A month earlier, a poll conducted for the Pew Research Center found 92 percent agreeing "completely" or "mostly" with the statement "I am very patriotic." Only 6 percent disagreed. The percentage agreeing completely (54 percent) was the highest it had been in the last twenty years.[8]

In extreme form, patriotism promotes insensitivity to other people who may hold different values. It also prevents the constant self-examination that is required for more peaceful relationships with others on the planet. But even short of bellicosity, the dominant current of U.S. patriotism sustains two crucial beliefs: first, that American values are universally applicable; and second, that the United States is a force for good in its relations with the rest of the world. A Pew Global Attitudes survey found 79 percent agreeing with the statement "It's good that American ideas and customs are spreading around the world." When this assumption is challenged by foreigners who are skeptical of American intentions, a wide segment of the public becomes confused, perplexed, and sometimes angry. One response is to blame those who do not automatically see Washington's decisions as a force for good. The widespread condemnation of France for its (poorly understood) position on using force against Iraq provides a case in point. Here patriotism blends with a peculiarity of American nationalism, namely, that it fails to recognize itself as a form of nationalism but instead sees itself as a mission that will benefit all. There is also a distinctly religious component to the perception that the international role of the United States is essentially benign. President Bush certainly played upon this tendency, as in his October 7, 2001, announcement of the initiation of the bombing of Afghanistan, which also asked, "May God continue to bless America." The confluence of love of country, loyalty to its leaders and to its military, and presumption of innocent intent forms a type of identity politics—although it would never recognize itself as such. This form of patriotism has often been enlisted in support of war.[9]

A willingness to serve in the armed forces is one concrete embodiment of patriotism. But a distinct feature of the movement toward conditional war is that the public no longer supports conscription. Patriotism remains a strong social force, but most of the population is no longer willing to share in the national call to service. Since 1973, the Pentagon has relied upon an all-volunteer military. Until 2004, the system worked reasonably well, although, as with the previous reliance on conscription, the military was disproportionately working and lower middle class. At the start of the 2003 war with Iraq, of the 535 members of Congress, only one had a son or daughter in Iraq.[10] Another important consequence of the volunteer military has been the significant increase in the number of women, who now make up close to 15 percent of the armed forces.

Periodically over the last twenty years, Gallup has asked, "Do you think the United States should return to the military draft at this time, or not?"[11] In the early 1980s, a majority of Americans favored returning to the draft, but by June 1998, support had dropped dramatically, to only 16 percent of the population. Gallup did not ask the question immediately after September 11 but in January 2003, the number in favor of returning to the draft had increased slightly to 27 percent of the population. Declining support for the war in Iraq was paralleled by a similar downward trend in support for conscription, with only 17 percent in October 2003 and 14 percent in October 2004 expressing their support. An Annenberg Public Policy Center poll conducted just before the 2004 election found less than a quarter of the population supporting a return of the draft.[12] In 2005, as more branches of the armed forces reported failing to meet their recruiting goals, seven in ten Americans still opposed reinstatement of the draft.[13]

Despite the reports of newfound patriotism among college students, this segment of the population was particularly opposed to the possibility of forced military service. A poll conducted by the Harvard University Institute of Politics during October 2002 found that only 7 percent strongly supported reinstating the military draft, 22 percent were somewhat in support, 28 percent were somewhat opposed, and 39 percent were strongly opposed (5 percent did not know). When asked if they would favor conscription if the size of the U.S. forces needed to be increased, two-thirds still replied negatively.[14] A similar pattern was found in a poll of African American voters who were asked, "Do you favor or oppose reinstating the military draft to provide soldiers for the Iraq conflict?" Only 15 percent favored the option compared to 82 percent in opposition.[15]

National security officials have maintained that a draft is not necessary to provide the necessary troops, and that a professional army performs better and is less costly to train in the long run. David S. Chu, the under secretary of defense for personnel and readiness, found the current American military better educated than the general population, noting that "over 90% of new recruits [have] a high school diploma, while only 75% of the American youth do." Chu also says that "today's high-technology military also benefits from personnel who are committed to staying in the service for several years, allowing the armed services to reap full benefit from their costly training. During the draft, soldiers were required to stay in the service for only two years. But Pentagon studies show that current recruits need one to three years to reach full competency in combat or support skills." Additionally, a draft would cause a loss of morale within the military: "The most important thing about a draft is that the people you draft, by definition, don't want to be there. The great strength of the volunteer force is the ranks of people who all made a positive, voluntary decision that this is what they want to do."[16]

The wars in Afghanistan and Iraq have led to a recruitment and retention crisis in the military and prompted some battalion commanders to hesitate before dismissing new recruits for drug and alcohol abuse, poor fitness reports, or pregnancy. By early 2006, the army had eased enlistment restrictions on weight, age, health, and education in order to improve its chances of meeting recruitment goals. The year before, recruits who tested positive for marijuana use had to wait six months before retaking the test. In 2005, the waiting period was reduced to forty-five days.[17] The reserve and National Guard were deployed and at times made up almost 40 percent of the total number of troops in Iraq. Tours of duty have been extended, both for regular forces and for reservists and National Guard members, by "stop loss" orders, which have been described as a "backdoor draft." People in their late forties and fifties have been placed in dangerous situations and the staffing of many businesses and first responders, such as police and firefighters, have been stretched thin by the extended deployment of key members. Many important military functions such as the delivery of fuel, the preparation of meals, and some maintenance and security functions have been outsourced to private contractors, thus effectively augmenting the actual size (and cost) of the U.S. effort. Despite these methods of retaining and substituting for military personnel, signing bonuses of up to $30,000, and an aggressive strategy of targeting minority teens, in early 2005 the army managed to garner only about 70 percent of its planned new recruits.[18]

Many military leaders, and even Secretary of Defense Donald Rumsfeld's own Defense Advisory Board, have maintained that the number of troops in Iraq was far too low. An early 2006 report prepared for the Pentagon concluded that the army could not sustain sufficient troop deployments to defeat the insurgency and that a decision to begin to reduce the force in Iraq over the forthcoming year was driven in part by a new appreciation that the military was overextended.[19] Meanwhile, some strategists had been arguing that the Pentagon, in order to match the 1:50 troop-to-civilian ratio of the more successful peacekeeping efforts of NATO in Bosnia and the United States in Kosovo, would have had to triple the number of troops in Iraq to over 500,000 if the insurgency was to be controlled. But without a draft, it is difficult to see how the additional troop levels could be achieved. An army colonel at the Pentagon, speaking off the record, said, "The military right now is stripped down pretty thin. If the President decided we needed to go somewhere other than Iraq, it doesn't take a mental giant to figure out that we don't have the people to do that."[20] Recruitment goals became harder to meet. Traditionally, African Americans have provided a disproportionate number of soldiers and have made up nearly 25 percent of the army but since 2000 that representation has fallen. In early 2005, African Americans made up 13.9 percent of army recruits and 18.4 percent of the army reserve recruits.[21] More-aggressive measures to get students "to volunteer" were used in working-class schools. At one, McDonough High in Pomfret, Maryland, recruiters chaperoned dances, taught drills at a junior ROTC class, and distributed mugs, brochures, and key chains in the cafeteria. Every prospect was called at least six times by the army alone.[22] Army recruiters reported that they felt pressure to bend the rules in attempting to encourage new enlistments. At some schools, these activities prompted protests against the war in Iraq and the possible return to the draft.

Ironically, it has been two liberal members of the House of Representatives, Charles Rangel (D-N.Y.) and John Conyers (D-Mich.), who have taken the lead in proposing a reinstitution of the draft. Their main point was to raise the issue of the need to share more equally the sacrifice of going to war. The proposal was quickly rejected by Rumsfeld, who claimed that draftees added "no value, no advantages really to the United States armed services over any sustained period of time." It was later pointed out that 21,000, or 35 percent, of the 58,000 killed in Vietnam were draftees, and Rumsfeld was forced to apologize to the American Legion.[23] During a public address, Rangel argued that his bill "should be subject to hearings and to expert testimony. The Administration should come and tell us about our manpower needs, about recruitment and retention, about the extent to which our troops are overextended. And they should give us their views about shared sacrifice. If they did all of those things in a serious way, they would have to admit that my bill is an option."[24]

There is something deeply unsettling about the willingness of some parts of the public to support war but not accept the need to distribute the costs of commitment equally throughout the population. In an all-volunteer army the actual fighting will be done by those with less money and with darker skin. "Pulling a trigger," one observer notes, "is what Jose, Tyrone, and Bubba do, not early admissions students at better universities."[25] One can respect the reluctance to be drafted, or disapproval of decisions that place sons or daughters in dangerous situations. But the disparity between private sensitivity toward the costs of war and public support for war policies that may demand sacrifice is ultimately unsustainable in a democratic society. Meanwhile, Type II opposition to war mobilization via a draft means that the Pentagon may at times have difficulty securing enough troops. One result is an inequitable distribution of risk. Another is that opposition to conscription continues to serve as an important check on militarism.

Enemy Images and Muslim Americans

Militarism often generates enemy images that justify the need to threaten and actually use force. Highly militarized societies, such as Nazi Germany or Imperial Japan, systematically mobilized their populations to see other nationalities and specific social groups within their own countries as dangerous threats. While not as fully militarized as the Axis powers, the United States still made full-scale enemies out of the Japanese. Propaganda depicted the Japanese as subhuman, helping make it possible to place 120,000 Japanese Americans—two-thirds of them U.S. citizens—in internment camps. An example of the racist thinking of the time is provided by a *Time* editorial published a few weeks after Pearl Harbor:

> There is no infallible way of telling [Chinese and Japanese people] apart. Even the anthropologist, with calipers and plenty of time to

measure heads, noses, shoulders, hips, is sometimes stumped. A few rules of thumb—not always reliable.... Japanese—except for wrestlers—are seldom fat; they often dry up and grow lean as they age. The Chinese often put on weight. The Chinese expression is likely to be more placid, kindly, open; the Japanese more positive, dogmatic, arrogant. Japanese walk stiffly erect, hard-heeled. Chinese, more relaxed, have an easy gait, sometimes shuffle.[26]

References to "Japs" and "the Nips" were common in the mainstream press and from public officials, and there was little effort to distinguish between citizens and leaders in Japan. These practices contributed to the brutal treatment of Japan at the end of the war, not only in the atomic bombings of Hiroshima and Nagasaki but also in the "conventional" bombing of Japanese cities, which were firebombed, causing the death of hundreds of thousands.

The transition from mobilized to conditional war, and the process in which Americans are becoming more peaceful, has made it more difficult to construct an enemy out of entire peoples. Military force is now focused against evil regimes rather than the nation as a whole. Indeed, a justification that has accompanied every military intervention after the cold war is that the population will welcome U.S. troops. Domestically, a parallel process is under way. Racial, ethnic, and religious discrimination and other forms of targeting internal "others" is also more limited and is balanced by counterexpressions of tolerance and cultural pluralism. This process is not perfect. Discrimination against Muslims, both by government agencies and by parts of the public, is evident at airports, in visa applications, and in many areas of daily life. The torture conducted in Guantánamo Bay, Abu Ghraib, and other detention facilities stands at the apex of a broader tendency to challenge the rights and to deny respect to many Muslims. Conditional war is still war and the vicissitudes that accompany that system of violence have not been transcended. The challenge is to recognize that discrimination continues to take place without losing sight of the opposing tendencies that make the practices of mobilized war more difficult to follow. The United States continues to harbor different currents of xenophobia, prejudice, and racism. Numerous acts of outlandish violence and disrespect have occurred since 9/11. But these ugly parts of the landscape should be viewed against other, more tolerant patterns that suggest that internal targeting of enemies by the population as a whole has eased and that this feature of militarism is declining as a result.

An undeniable surge in hate crimes against Muslims and others who appeared to be from the Middle East followed September 11.[27] In 2000, 28 hate crimes based on religious bias against Muslims were reported to the FBI; in 2001, that number jumped to 481—concentrated in the last three months of the year.[28] The FBI's 2001 Uniform Crime Reporting Program stated that anti-Islamic hate crimes had become the "second highest reported among religious-bias incidents"—they were "previously the second least reported."[29] Religious-related hate crimes against Jews far outnumber those against Muslims, a feature of American intolerance that continued after 9/11 even though the "hate crime gap" between the two groups shrank significantly after the terrorist attacks. In a typical year more hate crimes are committed against Jews than against Catholics, Protestants, and Muslims combined. Even in 2001, when hate crimes against Muslims skyrocketed, more crimes were committed against Jews than all of the other religions put together. The fact that there are not nearly as many reported hate crimes against Muslims as against Jews is not exactly a cause for celebration. What is somewhat more reassuring is the decline in hate crimes committed against Muslims, which fell from 481 in 2001 to 155 in 2002.

Civil rights organizations, including the National Asian Pacific American Legal Consortium (NAPALC), and the Council on American Islamic Relations (CAIR), have disputed the relatively low FBI figures. NAPALC and CAIR suggest that the federal agency's data understates the true magnitude because the FBI reporting is dependent on information submitted by some 11,909 law enforcement agencies across the country. The FBI does not conduct its own investigations, and many states underreport hate crimes to the national agency. In 2003, for example, Alabama, Louisiana, Montana, and Mississippi reported 10 or fewer hate crimes of all types, figures that strain credibility. As explained by FBI spokesman Paul Bresson, "The crimes themselves are investigated by local and state police or the county police" and not by the agency itself. "We don't really know why," Bresson added, "the numbers are what they are. We pay more attention to ensuring the numbers reported to us are tabulated correctly, that they are collected in accordance with our hate crime collection policies so that they are all in uniformity and that they, after a while, will lead to some meaningful comparisons you can make from year to year."[30] In 2002, NAPALC and its affiliates documented 275 bias-motivated hate crimes against Asian Pacific Americans, a number that is almost double that offered by the FBI. Yet this figure was also lower than the 507 reported in 2001 and 392 reported in 2000. The pattern seems to be as follows: (1) an increase in hate crimes after 9/11; (2) more hate crimes against Muslim groups and those mistakenly thought to be Muslim than contained in official figures; and (3) partial "recovery" following 9/11 to lower (but still too high) levels.

Beyond hate crimes, which are committed by relatively few in-dividuals, lie other forms of discrimination and prejudice toward Muslims. In a poll carried out during late July and August 2002, 57 percent of American Muslims reported experiencing some form of bias after September 11; 87 percent reported knowing of a Muslim who had experienced bias.[31] Discrimination most often took the form of verbal abuse, religious or ethnic profiling, or workplace dis-crimination. Forty-eight percent of respondents thought that their quality of life had declined after September 11 and only 16 percent responded that it had improved. (The improvement was most often attributed to receiving respectful questions about Islam from non-Muslims.) Other daunting findings include an October 2004 poll of all Americans that found one of four agreeing with stereotypes such as "Muslims teach their children to hate" and "Muslims value life less than other people." In addition, 32 percent responded negatively when asked what they thought after hearing the word "Muslim."[32] CAIR held the Bush administration partly responsible for the increase in incidents of anti-Muslim discrimination, argu-ing that government policies introduced after September 11, 2001, especially the Patriot Act, created hostile conditions for Muslims living in the United States. Twenty-three percent of the incidents collected by the group involved interactions with government agen-cies. These actions included "intimidating" interviews conducted by the FBI, requests for mosque membership lists, and raids on Muslim homes and businesses.

The media also played a significant role in the development of anti-Muslim prejudice and discrimination. A Columbia University study released in October 2004 found that the number of newspa-per articles insinuating that American Muslims support terrorism increased from 4 percent in the six months after 9/11 to 14 percent in articles published around the first anniversary.[33] In addition, the media reinforced other stereotypes of Muslims, including "women as victims" and "men as brutal and war-mongering." Radio talk shows are particularly instrumental in furthering bias. In April 2004, Rabiah Ahmed, CAIR's communications director, contended in a press release that anti-Muslim attitudes and recent hate crimes could be attributed to negative representations of Islam and calls to violence on the radio: discriminatory messages "[harm] our nation by fostering a climate of intolerance and bigotry."[34] One of the more extreme examples came from Michael Graham, a talk show host at 630 WMAL-AM in Washington, D.C., who on April 1, 2004, said, "I don't wanna say we should kill 'em all [Muslims], but unless there's reform [within Islam], there aren't a lot of other solutions that work in the on-the-ground struggle for survival." WTKK-FM (Boston) host

Jay Severin also offered the following insight: "I've got an idea, let's kill all Muslims." In response, CAIR began a radio campaign entitled "Hate Hurts America," which proposed methods of combating such attacks, including filing complaints with the Federal Communications Commission and advertisers.

A report of the Media and Society Research Group at Cornell University provides still more sobering news.[35] Nearly half of those surveyed in the fall of 2004 believed that Islam is more likely to encourage violence than other religions. And nearly half agreed with a question asking if at least one form of restriction should be placed on the civil liberties of Muslim Americans.[36] These pessimistic findings are concentrated in particular segments of the public. For example, Republicans and Christians who described themselves as highly religious were more likely to support the curtailing of civil liberties than Democrats or those who are less religious. Christians with high levels of religiosity were almost twice as likely as the rest of the respondents to agree that the government should have more power to monitor Internet activities. In addition, respondents who depend on television for their news are also more likely to feel personally in danger of another terrorist attack and more willing to limit the rights of Muslim Americans. "Elected representatives, government officials and other opinion leaders," said CAIR executive director Nihad Awad in response to the study, "must finally recognize that Islamophobia is a growing phenomenon in American society that must be urgently addressed."[37]

This record is certainly alarming but the majority of Americans are not party to the "enemy-within" aspect of militarism. Most continue to show respect for Muslims. "How Americans Responded," a survey conducted by the Institute for Social Research at the University of Michigan shortly after the September 11 attacks, did not support the contention that Americans were engaged in widespread prejudice against foreigners.[38] In fact, the institute found more than 80 percent either "agreeing" or "strongly agreeing" that immigrants made Americans open to new ideas and culture. The report describes Americans "rallying around each other, concerned and even distrustful of some groups of foreigners … [but also exhibiting] a kind of patriotism of mutual support more than a jingoistic reaction to all foreigners or even immigrants." The post–September 11 environment also includes numerous expressions of support for the Muslim community, and many individuals bought books or otherwise tried to educate themselves about Islam. Many efforts, often organized through religious organizations, created celebrations of ethnic and religious pluralism and tolerance. The media's coverage of these events has been sparse at best and, as a result, the public has not often had an opportunity to reflect on its own, more peaceful, tendencies. One poll found that 79 percent of American Muslims experienced acts of tolerance or kindness from acquaintances who follow other religions.[39] Nihad Awad noted that extreme prejudices are held by only a minority of Americans and combating such biases is feasible: "The results of this survey show that while we have all gone through a traumatic year in our nation's history, there is hope for the future if Americans who support and practice tolerance challenge the vocal minority who seek to divide our nation." An October 2004 poll of all Americans found half having positive beliefs about Muslims, including "Muslims have family-oriented values" and "Muslims have contributed to civilization."[40]

Following September 11, political leaders in both parties reminded the population of the need to distinguish between terrorists and people from the Middle East and South Asia. One might counter that the wars in Afghanistan and Iraq have helped create a climate that encouraged the mistreatment of people from those regions. Certainly the treatment of prisoners in Guantánamo Bay, indiscriminate efforts on the part of the FBI to interview thousands of men who had recently arrived in the United States from the Middle East, and the targeting of Muslims at airports all contributed to the idea of an imminent threat. Representative John Cooksey (R-La.) could still argue that any "person 'wearing a diaper on his head' should be subject to more scrutiny when traveling on airlines."[41] Similarly, Representative Peter King (R-N.Y.) could appear on a nationally syndicated radio program and claim that the vast majority of American Muslims were "an enemy among us," that "80–85 percent of mosques in this country are controlled by Islamic fundamentalists," and that "no (American) Muslims" cooperate with the U.S. government in the war on terror.[42] But these extreme views were isolated when measured against the beliefs of most of the public.

A comparison of editorials from the *Los Angeles Times* published in the thirteen weeks following Pearl Harbor and in the eleven weeks after September 11 found that almost one-third of the editorials during the earlier period supported ethnic profiling or reasserting a traditional perspective of what it means to be an American. No editorial did so following September 11. In fact, 20 percent of the editorials in the more recent period highlighted the value of multiculturalism, compared to only 2 percent during the World War II period. The 2001 editorials referred to the United States as "a nation of immigrants" that "celebrated diversity" and highlighted the "evolution of American ethnic identity."[43]

Local leaders demonstrated a willingness to prevent discrimination and develop tolerance. Many organized a broad range of community events including educational efforts and acts of solidarity that exemplified Type I explicit peace activity. On September 13, 2001, approximately five hundred people held a vigil outside the city hall in Portland, Maine, to express their support for the Muslim community. Community leaders warned against prejudice and asked the audience to uphold instead the values of tolerance and respect. Tom Ewell, director of the Maine Council of Churches, emphasized the necessity of unity after the disaster of September 11: "We stand together, shoulder-to-shoulder, as Jews, Buddhists, Christians, Hindus, Muslims, Ba'hai and adherents of other religious traditions. In this time of crisis we are joined simply by our common humanity in the aftermath of the terrible tragedy of yesterday's attack."[44] Similarly, organizers of an interfaith vigil outside the Islamic Center Mosque in Denver, Colorado, on September 22, 2001, were hoping to draw three hundred participants but were greeted with a crowd of three thousand. Forty different religious groups contributed to the event. Some community activities took the form of adopting Muslim practices. "Scarves for Solidarity" became a worldwide movement and a method of communicating respect for the Muslim community, particularly women. On February 20, 2002, events in thirty cities commemorated the National Day of Solidarity with Muslim, Arab, and South Asian immigrants. Activities largely organized by college groups and local activists included speeches, rallies, art exhibits and cultural performances, marches, wearing/distribution of blue triangles (the day's emblem), film showings, candlelight vigils, and coffeehouses.[45] An event planned by the Bill of Rights Defense Campaign in Syracuse, New York, on February 26, 2004, included the opportunity to don a shawl and wear tags with the words "In solidarity with the Muslim and Arab communities." The event also included a vigil and an interfaith gathering at a local mosque.[46]

Talk show host Oprah Winfrey sponsored another type of peace-education event. Her "Islam 101" presented basic information about the religion and dispelled several misconceptions.[47] Winfrey also developed a section on her Web site that included interviews with prominent Muslims, a profile of an American Muslim woman, and information on the basics of Islam and the origin of the Qur'an. Many viewers responded enthusiastically to her series. CAIR's director of communications noted an "increase in U.S. media and public outreach to learn more about the fundamental tenants, history, and practices of Islam." Editorials posted in conservative journals such *National Review* and weblogs such as frontpagemag. com disputed Oprah's presentation of Islam as a peaceful religion. But the majority welcomed these efforts. TV networks rebroadcast the much praised documentary *Islam: Empire of Faith* in part due to popular demand.

Another feature of popular culture promoting tolerance was the involvement of celebrities in public service announcements. Disturbed by the post-9/11 discrimination against Arab and Muslim Americans, actress Mary-Louise Parker organized a campaign against discrimination that included the Advertising Council, the National Crime Prevention Council (NCPC), and Seeking Harmony in Neighborhoods Everyday (SHiNE). Responding to a question posed by *Cosmopolitan* magazine about her decision, Parker said: "After September 11, I heard and read of so many innocent Arab Americans who had been attacked or who were living in fear. I became frustrated because I felt that this country is a place where people should be able to feel safe. So these ads serve as a gentle reminder to people of what America stands for."[48]

The ads starred celebrities such as Dennis Quaid, Mia Farrow, Shannon Elizabeth, and Steve Buscemi. Each spot featured the celebrities looking directly at the camera and saying, "Don't pick the wrong fight" and "Stop the hate." Commenting on the campaign, Jack Calhoun, president and CEO of NCPC, stated:

> We are a caring nation of people who must not tolerate hate crimes perpetrated against individuals for ethnic, religious, or cultural differences. We have seen some awful instances of hate crimes but these are outnumbered by the examples of concern and caring for people of all backgrounds. This ad is a powerful reminder that though we may be different, we are united as Americans. It is my hope that the events of September 11th do not paralyze our country in fear and hate, but spur us to a new commitment to connect with each other, our families, and our communities.[49]

Gauging the level of tolerance for Islam within U.S. popular culture is a classic instance of looking at a glass that is either half full or half empty. On one side lie hate crime, prejudice, ignorance, and government practices taken in the name of antiterrorism that only contribute to continued discrimination. For some citizens, war in Afghanistan and Iraq has intensified already existing xenophobic tendencies within the United States. On the other side lie respect for difference, a desire to learn more, and the remarkable pattern in which local interfaith coalitions have formed to respond to acts of hatred. These more moderate tendencies underscore an ability to distinguish between the perpetrators of a specific crime and the adherents of a major religion. The strength of the tolerant current varies significantly, and some expressions of support are deeper and more sincere than others. Celebrities making public service announcements and advertising councils are not the equivalent of community leaders and local public officials who resist enemy images and discriminatory behavior on a daily basis. But in some ways, this variation is precisely the point. Type I explicit opposition to war is more likely to be principled in its inclusion of Muslim Americans among the "we." But Type II nonacceptance of the tendency of war to create and then stigmatize an Other are crucial as well. Respect for multiculturalism has certainly not eradicated prejudice. Nonetheless, a significant spectrum of opinion has been created that opposes the creation of internal enemies of entire peoples or religions in the United States.

Militarism and Conditional War

For most of this book, I have emphasized the differences between mobilized and conditional war. There are also continuities that reflect that both forms of organized violence are still in fact war. All wars have negative impacts on democratic processes, the status of women, and the mental health of those who do the fighting. While I am cautiously optimistic on the boundaries of conditional war for intergroup relations within the United States, it is also impossible to pass over the ways that the war in Iraq has fueled international tension between Muslims and the United States and Europe. During Operation Iraqi Freedom, rioting took place in several suburbs in France, anti-Muslim behavior in the Netherlands followed the stabbing death of a maker of documentary films, and an enormously volatile situation followed the publication of cartoons in newspapers in Denmark and elsewhere in Europe that were considered blasphemous because they depicted Mohammed in bodily form. Each example has its own specific explanation and unique dynamic. In France, high Muslim unemployment was important, and the cartoon furor was fueled by deliberately provocative journalists and politicians such as an Italian government minister who wore the drawing on his shirt. But the depth of the controversy is also difficult to understand without an appreciation of the war's broader impact on Islam as a whole. Here a broad-based, systematic feeling of being under attack is being created on a significant scale. In this regard, the features of conditional war that limit the connections between the public and the war system within the United States can be contrasted to a possible remobilization of enemy relations in the international arena.

Many cultural practices in the United States continue to provide support for military policies. Traditional patriotism resonates strongly, perhaps more than in any other developed country. The strong tendency to hold the military in high regard also tends to sustain government policies that rely on military force. Yet, in contrast with mobilized war, in conditional war the connections between the war effort and popular culture have become weaker. Conventional patriotism and support for troops are balanced by counterarguments over the meaning of patriotism and by the fact that relatively few people are willing to join the military. The labeling of enemies and the search for them within the country also continue. But this process also meets the countercurrents of tolerance and multiculturalism. The "acceptable" targets of hate must be individual perpetrators of crimes, not entire peoples—though Washington may make decisions and create an atmosphere in which these constraints are partially undermined. And finally, the majority of the public is not willing to participate in systematic campaigns against lightning rods of antiwar opposition such as the Dixie Chicks. This situation is far from the nonviolent vision of peace advocated by Leo Tolstoy, Mahatma Gandhi, and Martin Luther King Jr. It also falls short of what most Type I opponents of war would regard as a peaceful culture. But the country has also moved far from the deliberate internal targeting that occurred during World War II and the McCarthy period of the cold war. Contemporary popular culture in the United States contains important elements of resistance to militarism as well as the potential to build more explicitly peaceful alternatives.

Chapter 8

Managing Casualties

In December 1968, Colonel George Patton, son of the famous World War II general, sent out Christmas cards from his headquarters in Vietnam. This ritual holiday greeting often features a family portrait of smiling children, proud parents, and perhaps a favorite pet. But this time Patton included a color photograph showing a section of bare dirt with a background of trees and thick jungle undergrowth that highlighted the foreign setting. In the middle of this area lay dozens of dead Vietnamese stacked together in a giant pile and made ready to be carted off by a soon-to-be-arriving helicopter. The card read, "From Colonel and Mrs. George S. Patton III" and it wished the recipient "Peace on Earth."[1]

Imagine the brouhaha that would follow if General Norman Schwarzkopf had sent a similar greeting from Iraq following the 1991 Gulf War, or if General Tommy Franks had distributed triumphal Easter cards featuring dead Iraqis following the fall of Baghdad in 2003. Both military leaders were celebrated for their victories, but would either have been able to keep his command if he publicly reveled in the concrete results of his work? The reluctance to show American bodies to the U.S. public is well documented. But it has become more difficult to show the other side's pain as well.

This chapter examines two public concerns with conditional war. The first is minimizing U.S. casualties: the United States may go to war but soldiers cannot die in significant numbers. The goal is zero casualties, one that is almost impossible to achieve, although, significantly, it was attained once, during the 1999 air campaign against Serbia. In Type II opposition, the public may withdraw its support whenever casualties rise beyond "small." The boundary of small fluctuates and can change in the middle of the operation itself. For example, casualties are less likely to become a policy constraint when pursuing those thought to be responsible for September 11. On the other hand, sensitivity will increase where success is uncertain and where the mission does not have strong support. Despite this variation, the overall range of "acceptable casualties" is far less than it was for mobilized war, and Pentagon operations are planned with this sensitivity in mind.[2]

A second public concern with conditional war is the reduction of perceived noncombatant casualties on the other side. The public's increased sensitivity to costs means that the military cannot fight in ways that appear to produce significant "collateral damage." Evil leaders such as Saddam Hussein or Osama bin Laden can be targeted. It is also permissible to kill their immediate supporters such as the Iraqi Republican Guard or al Qaeda recruits. But conditional war cannot be pursued in ways that look like indiscriminate killing. New technology has increased the accuracy of many weapons and improved the flow of information to those who target them, in theory making it possible to separate combatants from noncombatants more reliably. But this technology also raises the public's expectation that this distinction will be preserved. The United States is obliged to fight in ways in which "force protection" is a crucial and sometimes predominant goal, and in which harm to innocents in the combat area is avoided as much as possible. The public expectation is that neither U.S. soldiers nor "enemy" civilians should die. Both goals are genuine even though the Pentagon is significantly better at achieving the first than the second.

The goal of mobilized war was attrition: destroying people and resources to the point that further resistance was either impossible or seemed futile. Consider the sacrifice made by U.S. troops during World War II. Table 8.1 shows the casualty figures, both dead and wounded, for U.S. infantry divisions after D-Day and during the subsequent march toward Germany. The percent dead for each division ranges from 15 to 20 percent, while the proportion wounded is between one-half and two-thirds. It was the lucky man who escaped unscathed.

During World War II, the United States followed a strategy of attrition, which produced casualties and called for sacrifices that were impossible to hide. Media coverage of the war may not have been graphic in its description but the pain and loss were well understood. Archibald McLeish said at a dinner to honor Edward R.

Table 8.1 Casualty Figures for U.S. Infantry Divisions
in Northwestern Europe during World War II

Division	Months	Battle Casualties		Percentages	
		Dead	Wounded	Dead	Wounded
4	11	4,834	17,371	18.1	65.1
29	11	3,786	15,541	15.9	56.3
30	11	3,516	13,376	16.5	62.7
79	11	2,943	10,971	16.1	59.8
83	11	3,620	11,807	19.2	62.5
90	11	3,930	14,386	17.3	63.2
5	10	2,656	9,549	15.9	60.3
8	10	2,820	10,057	16.3	45.3
35	10	2,947	11,526	15.6	61.0
28	9	2,683	9,609	16.1	57.7
80	9	3,480	12,484	17.0	61.1

Source: John Ellis, *Brute Force: Allied Strategy and Tactics in the Second World War.* London: Andre Deutsch, 1990, 538–39.

Murrow and his reporting from England during the early days of the war: "You laid the dead of London at our feet and we knew that the dead were our dead, were mankind's dead. Without rhetoric, without dramatics, without more emotion than needed, you have ended the superstition that what is done beyond three thousand miles of water is not really done at all."[3]

The best-known correspondent in World War II was Ernie Pyle, whose moving writing connected the troops and the home front. Pyle recognized the human cost of war. In December 1943, he submitted the following dispatch from Italy:

I was at the foot of the mule trail the night they brought Captain Waskow's body down. Dead men had been coming down the mountain all evening lashed on the backs of mules. I don't know who the first one was. You feel small in the presence of dead men and ashamed to be alive and you don't ask silly questions. Then a soldier came and said there were more bodies outside. Four mules stood there in the moonlight. The four soldiers who led them stood there waiting.

"This one is Captain Waskow," one of them said quickly. Two men unlashed the body and lifted him off and laid him in the shadow of the old stone wall.

The men stood around and gradually, one by one, I could sense them moving closer to Captain Waskow's body. One soldier came and said out loud, "God Damn it."

Another came and looked down into the dead captain's face and then spoke directly to him as if he were alive, "I'm sorry, Old Man."

Then a soldier came and he too spoke to his captain and he said not in a whisper but awfully tenderly, "I sure am sorry, sir."

Then the first man squatted down and took the captain's hand and he sat there for a full five minutes holding the dead hand in his own and looking intently at the man's face. Finally he put the hand down and gently straightened the points of his shirt collar and then he rearranged the tattered edges of the uniform around the wound, then he walked away down the road in the moonlight all alone.[4]

President Roosevelt probably approved of Ernie Pyle; of a contemporary equivalent describing the losses in Iraq, President Bush would not approve.

The Body Count

During the Vietnam War, the Pentagon used the "body count," or number of enemy soldiers that were killed in a particular battle, or during the previous week or month, as its best measure of progress. The claim that United States was winning the war was based on official calculations purporting that National Liberation Front guerrillas or North Vietnamese soldiers were being killed at a far greater rate than Americans. The infamous search-and-destroy strategy tried to entice opposing forces into a battle and then kill them with a combination of U.S. ground troops, artillery, and munitions delivered by air. Washington would win when it killed a sufficient number to reach a magical "breakpoint" that would erode Hanoi's resolve or where the birthrate in the North, or in the areas of South Vietnam controlled by the NLF, could not match the number killed by U.S. forces. The inability of the Pentagon to achieve the required kill rate was one of the factors that prompted then secretary of defense Robert McNamara to conclude that the war could not be won.

The body count, however, became a subject of ridicule. The antiwar movement, increasingly the press, and even the military itself dismissed the significance of the numbers. The body count was not considered an appropriate measure for a war that was supposed to be over the "hearts and minds" of the Vietnamese and because the numbers themselves were grossly inflated. Did a higher body count mean that the military was winning, or that the revolutionary forces had succeeded in recruiting more soldiers that could be thrown into battle? Perhaps junior officers were padding the figures to claim success for their units and promotion for themselves? Did more bodies mean that the United States controlled more territory or was in any other way coming closer to determining the outcome of the war?

Donald Kinnard's postwar survey of generals who served in Vietnam asked about the value and accuracy of the body count and revealed considerable unease among the military's leadership. The questions, with percent agreeing with each option, were as follows:

One important indicator was the kill ratio. Was this:

1. a valuable indicator and necessary in managing the war (4)
2. a rough device that was better than others (35)
3. a misleading device to estimate progress (55)
4. other or no answer (6)

The kill ratio was based upon body count. Was the body count

5. within reason accurate (26)
6. underestimated (3)
7. often inflated (61)
8. other or no answer (10)

An open-ended question on the body count produced a stream of commentary: "The immensity of the false reporting is a blot on the honor of the Army." "The bane of my existence and just about got me fired as a division commander. They were grossly exaggerated by many units primarily because of the incredible interest shown by people like McNamara and Westmoreland. I shudder to think how many soldiers were killed on a body-counting mission—what a waste." "A fake—totally worthless." And finally, "Gruesome—a ticket-punching item."[5] The substantial loss of life, fifty-eight thousand Americans and more than 2 million Vietnamese, all for a Washington defeat, became one of the key memories of the war.

The post-Vietnam period was one of relative caution for the use of military power, especially because the public was reluctant to approve of overseas commitments of force. Many factors contributed to this "Vietnam syndrome," but the anticipated reaction of the public to the death of still more American troops was among the most important. In their own ways, Presidents Carter and Reagan tried to rebuild the status of the United States as world leader but each president also generally respected the need to avoid the further deaths of military personnel. In 1980, Carter made a failed effort to rescue hostages who had been captured by the new Iranian government. And Reagan sent troops to Lebanon in a peacekeeping mission and later to Grenada to overthrow the government. Though U.S. troops died in each operation, the overall reluctance to commit ground troops against any but the weakest opponent remained intact. Possible military intervention against Nicaragua's Sandinista government, for example, was ruled out in favor of the surreptitious and illegal funding of a local proxy army known as the *contras.*

In 1984, Reagan's secretary of defense, Caspar Weinberger, presented a new "doctrine" that attempted to balance the new constraints with the traditional requirement that U.S. foreign policy rely on the threatened and actual use of force.[6] Weinberger outlined six tests that were read as limiting the conditions under which the military could be used. The secretary of defense said that the United States "should not commit forces to combat overseas unless the particular engagement is deemed vital to our national interest or that of our allies," but once troops were committed, the use of force should be "wholehearted and with the clear intent of winning." Weinberger called for "clearly defined political and military objectives" and continued reassessment of the "relationship between these objectives and the forces we have committed." Perhaps the most important requirement was for "reasonable assurance that we will have the support of the American people and their elected representatives in Congress." The final criterion was that military force should be committed only "as a last resort."

Weinberger's emphasis on invincible force and the call to avoid the danger of a "gradualist, incremental approach, which almost always means the use of insufficient force," sounds like a demand for overwhelming military superiority. But Weinberger's position can also be read as restricting the arenas where military force could be applied and, most of all, as an argument against employing forces almost indiscriminately, for this approach would "surely plunge us headlong into the sort of domestic turmoil we experienced during the Vietnam war without accomplishing the goal for which we committed our forces. Such policies might very well tear at the fabric of our society, endangering the single most critical element of a successful democracy: a strong consensus of support and agreement for our basic purpose." Vietnam, the public's sensitivity to casualties, and the prospect of eroding support were affecting the way that government officials thought about the circumstances in which they could apply military force.

Only a few weeks later, Reagan's secretary of state, George Shultz, gave a speech at Yeshiva University that many felt took as a reply to the Weinberger doctrine.[7] Military force continued to be important. "Power and diplomacy," argued Shultz, "must always go together or we will accomplish very little in this world." And diplomacy, according to the secretary of state, that is not backed by strength will be ineffectual and possibly even dangerous. The speech, as many commentaries noted, did not mention any political restraints on the use of American strength. In fact, Shultz maintained that "there is no such thing as guaranteed public support in advance" of the use of force. Great powers are not freed from the necessity of making choices. The United States "must bear responsibility for the consequences of its inaction as well as for the consequences of its action," Shultz argued. Furthermore, "We must use our power with discretion, but we must not shrink from the challenges posed by those who threaten our ideals, our friends, and hopes for a better world." Unlike Weinberger, Shultz did not want to accept the constraints offered by public opinion.

Where military force was used, the public was shielded from the scenes of combat. The Reagan administration organized the press into tightly controlled pools during the 1989 invasion of Panama so that no bodies were shown to the public. The Bush administration used a similar system during the first Persian Gulf War, which consisted of a long period of bombing before a ground invasion which lasted only a hundred hours. While President George H. W. Bush claimed that the military operation left "the Vietnam syndrome dead and buried in the sands," post–Desert Storm policy discussions continued to focus on the public's reluctance to accept losses. Bush continued to act cautiously, refusing to commit combat troops to the overthrow of Saddam or to stop ethnic cleansing in Bosnia, and he only reluctantly did so in the effort to reduce famine in Somalia in the last two months of his term.

This continued caution was reflected in yet another formulation, the Powell doctrine, which in many ways accepted the constraints elucidated by Weinberger, whose protégé Colin Powell was. The Powell doctrine was similarly understood within the Pentagon as cautious in its argument that military force be used only as a last resort and where there is a clear threat to national security. The military should be committed only when overwhelming force was to be used to accomplish a clearly defined mission supported by the public, with explicit rules of engagement and a strategy for eventual departure. The doctrine was never made formal, but in a *Foreign Affairs* article, Powell wrote, "We owe it to the men and women who go in harm's way to make sure that this is always the case and that their lives are not squandered for unclear purposes."[8]

In Vietnam, the United States allegedly fought with one hand tied behind its back. (Of course, the one hand that was used did considerable damage and no one has yet been able to explain how the use of a second would have made a difference in a war fought essentially over political will.) Now a pillar of the military establishment was arguing that the United States could not use military force unless fully committed. The capacity of the military—new weapons, better training, improved leadership, renewed esprit de corps—grew in the post-Vietnam recovery years. But the argument over the rules governing the actual use of this new force continued to engulf the Pentagon throughout the 1990s. Behind the political battles lay public sensitivities to the loss of life.

Elites concerned with strengthening the traditional link between U.S. foreign policy and military force were displeased. Just as Shultz responded to Weinberger in the 1980s, Powell's desire for caution met 1990s critics. Pentagon consultant Edward Luttwak complained about the implied constraints in a widely cited article in which he wrote:

> Great powers were states strong enough to successfully wage war without calling on allies. But that distinction [between great powers and others] is now outdated, because the issue today is not whether war can be made with or without allies but whether war can be made at all. Historically there have been tacit preconditions to great power status: a readiness to use force whenever it was advantageous to do so and an acceptance of the resulting combat casualties with equanimity, as long as the number was not disproportionate.... Great powers normally relied on intimidation rather than combat but only because a willingness to use force was assumed. Moreover, they would use force undeterred by the prospect of the ensuing casualties, within limits of course. Parents who commonly approved of their sons' and daughters' decisions to join the armed forces, thereby choosing a career dedicated to combat and its preparation just as a fireman's career is dedicated to the fighting of fires, now often react with astonishment and anger when their children are actually sent into potential combat situations.[9]

Luttwak's particular explanation of this development—lower birthrates and smaller families, which cause parents to value each individual child more—is rather dubious. But his frustration indicates that the Vietnam syndrome was far from being buried in the Persian Gulf sands. The restriction imposed by anticipated casualties has been echoed by many others closely linked with the exercise of U.S. global power. For example, a national security official who had worked in both the Department of Defense and the CIA stated in an interview that: "As a group, the string of presidents, and senior national leadership, uniform and civilian, including senior members of congress are risk averse. I don't mean to imply cowardice but the size of the stakes has to rise a considerable way for this group to be willing to take what it views to be risks. They need to be more open-minded toward the use of force and the possibility of casualties." This official went on to say that risk aversion jeopardized the existing structure of global relations, which works largely to the benefit of the United States. When asked about the requirement to have an exit strategy, this same official replied: "I don't think it is possible to have a firm exit strategy. The hard-line requirement that you have an exit strategy is, I think, excessive. I don't think that most international situations can bear that weight. There is a big distance between jumping out into the dark and having a full-blown exit strategy and we need to explore that in-between area. If we can at least picture the circumstances in which we could say that the mission has been accomplished and that we can leave, that would be enough. But there would be no guarantee." This remarkably candid assessment of the importance of risk (i.e., potential loss of U.S. soldiers) for the exercise of U.S. global power also shows how Type II opposition (the nonacceptance of this loss) can restrict Washington's options to impose its will.

The military's hesitation to commit forces in situations other than in narrowly defined matters of national security prompted a now famous exchange between U.S. ambassador to the United Nations Madeleine Albright and then chair of the Joint Chiefs of Staff Powell. In Bosnia, journalists documented the displacement and widespread killing of civilians and the existence of camps where systematic rape and other crimes against women were carried out. Despite having knowledge of these crimes, the United States and Europe were reluctant to commit their militaries to an effort to stop the atrocities. Powell advised restraint. Getting in was easy, he argued, but the Serbs might respond in ways that would require Washington to increase its commitment. The military could get bogged down, troops could become more vulnerable, force protection could be difficult to provide, all without a clear exit strategy. It could become another Vietnam.

Albright, growing increasingly impatient with the failure of the West to respond to war crimes in the Balkans, asked Powell, "What's the point of having this superb military that you're always talking about if we can't use it?" The general's reply, "American GIs are not toy soldiers to be moved around on some sort of global game board," is said to have elevated his hero status in the Pentagon.[10] "I thought I would have an aneurysm," Powell later said.

The Clinton administration saw the public as well as the military as reluctant to accept significant casualties. An official with experience in both Democratic and Republican administrations later stated that "there was a concern in the Clinton administration that even relatively modest casualties would completely undermine public support for operations and cause them to be withdrawn as they were in Somalia, and the operation would crumble overnight. The feeling was that even two or three casualties could lead to an irresistible call to leave." Many Clinton officials were extremely reluctant to involve the Pentagon in Bosnia. Somalia provided a negative lesson and Clinton turned his back on the genocide in Rwanda. Clinton was also slow to become involved in Haiti, in part because he read the public as unwilling to support military intervention in support of the return of deposed president Aristide. Eventually, Clinton did intervene but only after strong pressure from the Congressional Black Caucus and only with orders that made force protection a high priority. U.S. military forces did not, for example, try to disarm the anti-Aristide militia for fear of provoking hostilities.

The Clinton administration's 1999 decision to use force against Slobodan Milosevic is perhaps the clearest example of the elevation of force protection to the most important strategic priority. On the eve of the bombing campaign, the president promised that no ground troops would be deployed in the effort to prevent Serb ethnic cleansing in Kosovo, and NATO commanding general Wesley Clark ordered his staff to prepare an air campaign against Serbia whose first principle would be to ensure "no loss of aircraft."

In 2001, President George W. Bush came to office determined to change this casualty constraint. The administration intended to free itself not only to threaten but also to use military force. Many leading officials were determined to reshape the Middle East to conform more closely to U.S. managerial interests. Saddam had to be removed, access to oil guaranteed, and "democracy" used as a wedge to enhance American influence. At the same time, the new administration had no intention of intervening in the humanitarian emergencies in which Clinton had dabbled without producing a coherent policy. Bush specifically excluded the military from "nation-building" missions. But regaining the freedom to use force would require a different attitude on the part of the public and even from a large section of the military toward anticipated casualties.

The Casualty-Aversion Thesis

A key element of conditional war is that the public has become less willing to support military force when there is a significant prospect of casualties. In some cases, war support may be secured but approval will evaporate if the scale of the hostilities resurrects Vietnam themes of quagmire and loss. Type II sensitivities toward casualties will force political and military leaders to manage war to keep perceived losses low or risk withdrawal of public support.

This argument is challenged by a series of studies, largely from political scientists, that have argued that support will not disappear if casualties occur—at least not in any simple or automatic way.[11] In their terms, the public is not "casualty averse." (There is something particularly annoying abut the use of medical terms that convey pathology, such as "aversion" or Vietnam "syndrome," to describe the reluctance to accept casualties. The implication is that the attitude is some kind of sickness from which the public will hopefully "recover.") Using polling data, this revisionist school sees the public as supporting military missions, even where casualties occur, as long as these operations are regarded as important, are clearly explained by the president, are supported by Congress, and where there is a good chance of eventual success. In fact, the public's tolerance for fatalities can be greater than that of either civilian or military leaders. "The available evidence," writes one member of this group of political scientists, "identifies a significant disparity in casualty tolerance between the leadership and the average citizen, with the latter more willing to accept combat losses—depending on the circumstances."[12] Conversely, missions that lack a clear moral urgency or strong national interest are beset by significant divisions within government, and are tarnished by uncertainty will be met by declining public support if casualties occur. But if the mission is credible, the public will stick it out.

Until the George W. Bush administration, post-Vietnam civilian leaders did see the public as casualty averse. For example, in a series of 1996 interviews conducted in Washington on peacemaking in Bosnia, a congressional staff member said of the public: "If it suddenly heats up and we have people engaged in firefights and start getting a weekly death toll, then I don't think they'd like it at all." Another congressional staff member said, "God forbid something does happen in Bosnia ... and you sustain a number of U.S. casualties—I don't even think it has to be .... [e]leven.... I don't know what the magic number would be." And an official in the executive branch thought that if "one American soldier dies we're all in trouble. I think the biggest worry some people have in the political system is somebody getting popped in Bosnia." Similarly, a senior defense official told the *Washington Post* after Kosovo: "We have gotten into this mentality where we feel the American public will cut and run if we have any casualties, and therefore we have to operate in a manner that absolutely minimizes military losses."[13] And a 1999 survey conducted by the Triangle Institute in North Carolina found civilian and military elites and the American public all strongly agreeing with the statement, "The American public will rarely tolerate large numbers of U.S. casualties in military operations."[14]

Somalia is often taken by the revisionist school as the most important point in the formation of the perception that the public has become casualty averse because the death of eighteen Army Rangers in a disastrous attempt to capture warlord Mohammed Farah Aidid was followed by the withdrawal, six months later, of U.S. troops from the country. The incident was significant for U.S. policy in general and its effect was reflected in Clinton's reluctance to enter Haiti to restore President Aristide to office and his administration's failure to respond at all to the genocide in Rwanda that claimed the lives of some eight hundred thousand people. Casualty-aversion revisionists argue that polls following the "Blackhawk down" incident in Somalia did record a drop in support but only a minority favored withdrawal. Several members of the school have even reargued the Somalia case, maintaining that had the White House tried to mobilize support for hunting down Aidid and punishing him, then public support for the mission was available despite the casualties.[15]

Articles revisiting public attitudes toward possible losses were published in major newspapers and leading foreign policy journals and were generally reassuring to the political mainstream because of its main message: there was no need for Washington to refrain from military action because of false assumptions regarding public demand for a cost-free policy. Certainly, there was no need to fear a "Mogadishu line" whereby opposing leaders think that they can force U.S. forces to leave by inflicting a relatively small number of casualties such as in Somalia. In 2002, a "senior official" in the Bush administration "approvingly mentioned" the Triangle Institute study and its argument that "the 'mass public' is much less casualty averse than the civilian elites believe." The official went on to note that "the study showed that the public would tolerate thirty thousand deaths in a military operation to prevent Iraq from acquiring weapons of mass destruction."[16] Tactical setbacks will not produce a "cut-and-run" response as long the original intervention is defended in forceful terms and as long as the public thinks that success is still probable. Washington can retain the option of using military force even though casualties could be a consequence. The revisionists were greeted warmly because they were arguing that the time-honored pursuit of foreign policy objectives through military force would be supported by the public if it were done right. The revisionists on casualty aversion were not revisionist at all with respect to the use of force.

The revisionist school relies almost exclusively on polling data to support the argument that the public is not as casualty averse as political and military leaders believe. Polls can be an important source of information, but the responses are often conditioned by the specific phrasing of the questions and by the timing or immediate context of the survey. For example, polling questions designed to measure support for a particular military mission that also mention potential casualties yield approximately 10 to 15 percent less support than questions that do not mention casualties.[17] Prewar attitudes toward the prospect of attacking Iraq found support dropping from roughly two-thirds to half when casualties are included in the question. There is also a high rate of refusal on questions aimed at tapping the depth of casualty aversion. The Triangle Institute found 30 percent of the sample leaving blank a question designed to measure acceptable casualties in a variety of scenarios. Most questions had a refusal rate of only 5 to 20 percent. A UK survey that asked respondents how many British lives they were willing to lose to protect Albanian Kosovars produced a similarly high percentage who refused to answer the question.[18] It is almost as though the public exhibits casualty aversion when asked to answer polling questions about casualty aversion.

But the main difference between the revisionist critique and my own focus on public sensitivity to war costs lies in their very different picture of social life. Polling tends to look at public opinion as an objective "thing" that can be captured and measured. The goal is to represent the public on a single, quantifiable dimension.[19] By contrast, the concept of Type II nonacceptance of war allows for ongoing tension between constraints and support in more than half the public. The result is a fluid political and cultural force field that encompasses contradictory tendencies. When a military mission does not go well, and when more than a "small" number of casualties are sustained, the force field morphs into a critical filter for public perceptions of war. That filter is composed of more-critical Vietnam themes. Polls are useful and many have been cited in this book. But they provide only an insight into the changes taking place in the overall set of social relationships between the public and war. Wars have different, often complex meanings that are rarely captured by the formulation of a survey question. Polls are not particularly good at capturing contradictory or multisided understandings; nor, as shown by the "finding" that the public might be willing to tolerate the loss of thirty thousand soldiers in Iraq, do they reveal the possible speed with which war support can be replaced by underlying opposition. As one former Clinton official eloquently responded when presented with an example of polling data that supported the revisionist thesis: "That's bogus. You walk up to a person and ask, 'How many casualties are you prepared to accept to go do X?' Then you get a number. I think it's ridiculous; it's out of context. You ask a group and they average a thousand. The next day you see the pilots paraded in the streets and the effect is electric. That's the reality of it."

Other academic studies are relevant for gauging public support for military missions, at least by public willingness to tolerate casualties. Bruce Jentelson examines the importance of "principal policy objectives" and finds that certain types of missions such as "foreign policy restraint" and "humanitarian intervention" are more likely to be supported by the public than attempts to influence "internal political change."[20] Richard Eichenberg finds that successful missions create a "halo effect" that provides for support even where casualties occur.[21] All of these studies recognize that the range of acceptable casualties is now several orders of magnitude lower than for most of the cold war. (The numerical threshold normally used by political scientists to develop a database for studying war is a thousand battlefield deaths. Above that number, the case counts as a war. Below that level, it does not. Until the war in Iraq, in not one single post-Vietnam case have casualties reached a thousand U.S. dead. From the standpoint of conventional studies the United States has not even engaged in a war since Vietnam, although clearly war has not disappeared from American politics and foreign policy.)

Jentelson's focus on type of mission provides an important overlap with the argument that Americans are becoming more peaceful in the joint recognition that Americans are more willing than is usually recognized to risk casualties to stop genocide or to come to the support of victims of humanitarian emergencies. A July 1994 poll conducted by the University of Maryland posed a hypothetical scenario in which respondents were asked to imagine that twenty-five to one hundred U.S. troops are killed in a peacekeeping mission in Haiti and that the pictures of the dead bodies are shown on television. They were then asked if they would want to withdraw all troops, strike back hard at attackers, bring in reinforcements so that future attacks could be met with overwhelming force, or stay the course. Only 21 percent favored withdrawal, while a majority favored a stronger response with 34 percent opting for reinforcements and 24 percent wanting to strike back hard. Similar responses were found for a hypothetical intervention in Rwanda and in favor of peacekeeping missions in Bosnia.[22] A 2004 survey conducted by the Chicago Council on Foreign Relations found the public more supportive of the use of UN military force to prevent "severe human rights violations such as genocide" than of any of the other four possibilities.[23]

These precise numbers and exact proportions need to be treated with caution. What can be said is that military leaders are more willing than civilian leaders and the public to accept higher casualties for realpolitik military missions, or those taken in the name of classic security concerns such as the defense of traditional allies. For humanitarian missions, however, the pattern is reversed: the public is more likely than civilian elites and especially the military to accept casualties in these circumstances. A 1995 poll found only 43 percent retrospectively supporting the attempt to resolve the civil war in Somalia with military force while a full 82 percent agreed with the original, humanitarian side of the mission. Similarly, the Triangle Institute survey found that respondents who "view human rights as an important goal for U.S. foreign policy tend to be more willing to tolerate casualties in Congo and Kosovo scenarios." When asked about support for a hypothetical mission in defense of a democratic government in Congo, more than a quarter of the population stated they would accept more than five hundred casualties, compared to only 7 percent of the civilian elite and 3 percent of military officers.[24] More than 40 percent of military officers stated that *no* casualties would be acceptable. Overall, with regard to nontraditional missions, military officers' estimates of acceptable casualties are a quarter to a half of those offered by civilian leaders. But the issue of casualties is posed more recently in Iraq, an operation that would only with great difficulty qualify as an example of humanitarian intervention.

Iraq and U.S. Casualties

About 400,000 Americans were killed in World War II, 54,000 in Korea, and 58,000 in Vietnam. In the post-Vietnam conflicts, 43 were killed in Somalia, 383 in the first Gulf War, none in Kosovo, 23 in the invasion of Panama, and another 19 overthrowing the government of Grenada, and 265 marines in Lebanon when their barracks were blown up. World War II, the Korean War, and the Vietnam War resulted in far more casualties than the later conflicts. As of March 1, 2006, 266 soldiers had died in Afghanistan and more than 2,300 in Iraq.[25] Despite the prediction of some political scientists that the public was not casualty averse, the behavior of the Bush administration shows that conditional war requires management of public perceptions so that casualties appear low. An interview with a Pentagon official conducted in the summer of 2003 illustrates the sensitivity to the loss of even one soldier a day:

OFFICIAL: Yesterday on NPR there was a report that we've averaged more than one death a day since the end of April.

JOSEPH: Is that a difficult story for you?

OFFICIAL: News, to be effective, has to communicate why it's different than what you would expect. If it's not different than what you expect, it's not news. If what you expect is zero, anything more than zero is news. If one is news, then that person is going to be on the front page of the *New York Times,* and we're going to know that his name is Bill Smith. In World War II, there were hundreds of deaths, so the standard wasn't zero. From a communication standpoint, it's very difficult when the standard is zero. It's perfection, literally perfection.

If the expectation is zero, one can certainly understand the later frustration of military spokesman Lieutenant Colonel Steve Boyland, who sent an e-mail to journalists asking them to downplay the significance of passing the fall 2005 threshold of two thousand dead: "When you report on the events, take a moment to think about the effects on the families and those serving in Iraq. The 2000 service members killed in Iraq supporting Operation Iraqi Freedom is not a milestone. It is an artificial mark on the wall set by individuals or groups with specific agendas and ulterior motives."[26]

Should casualties be hidden from view? President Bush wrote private letters to the families of those killed in Iraq and Afghanistan but did not appear in public ceremonies to commemorate the fallen. Save for a few carefully chosen photo ops with the president, the more than seventeen thousand wounded by official count in early 2006 have also disappeared from the vision of the executive branch. The official explanation for this studied reluctance is respect for privacy. But the nonrecognition also forms a key piece of war management in a context where war support can be more easily overturned. A more public acknowledgment of the losses and honors for those who made the sacrifice would also engage the population in its own assessment of whether the losses were worthwhile. Instead, the Pentagon has enforced a ban on photographs of coffins and body containers returning through Dover Air Force Base. The policy began during the 1991 Gulf War and continued during the Clinton administration, although exceptions were made for the victims of the 1998 terrorist bombing of the U.S. Embassy in Kenya and the 2000 attack on the USS *Cole* in a Yemeni harbor. The Pentagon went back to a total ban in November 2001, shortly after the bombing campaign began in Afghanistan. In March 2003, Bush issued a directive stating that there would be no coverage of "deceased military personnel returning to or departing from" air bases.[27] In 2005, in response to a lawsuit filed under the Freedom of Information Act, the Pentagon released a limited number of its own pictures. News organizations are still prevented from taking their own photographs. Defense Department officials maintain that the restriction is necessary to protect mourners and to ensure their privacy. Antiwar activists have always criticized this policy and have created many exhibits that attempt to concretize the human toll. What is interesting is how many military families also oppose the Pentagon's inclination to hide the dead.

A Department of Defense regulation prohibits taking or distributing images of caskets or body containers holding the remains of soldiers who die overseas. Some photographs are now available after a successful Freedom of Information Act request (http://www.honorthe-fallen.com/gallery).

An October 2004 study found a military sample overwhelmingly in opposition to the Pentagon's restriction. Fifty-one percent thought that permitting the photographs would increase respect for their sacrifices while only 8 percent felt that it would have an opposite effect.[28] At least one mother protested her son's death in Iraq by inviting the media, against regulations, to film the return of his casket.[29] Family members of fourteen National Guard soldiers from Louisiana who had been killed in Iraq invited the press to cover a ceremony that included flag-draped coffins. There are other signs that the Pentagon's policy is aimed more at the public than at preserving respect for soldiers and their families. The 2003 year-end issue of *Army Times* reprised the famous 1969 issue of *Life* by using eight pages to run photos of the then 506 soldiers who had been killed in Afghanistan and Iraq. Conservative media outlets may have criticized the decision of Ted Koppel and ABC's *Nightline* to read the names and show the pictures of the then more than 500 who had been killed in Iraq but military families themselves did not protest.[30]

These families wanted public respect for their sacrifice, but honor requires shared acknowledgment of loss. Instead, the White House preferred that casualties remain a private matter.

But casualties became a growing concern to the military itself, especially to ground troops and many of those who commanded them. Even before the war began, General Eric Shinseki, the army's chief of staff, warned in congressional testimony that on the basis of the Bosnia and Kosovo experiences the peacekeeping stage of operations in postwar Iraq would require three hundred thousand to four hundred thousand troops. Almost immediately, Rumsfeld announced Shinseki's early retirement. While the level of casualties had not approached those of the Vietnam War, senior military officers in Iraq began to worry, as early as spring 2004, that history might be repeating itself in Iraq, particularly in the pattern of being able to win the battle at the tactical level yet lose the war at the strategic level. Many blamed the civilian leadership at the Department of Defense for failing to heed the past lessons. "I lost my brother in Vietnam," said army colonel Paul Hughes, who served as the first director of strategic planning for the U.S. occupation authority in Baghdad. "I promised myself, when I came on active duty, that I would do everything in my power to prevent that [sort of strategic loss] from happening again. Here I am, 30 years later, thinking we will win every fight and lose the war, because we don't understand the war we're in."[31] According to retired general William Odom, "I've never seen it so bad between the office of the secretary of defense and the military. There's significant majority believing this is a disaster. The two parties whose interests have been advanced have been the Iranians and al-Qaida."[32] In December 2005, in a speech that received wide coverage, Democratic representative and former marine John Murtha called for withdrawal from Iraq within six months. The war in Iraq, Murtha argued in a letter to his colleagues, "was not enhancing the War against Terrorism, it is hurting the prospect for winning it."[33] In January 2006, a Pentagon report concluded that the army could not sustain the pace of troop deployments long enough to defeat the insurgency. "The Army," stated author Andrew Krepinevich, had become a "thin green line" that could snap unless some form of relief was provided.[34]

The military leadership had ignored its own Vietnam postmortem. Iraq violated virtually every lesson, including most of all the need for a clear exit strategy. Iraq had become a war of attrition against the insurgency and the process exceeded the boundary line of acceptable losses for conditional war. There were differences from Vietnam; there the revolutionary forces were grounded in nationalism and a need for land reform and other measures of social justice. In Iraq, the insurgency reflected more a feeling of desecration, lost honor, and the failure of the United States to make good on its promises to bring democracy and economic stability. Greedy landlords, the abusive Saigon government, and foreign occupation motivated the Vietnamese to resist. Foreign occupation also played a role in Iraq but Abu Ghraib and Guantánamo Bay also shamed the Muslim public and motivated many to fight. In both cases, the Pentagon became locked into a tunnel with no light at the other end.

U.S. troops in Iraq did not show any of the signs of active or passive mutiny that many of their counterparts did after 1968 in Vietnam. But by the end of 2004, 5,500 servicemen had deserted since the start of the war.[35] Possibly to avoid public attention to the growing tendency, the army took a good-riddance stance favoring quick discharge rather than prosecution. Many soldiers—and many press reports—noted the slow pace of providing body armor to all ground troops and armor plates to additional protection to the soldiers in the Humvees that many used for patrol and transportation. Recruitment and retention problems became worse and morale declined in the field. In March 2006, only one soldier in five wanted to heed Bush's call to stay "as long as they are needed." Almost three-quarters thought that the United States should leave Iraq within a year and nearly one in four thought that they should leave immediately.[36] The Vietnam War saw growing antiwar sentiment within the military, and on their return to the States a significant number of veterans joined the antiwar movement. When the Iraq war began, a small group of military families mobilized in opposition but their number quickly grew. Cindy Sheehan became the public face of Gold Star mothers opposed to the war but groups such as Military Families Speak Out experienced rapid growth and included more than a thousand members by the end of 2005. Both leaders and enlisted personnel were turning against the war.

Their Casualties: "The Chick Got in the Way"

"The chick got in the way." That was the sergeant's explanation for why his unit shot and killed a woman who was standing close to some Iraqi soldiers on a Baghdad street corner in April 2003. The sergeant's rationale was caught by an embedded reporter, Dexter Filkins of the *New York Times*.[37] The words are crude, rude, callous, and shocking, and most will recoil from their insensitivity—even allowing for a certain level of linguistic permissiveness granted by the circumstances of combat. One does not refer to a Muslim woman as a "chick"—particularly a woman whom you just killed.

Collateral damage is inevitable in war and it is difficult to pass ultimate judgment on this particular incident other than to blame war itself. The woman appeared to be an unfortunate victim caught in crossfire between Iraqi soldiers and U.S. troops. It is possible that the sergeant later felt remorse. Perhaps he is even now haunted by the episode despite his cavalier dismissal at the moment. While these details remain elusive, it is possible to ask why the public was not able to read—or see—many more examples of similar incidents that led to the loss of innocent life. Embedded reporting was supposed to bring the public closer to the face of battle and show combat more realistically. The fact that a female civilian was killed by U.S. troops while an embedded reporter was around was certainly not unique. And the words used at the moment were certainly not unusual. What was different about this early period of the war is that the account of the episode appeared in the *New York Times*.

During the march to Baghdad, at least some newspapers, some of the time, did chronicle civilian deaths. Examples include the *Pittsburgh Post-Gazette* ("Civilian Death Toll in Battle for Baghdad at Least 1,100"), the *Los Angeles Times* ("Dead on Arrival; at one Baghdad trauma center, its morgue overflowing, the battle toll is measured in body bags and blood"); the *Washington Post* ("Hospitals Overwhelmed by Living and the Dead"); and the *San Francisco Chronicle* ("Hundreds in Iraqi Town Hospital: Wards filled with many civilians, some apparently the victims of cluster bombs").[38] While significant, these headlines and their accompanying stories were also relatively rare. The tendency of conditional war is to avoid the presentation of death and injury not only to U.S. troops but also to civilians. Conditional war has created a new need to incorporate public sensitivities toward both into strategic decisions. Actual civilian losses might well be significant (see below for details), but the public cannot know that collateral damage and even large-scale killing of ordinary soldiers are taking place. Civilians are also killed, but in conditional war their numbers must be perceived as "small" and "exceptional," or Type II opposition will develop. The media have been a reasonably good partner of the Bush administration in establishing filters that keep information out. In Afghanistan and Iraq, the public was not able to read and see much about "chicks getting in the way." But there are too many alternative sources for this strategy to be perfect. Independent bloggers, Arab outlets, established media from other countries, and American reporters with integrity can file reports that reach the public and force the Pentagon to plan its operations so that officials appear to be doing everything they can to keep the loss of innocent life "low."

Rear Admiral James A. Winnefeld (ret.) provides a recent example of how the possibility of collateral damage affects strategic thinking:

1. The only sure way to eliminate civilian casualties is to not conduct attacks.
2. ROE [rules of engagement] designed to limit enemy casualties usually come with a price: (a) degraded effectiveness and efficiency of own force application; (b) endangerment of own forces tactically; and (c) lengthening a campaign with the probability of even greater civilian casualties.
3. There is an asymmetry between an enemy who pays little heed to casualties among his civilian population (and indeed sees political advantage in exploiting such casualties) and an attacking force that puts a high premium on avoiding civilian casualties. The political and military advantages accrue to the former.[39]

Winnefeld sounds frustrated with the "asymmetry" but also clearly recognizes that prospective civilian casualties can undermine political support or force a change in the rules of engagement for an intervention that has already been undertaken. The Pentagon is forced to adjust.

One approach is to pretend that civilian casualties are not taking place. During the 1991 Gulf War, the Pentagon refused to offer public estimates not only of how many Iraqi civilians had died but also of how many Iraqi military had been killed. "It's not really a number I'm terribly interested in," replied Colin Powell, then chairman of the Joint Chiefs of Staff, when asked about the number of Iraqis killed during the Gulf War.[40] Shortly before the conflict, then secretary of defense Dick Cheney fired air force chief of staff Mike Dugan for disclosing contingency plans that called for massive air raids on Baghdad and elsewhere in Iraq and "decapitation" targeting of Saddam Hussein, his family, and his mistress.[41] Shortly afterward, the Census Bureau attempted to fire a staff demographer who offered her own assessment of civilian casualties during the war and in the immediate aftermath.[42] More recently, Washington had a difficult time determining how to prove to a skeptical Iraqi public that its forces had killed Saddam's sons, Uday and Qusay, after a raid in northern Iraq. On the one hand, showing the bodies would have reassured many that Saddam's influence was indeed on the wane. On the other, the sight might have backfired by jarring Muslim sensibilities. For everyone, there was something unseemly about parading the deaths for U.S. and global audiences. The awareness and anticipated emotional reaction to death, especially of innocents, underscores the significance of the often-quoted statement "We don't do body counts" offered by General Tommy Franks, the former head of CENTCOM.

Officially, the Department of Defense does not count the number of Iraqis killed in the war. "We don't track them," a Pentagon official told a Washington reporter. An official at the U.S. Army Center of Military History stated that the issue of enemy fatalities "is a bit sensitive to our people. We just don't face up to how many people were lost."[43] Several months into the war, the new Iraq health ministry ordered a halt to its own count of civilians killed. The minister making the announcement, Dr. Nazar Shabandar, said that the U.S.-led Coalition Provisional Authority "doesn't want this to be done."[44] Yet the Pentagon does know at least something of the extent of civilian losses. Shortly before the March 2003 launch of Operation Iraqi Freedom, the Pentagon provided a secret estimated body count to Bush and his principal advisers.[45] In December 2005, a now unpopular President Bush, under siege for his policies in Iraq, slow reaction to Hurricane Katrina, and willingness to appear only before sympathetic audiences, took the unusual step of taking questions that had not been prescreened from an audience that had not been preselected. The first was unusually blunt: "I'd like to know the approximate total of Iraqis who have been killed. And by Iraqis, I include civilians, military police, insurgents, [and] translators."[46]

Bush's response was also unusually precise and accurate: "How many Iraqi citizens have died in this war? I would say 30,000, more or less, have died as a result of the initial incursion and the ongoing violence against Iraqis."

White House press secretary Scott McClellan immediately said that Bush was "citing public estimates" and that there was "no official government estimate."[47] But Bush's reply shows that the White House was in fact keeping track of casualties—or at least keeping track of the work of Iraq Body Count, an antiwar research group that prepares its estimates by compiling press reports from around the world. The large figure, approximately ten times that of the toll of September 11, raises the question of whether the United States is in fact preparing and fighting in a different way.

To retain war support, the military's desire to distinguish between combatants and noncombatants is sometimes reflected in the war fighting plans.[48] As one Pentagon official explained in an interview about the planning that preceded Operation Iraqi Freedom:

OFFICIAL: The effort put into the avoidance of civilian casualties and the reduction of collateral damage was astonishing and unprecedented in the history of warfare. People were going to ridiculous lengths to make sure that when the smoke cleared we didn't have a lot of civilian casualties or that we had not wiped out the infrastructure that these folks were going to need to get back on their feet.

JOSEPH: Could you give me a specific example?

OFFICIAL: Sure. When do you hit something? What time of day? There are plenty of targets which, if you hit them at such and such a time, there's nobody at home. There's others where, if you hit them at such and such a time, it's full of soldiers and if you hit them at another time it's going to be full of cleaning ladies. So, if the intent is to blow up soldiers, then that's when you want to hit it. If the intent is to blow up equipment and not hurt the civilians who operate it, then you probably want to do it in the middle of the night when the civilians are all gone home and gone to bed.

JOSEPH: So timing is one factor?

OFFICIAL Right. Another is the choice of weapon. There is a new warhead for the Hellfire missile which allows us to take out a floor of a building without damaging the superstructure. It is terribly useful because of Saddam Hussein's constant predilection for putting military targets in hospitals and schools. Frequently he would take a whole floor. It's very useful to be able to put a Hellfire through the window and blow up that floor without hurting the second grade up above or the sixth grade down below. And we do that.

JOSEPH: And you were pleased with the result?

OFFICIAL: Absolutely. To send 130,000, 140,000 people ten thousand miles away and have them conduct a campaign against what was at the time the most formidable military in the region and have them pull off a complete military victory in the classical sense in a couple of weeks isn't bad. I think it's an amazing achievement. But I've got to say, I don't think it's as amazing as the low casualty figures on the other team. This is a level of humanity which, frankly, I don't think has ever been injected into the planning process of a military campaign.

This description is both true and not true.

What is true is that in *some types of operations* the military is able to reduce the number of civilian deaths so that they *are relatively lower* than in World War II and Vietnam. Washington recognizes the potential impact of civilian casualties on public attitudes toward war and anticipates the counterarguments offered by critics. In some circumstances the military will try to fight in a more discriminating manner. Avoiding situations where civilian casualties are likely is becoming a more important rule for military operations. Unfortunately, it is also a rule that is often broken. The Pentagon is also concerned with the self-defeating aspects of killing noncombatants. "If you use a precision-guided missile to take out a house with a few terrorists in it," said Peter Khalil, former adviser to the Coalition Provisional Authority, "you will get them but you might get civilians too, and then the brothers and the husbands and the fathers will join the insurgency as a result."[49]

At the end of World War II, the Allies were not concerned with collateral damage; they bombed people in an attempt to break their will to fight. Now precision-guided munitions have made it possible to lower collateral damage while striking targets such as bunkers, antiaircraft sites, communication centers, and command posts. Significantly, the new technology has also heightened the expectation that the loss of innocent life can be avoided. Ironically, the same technology—sensors, microchips, miniature cameras, increased speed in processing information, and satellites—has also made it more possible to see this damage where there is a political and professional will to show it.

Bob Woodward's account of prewar planning for the war in Iraq mentions several instances where Bush and his advisers weighed the strategic impact of particular targets against the potential for collateral damage, operationally defined as carrying the possibility of killing thirty or more civilians.[50] Several targets were taken off the air force list for this reason. Yet, in the opening days of Operation Iraqi Freedom, the United States struck fifty targets that were suspected of holding "high-value" members of Saddam's regime. These attacks did not decapitate the government but they did lead to significant civilian casualties. In January 2006, U.S. aircraft struck several homes in Damadola, a remote village in northwest Pakistan near the border with Afghanistan. Several al Qaeda operatives were supposed to be present and possibly up to four were killed. But the bombing also took the lives of at least eighteen civilians. The incident received wide coverage in the United States and had an even greater political impact in Pakistan and the Middle East, where large demonstrations were organized to protest the loss of innocent life.[51] Though the Pentagon may take special care in some circumstances, every use of military force from the Gulf War to the current war in Iraq contains many examples of noncombatant deaths. Bunkers holding civilians have been struck and wedding parties bombed, precision-guided missiles, or PGMs, have been directed to the wrong coordinates, depleted uranium has entered the environment, and people in marketplaces have been killed by bomb debris. Civilians may not be deliberately targeted but there has been a significant loss of life nonetheless.

These photos show the two-sided nature of the U.S. occupying force in Iraq. The first shows a soldier trying to protect a child in a dangerous situation. His actions are taken probably at some risk to himself, yet his behavior is motivated more by the desire to protect

A U.S. soldier comforts an Iraqi child (Johan Spanner/Polaris).

a civilian than by self-preservation. I believe that many soldiers in Iraq would do the same. The second photograph shows civilians fleeing as a U.S. helicopter attacks a residential area in Baghdad. This particular image shows only their fear; other images of the same incident capture the tragic loss of life of innocent people and do so in a far more graphic manner.[52] Deaths of civilians at the hands of the U.S. military are usually—but not always—unintended. Yet they are an inevitable part of the occupation.

As an occupying military force, the United States is legally responsible for the safety of civilians living in the territory it controls. Under the Foreign Claims Act, Iraqis are entitled to financial compensation when U.S. forces kill or injure civilians or damage property during "non-combat related activities." Currently, the maximum compensation is set at $1,000 per injury and $2,500 per life. This compensation is not always received. Of the first 11,300 claims received, the United States denied compensation for 5,700.[53] In addition, the Pentagon does not accept responsibility for those who are killed or have their homes destroyed by coalition bombing. For example, civilians killed during the April and November 2004 battles for Fallujah are not eligible for compensation.

In addition, there continue to be combat situations where civilian casualties can be anticipated and where military force is still used.

*Civilians flee as U.S. helicopters attack Haifa Street in Baghdad,
September 2004 (Ghaith Abdul-Ahad).*

In these circumstances, usually involving densely populated cities,
checkpoints, and retaliatory fire during attacks against convoys,
efforts to discriminate between combatants and noncombatants
weaken and may dissolve entirely. The caution and care that are
sometimes displayed are removed and civilian casualties can easily
follow. The Pentagon will now try to avoid using its own troops in
urban warfare. "I wouldn't get sucked into the cities," said General
Anthony Zinni, former head of CENTCOM. "There would be lots of
casualties on our side, we'd kill a lot of civilians and destroy a lot
of infrastructure, and the images on Al Jazeera wouldn't help us at
all."[54] But, sometimes, the Pentagon does fight in cities.

A return to Fallujah helps clarify exactly what has changed and
what remains constant about conditional war and civilian casualties.
I ended chapter 4, which discusses the role of the media, by arguing
that coverage of the civilian casualties that had already occurred
and the prospect of creating still more ended a planned April 2004

invasion of the city, which was controlled by antioccupation forces. At least six hundred civilians had been killed and a soccer field converted to a cemetery to handle the rapidly accumulating dead.[55] The United States changed its plans because it could not follow actions that evoked the Vietnam era callousness of "destroying a town in order to save it." It looked like the rules had changed.

In November 2004, after the presidential election had been concluded, U.S. troops reentered Fallujah and military authorities were able to reestablish at least initial control of the city after heavy fighting. The operation was covered closely by the media and the sustained urban fighting was unusual for U.S. ground forces in Iraq. The Pentagon offered an explicit body count that included 1,200 resistance fighters killed and another 1,100 captured over six days of fighting. Fifty-one Americans and 5 Iraqis died with another 425 wounded. Large areas of Fallujah were damaged, and if the military didn't quite "destroy the town in order to save it," they certainly ended up wreaking considerable havoc. In an effort to hold down civilian casualties, residents had been warned to leave the city before the fighting began and perhaps as many as 80 percent did. This step no doubt lowered the number killed but may have also permitted many fighters and terrorist leader Abu Musab al Zarqawi to escape. Despite the evacuation, at least as many civilians from Fallujah were killed in November as in the aborted invasion the previous April.[56] There were repeated reports of U.S. forces firing on ambulances and emergency vehicles and halting the shipment of medical supplies to nearby hospitals and medical clinics where wounded Fallujah civilians had sought help. In response to a report on Italian state television that incendiary munitions had been used against civilians in Fallujah, some of whom had been burned to the bone, the Pentagon officially acknowledged that it had used white phosphorus munitions in the attack but denied that it had targeted civilians.[57] The March 2005 issue of *Field Artillery* contains the following description from the Second Infantry's fire support element: "White Phosphorous. WP proved to be an effective and versatile munition. We used it for screening purposes at two breaches and, later in the fight, as a potent psychological weapon against the insurgents in trench lines and spider holes when we could not get effects on them with HE [high explosives]. We fired 'shake and bake' missions at the insurgents, using WP to flush them out and HE to take them out."[58] According to the Chemical Weapons Convention, white phosphorus can be used legally as a flare or to produce smoke to obscure troop movements but it cannot be used directly against people, military or civilian. Use of the chemical weapon in "shake-and-bake" attacks to dislodge insurgents from foxholes was prohibited. During the fighting, a wounded and apparently unarmed insurgent was shot by a marine. The incident was caught by a CNN cameraman and the videotape was shown to audiences in the United States and throughout the world. In a manner that reflects the sensitivities of conditional war, the episode provoked a debate (or morality play) over whether the act was taken in legitimate self-defense or whether it was a war crime.

Pentagon attention to civilian casualties is thus inconsistent. At times, the prospect of casualties is sufficient to change the way that the United States fights. At other times, the toll of military force is the same as it ever was. In all cases, there is a new urgency to present warfare as being more discriminating than it has been in the past. The rules regarding the prevention of civilian casualties have changed and, imperfectly, the U.S. public and a global audience judge military performance by the new rules—rules that are all too frequently broken.

But what has been the actual toll of civilian casualties in recent wars? A quantitative summary is provided below but it is important to remember that the grim numbers are only an abstraction.[59] One specific incident involving a cluster bomb provides an example. Cluster bombs consist of a main casing, which opens in midair releasing submunitions or "bomblets," whose descent is slowed by parachute. Sensors detonate these bomblets a few feet off the ground, spewing shrapnel across a swath of territory. This shrapnel can kill soldiers, pierce tank armor, and destroy roads and some types of buildings. A significant number of cluster bombs are duds—at least 15 percent but perhaps as many as 30 percent. Unexploded bomblets left lying on the ground look like soda cans but remain armed and can detonate if moved. They are dangerous to anyone coming across them. That's exactly what happened to Rashid Majid and three of his sons when U.S. bombs set a neighbor's house on fire and they rushed out to help. Their tragic story follows:

> When the fire was out, the brothers—Arkan, 33, Ghassan, 28, and Nihad, 18—noticed that the street was littered with small gray cylinders, each about the length of a man's hand, with a white streamer attached to one end. Their friend Oday Shouki picked one up. So did Arkan.
>
> "Throw that away," Shouki's father warned. Startled, Shouki let go. There was a deafening bang. Arkan dropped the cylinder he was holding, and in the confusion, Nihad Majid recalled, his father stepped on it. Another bang.
>
> "The sound is still in my ears," said Nihad, who recently recounted the April 7 events his family now calls simply "the tragedy." Shouki, Arkan, and Ghassan were killed instantly. Rashid Majid, 58, died the

next day, leaving his eldest surviving son, Ayad, 32, to care for his mother, two sisters, his brothers' widows, and their five children.[60]

General Richard Myers, chairman of the Joint Chiefs of Staff, later said that warplanes had dropped nearly fifteen hundred cluster bombs in Iraq (and an additional but unknown number of cluster munitions fired by artillery, which are not technically "bombs" according to the Pentagon).

Who has been responsible for the deaths of Iraqi civilians? One could entertain an argument that all the deaths stem from the nature of the U.S.-led occupation. But in the immediate sense of committing the direct act of violence, a March 2005 calculation offered the following estimates of the then 25,000 civilian deaths: U.S.-led forces, 37.3 percent; criminal activity, 35.9 percent; antioccupation forces, 10.7 percent; clashes between forces, 5.1 percent; and 11 percent unknown.[61] Most of the civilian deaths caused by U.S.-led forces came during the first month of the war and during the two offensives in Fallujah, although subsequent, well-publicized incidents continued into 2006. After a long period of refusing to provide a body count, an October 2005 Pentagon report to Congress estimated that 25,902 civilian and security forces were killed and wounded by insurgents between January 1, 2004, and September 16, 2005. Iraq Body Count estimates that about three Iraqis are wounded for each one who dies. Given that ratio, about 6,500 Iraqis would have died from insurgent attacks over the twenty-one month period.[62] (The report, mandated by Congress, shows that the military has, despite public statements to the contrary, been tracking Iraqi deaths with some regularity.) In 2006, as the war continued to suck more and more of Iraq into its vortex, sectarian violence rose dramatically. The body count at the Baghdad morgue provided yet another quantitative estimate of this cost. According to director Dr. Faik Baker, the morgue recorded fewer than 3,000 violent or suspicious deaths in 2002, 6,000 in 2003, 8,000 in 2004, and more than 10,000 in 2005.[63] Dr. Baker had to flee to Jordan for his own safety after receiving pressure not to report the deaths.

Civilian Casualties

Iraq: Operation Desert Storm

Human Rights Watch estimated 2,500 to 3,000 Iraqi civilians killed; a study conducted by the Project on Defense Alternatives placed the number at 3,500.[64] (While the first Gulf War is often assumed to have been fought with precision-guided munitions, in fact more than 90 percent were "dumb" bombs with only a 25 percent success rate of reaching their designated targets.) A Census Bureau demographer offered the controversial estimate of 110,000 civilian deaths attributable to the Gulf War and its aftermath.[65] In addition to those killed either by coalition forces or by forces under Saddam's control, she estimated that another 70,000 died from health problems that followed the destruction of water and power plants by bombing attacks.[66] The U.S. Census Bureau itself had estimated 5,000 civilians killed during the war itself. The Bush administration's three-volume report on the war omitted all references to Iraq casualties. International sanctions applied against Iraq between 1992 and 1998 had a significant impact on Iraqi water, sewage treatment, and electrical power and have been linked to the deaths of an estimated 170,000 children.[67]

Somalia

Most civilian casualties in Somalia occurred during one battle in Mogadishu on October 3, 1993, which resulted in the death of 18 U.S. soldiers and several hundred Somalis. The warlord who was the target of the operation, Mohamed Farrah Aidid, later said that 315 Somalis were killed and 812 wounded, figures that the Red Cross called "plausible." A 1993 report from Human Rights Watch placed overall civilian casualties at between 600 and 1,000 Somalis. The United States attributed most of the deaths in this conflict to the Somali forces' practice of using civilians as human shields. Others noted the use of U.S. Cobra helicopters against large groups of people.[68] For example, after a U.S. attack on a hospital that was being used by Aidid's militia, the International Red Cross later found at least 54 deaths including many among patients. The legality of the attack was questioned by the UNOSOM (United Nations Operation in Somalia) justice division.

Kosovo: Operation Allied Force

Operation Allied Force was fought by air, and not a single NATO or American pilot was killed during the war. Most strikes used precision-guided munitions, and General Wesley Clark called the campaign "the most accurate bombing campaign in history." Yet Human Rights Watch found ninety incidents in which an estimated 500 civilians died.[69] (The Serb media more than doubled the estimated death toll to 1,200.)[70] A majority of the civilians died because of their proximity to military targets, but the Chinese embassy and nine additional targets including the Serb Radio and Television headquarters in Belgrade, a heating plant, and seven bridges that were not on major transportation routes were also struck. In addition, in seven confirmed and five likely incidents, the United States and Great Britain used cluster bombs that killed between 90 and 150 civilians. A midday attack on the Nis airfield killed 14 and injured 28. International criticism and anticipated negative reaction within the United States led to an unusual and unannounced White House executive order to cease the use of cluster bombs.[71] Unexploded cluster bomblets dropped during the early weeks of the campaign continued to inflict casualties after the bombing ended but exact numbers are difficult to determine.[72]

Afghanistan: Operation Enduring Freedom

On October 1, 2001, the Pentagon began a bombing program aimed at overthrowing the Taliban and destroying the al Qaeda network. Echoing Clark's words from two years before, General Tommy Franks called the bombing campaign "the most accurate war ever fought in the nation's history."[73] Nonetheless, U.S. bombing killed approximately 3,000 by the end of the year according to a compilation of world press reports made by Marc Herold of the University of New Hampshire.[74] Using a somewhat different methodology, the Project on Defense Alternatives and Human Rights Watch gave a lower estimate of 1,000 to 1,300. Even these lower figures suggest a rate of civilian deaths per bomb that is higher—perhaps by a factor of three or four—than that for Operation Allied Force in Kosovo.[75] One reason may be that cluster bombs in Afghanistan were shaped and colored similar to food drops. Another was faulty intelligence, which led to strikes against wedding parties and other social gatherings.[76]

Operation Iraqi Freedom

The current war in Iraq is by far the deadliest for civilians. As of March 1, 2006, estimates of civilian dead range from a conservative 33,000–37,000 as a direct result of combat or armed violence to almost 100,000 "excess deaths" from all causes. The smaller number is contained in the extensive database maintained at www.iraqbodycount.net. The larger figure is drawn from a 2004 study published in the British medical journal *Lancet* and conducted by a research group at Johns Hopkins University.[77] More recently, the *Lancet* database has been reanalyzed by the Geneva-based Graduate Institute of International Studies, which found an estimated 39,000 Iraqis were killed as a direct result of violence through mid-2004 (as opposed to a higher mortality without regard to cause).[78] (In World War I, about one civilian was killed for every ten soldiers; in post–cold war conflicts the ratio has been exactly reversed, with an average of ten civilians killed for every person in uniform. Without being able to offer a precise ratio, the war in Iraq conforms to the more recent pattern in which a disproportionate number of civilians die.)

Chapter 9

From Managing War to Making Peace

This book has focused on the process in which Americans are becoming more peaceful. I have divided the public into three parts: a dove constituency that rejects war out of principle, a middle group torn between sensitivity to war costs and war support, and a third cluster that provides consistent approval. The differences among these groups and with the media and government officials determine overall approval of or opposition to particular wars. Despite war management, these interactions reveal growing skepticism toward the use of armed force. Changes in the relationship between the public and war underscore a transformation in the social organization of war itself: mobilized war has been replaced by conditional war. A majority of the public may at times support conditional war, but the many questions and hesitations associated with war bring latent opposition to the surface when the boundary lines of acceptable conduct are crossed. Conditional war carries a tendency to become "like Vietnam" and thus provoke opposition. Iraq is a very good example of a war that has exceeded those boundaries.

War as acceptable policy is thus in a state of limbo. It certainly hasn't been abolished, but it cannot be pursued in the same way as in the past. War was never a good way to resolve differences but at least it held some advantages for those in power. With war they could often impose their will (while having others pay the price).

234

But the new rules of conditional war make it more difficult for war managers to succeed even on their own terms (although others still pay a price). It does not work as well—even for them. Iraq is also a good example of how compromised war has become, even when measured against securing the traditional goals of U.S. policy: maintaining access to important resources, supporting loyal political leaders, defeating oppositional social movements, and sustaining a safe climate for market-oriented behavior.

This chapter traces the implications of the new constraints on the use of military force. But it is first important to recognize that on many security issues the public sides with the dove beliefs of the first group. In this respect, Americans are not just becoming more peaceful—they are already peaceful.

Are Americans Already Peaceful?

The public certainly disapproves of U.S. nuclear policy. Washington currently possesses almost six thousand atomic weapons.[1] Even though this figure is significantly less than the peak arsenal of the cold war, the doctrine of possible first use of these weapons has never been removed. If there is a defense for the nuclear arsenal, it is that it could be used to deter or prevent an attack from another country that also has nuclear weapons. The purpose of nuclear weapons is to provide security by threatening a retaliation of such proportion that no opponent would use such weapons in the first place. A standoff is created when this situation is reciprocal. This stalemate, sometimes called "mutually assured destruction," is what most people think is the appropriate role for nuclear weapons. Atomic bombs aimed at others are only good for preventing others from dropping atomic bombs on you.

But the foreign policy establishment has always had broader, more ambitious intentions for atomic weapons. Each post-1945 American president, Republican or Democrat, cold war or post–cold war, has linked the threat to use nuclear weapons first to the conduct of U.S. foreign policy. In this regard, nuclear weapons are considered by Washington as "normal," or equivalent to other weapons, in that their planned use is part of "force projection" and is linked to the pursuit of political goals. This added agenda requires not just an ability to retaliate after a first strike but also to (not implausibly) use nuclear weapons first without suffering unacceptable retaliation in return. This more political use of atomic weapons, not only to deter an attack but also to exert leverage against others by threatening a first attack, has weakened nonproliferation measures. India and

Pakistan, North Korea and Iran are tempted to acquire nuclear weapons in part to respond to the United States' political as well as its military use of its arsenal.

To strengthen nonproliferation measures against nuclear weapons, a majority of the population would support a commitment by Washington not to use nuclear weapons against countries that do not themselves have nuclear weapons. A majority would also oppose trying to deter a chemical or biological attack by threatening retaliation with atomic weapons. About 20 percent of the population, roughly equal to the explicit peace sentiment in the country, think that the United States should *never* use nuclear weapons under any circumstances. Another 60 percent think that the Pentagon should use these weapons only in response to a nuclear attack.[2] Only 20 percent think that the United States should, in certain circumstances, use nuclear weapons even if it has not suffered a nuclear attack. This puts 80 percent of the country opposed to current U.S. policy.[3] Neither Republicans nor Democrats do much to inform the public about actual policy and still less to change that policy toward the minimal deterrence position that the most Americans believe should be the posture of the U.S. government. Reducing the number of nuclear weapons, lowering their alert level, and declaring that the United States will not use them first would enhance international stability and improve national security. These changes would also be firmly grounded in the beliefs held by a huge majority of the public.

The public is already peaceful on many other issues. A comprehensive poll conducted by the Chicago Council on Foreign Relations found strong support among the public for international treaties that have been rejected by the Bush administration. For example, 87 percent said that they favored a Comprehensive Nuclear Test Ban Treaty that would prohibit nuclear weapon test explosions worldwide; 80 percent favored a treaty that would ban all land mines; 76 percent favored an agreement on the International Criminal Court that would make it possible to try individuals for war crimes, genocide, or crimes against humanity if their own country failed to bring them to justice; and 71 percent supported the Kyoto Protocol to reduce global warming. When asked to choose between two possibilities on a policy on torture, the first that terrorists pose such an extreme threat that torture should be allowed to gain information that saves innocent lives, and a second that upholds rules against torture because it is morally wrong and that weakening the rules could lead to the torture of U.S. soldiers held prisoner abroad, only 27 percent chose the first option. Three-quarters favored the creation of a standing UN peacekeeping force, selected, trained, and commanded by the United Nations, and a majority favored giving the United Nations the power to regulate the international arms trade. Strict sovereignty is often held up as a strong priority of the public, yet two-thirds thought that the United States should be more willing to make decisions within the United Nations even if this means that the United States will sometimes have to go along with a policy that is not its first choice. A majority also believed that the United States should make a general commitment to accept the decisions of the World Court rather than deciding on a case-by-case basis whether it will accept the court's decision.[4]

On policy issue after policy issue, Americans are already peaceful—at least as measured against the priorities of their government. But polls showing support for individual dove policies are not equivalent to the political will to embrace an explicit peace program. The public is much more supportive of working with the United Nations, revamping energy policies, and reducing the size and role of the nuclear arsenal than is recognized by the political elite and media. Measured by approval of the International Criminal Court, a ban on antipersonnel land mines or child soldiers, and stiff taxes to limit the international arms trade, the size of the American dove constituency is far larger than the estimated 20 percent mentioned earlier in this book. But it is only through confrontation with the system of organized violence called war that the true measure of support for peace becomes known. Thus far, only a minority demonstrates a self-conscious choice to adopt as a matter of principle other methods of seeking security. War brings pain and loss—and multiple opportunities for political and military leaders to manage opinion by calling on enablers that also exist in most of the public.

War Opposition versus War Management

One of the most important war enablers, the strong tendency of the public to support troops in the field, can often be translated into broad support for the policy that put them there in the first place. Military operations that appear successful also create a halo effect that extends to the goals of the military mission itself. An atmosphere of crisis, especially one that produces widespread fear, makes it relatively easy to swing public opinion behind the national leadership and to produce support for actions that seem to have a good chance of reducing the threat. The Bush administration was especially adept at using fear of terrorism to gain support from much of the public for its military actions in Afghanistan and Iraq. Fear can also blind, and in the post–September 11 national mood, the "information" that sustained war in Iraq, namely, that Saddam Hussein posed a threat because he possessed weapons of mass destruction and nurtured connections to al Qaeda, was only partially dismantled by the revelations of high-level defectors from the national security bureaucracy and by official reports that found few facts supporting these assertions. All presidential administrations try to spin the public with respect to its war policies but the Bush administration has proven itself especially adroit in its management of the media. Its public relations expertise includes a policy to control certain types of photographs, reliance on sympathetic outlets such as Fox, and intimidation by labeling the media a "special interest" group. The administration embraced embedded reporting at a time when it contributed to patriotic celebration and perceived war success. When embedded reporting became more critical, the Pentagon favored the more traditional approach of controlling the flow of news and pictures to the public. This job was made easier by the media's inclination to censor itself or to avoid asking the more difficult and demanding questions. Many journalists were themselves caught in the halo effect or focused on the technical razzle-dazzle of the weapons and the sounds and sights of the battlefield as long as these did not include casualties. Traditional patriotism and faith that the country's intentions were essentially good also played major roles. Finally, support was provided by classic concepts of gender, such as that reassurance of being a strong man can be found in battle and that warriors are necessary to protect vulnerable women. Taken together, these enablers can make it possible to manage the public face of war and thereby retain support for the use of force.

But war management is not perfect, and war opposition, real and latent, is also influential. Publicly acceptable justifications for going to war have become more limited. The population will now support military force only where it appears to be in the self-defense of the United States or against the perpetrators of human rights violations on a massive scale. While the executive branch may subsume other political agendas within these two public rationales, the war must be managed in such a way that more traditional geostrategic motivations or hegemonic aspirations do not appear to dominate the goals of the operation. Casualties continue to be an important part of public perceptions, and the number must appear to be small even though the actual magnitude of that term is subject to renegotiation. Civilian casualties also play a prominent role in public perceptions of the rightness or wrongness of the battle, although here there is even more room for reconsideration of the meaning of small. Concern for the "others" is not nearly as strong as the concern with the loss of American life. Yet the Pentagon cannot conduct operations that appear to be indiscriminate, especially in comparison with the virtual absence of any obligation for the safety of civilians during World War II and Vietnam. Sensitivities are especially acute when photographs of the suffering appear in the public eye. Using the filter of "good taste," gatekeepers in both the Pentagon and the media often are exceedingly reluctant to show the sacrifice involved in war. The Bush administration shied away from time-honored icons of respect for the dead, such as flag-draped coffins, collections of snapshots of the fallen, or the reading of the names of those who have been killed. President Bush himself occasionally visited the wounded, but very few photographs of the presidential trips to Walter Reed Hospital appeared in the press. Public nonacceptance extends to the draft, which is opposed by the vast majority, and to war taxes.

The role of the media in highlighting war costs is uneven. At times, journalists appear to simply legitimate the war effort and show little of the distancing that is necessary for critical judgment and reflection. But at other moments, journalists take a more skeptical posture that introduces new information, to the dismay of public relations managers loyal to the administration. The balance between war enablers and constraints linked to the media varies considerably across different outlets. The press is different from television, cable television from the networks, and weblogs from more traditional sites. Fox News is different from everyone else. The careful reader (and perhaps Web surfer) is more likely than the astute viewer of television to acquire key information. Journalism's oscillating contribution to war constraints is borne out by the Bush administration's own occasional frustration with the coverage that it received and by Bush's own appeal to the public to ignore the "special filter."

Changes in the meaning of gender roles in popular culture and extraordinary changes in the position of women in the military have led to a less certain relationship between the meaning of "male" and "female" and support for war. The traditional masculine role and the need to protect vulnerable women are still used to help legitimate war. But the gender-defined aspects of the situation have become more complex. For some of the public, the movement of women into the military, and, within the military, into more dangerous roles, has been met with respect and approval. But greater acceptance for women as soldiers and women as warriors appears in the midst of important countercurrents. Many continue to worry about the cultural and personal implications of training women to be placed in harm's way or to kill. Whether the public will accept female casualties on any significant scale is still an open question. Meanwhile, the vulnerability of women on the battlefield is matched only by the continued record of sexual abuse meted out by their own male comrades in arms. How is it possible to square the increased formal equality of women within the military with the continued record of rape and other forms of sexual assault? At the same time, compassion for the plight of women in humanitarian emergencies, or at the hands of patriarchal political and religious leaders, has been used selectively to increase public approval for the use of armed force. Paradoxically, stronger recognition of the importance of some types of human rights can also provide war support. This contradictory mix of gender-related war enablers and constraints adds other layers of uncertainty to the social legitimacy and perceived effectiveness of war.

The collision between war opposition and war management structures conditional war, which entails many expectations and a different set of ground rules: low casualties to U.S. soldiers, low levels of collateral damage to civilians, reduced influence of enemy images, lack of a draft, military missions based only on self-defense or humanitarian intervention, absence of a call to sacrifice or otherwise embrace the war effort, and lower economic costs. Military interventions may in fact exceed these constraints. Where this is the case, conditional war will look like Vietnam. Vietnam became a quagmire, military strategies were ineffective, people were killed to no good purpose, and winning and losing were harder to measure. The media became more skeptical of Vietnam, it was more difficult to distinguish friend from foe, and the effort was increasingly tainted by corruption and scandal. Troop morale dropped and any honor that was originally associated with the enterprise was lost. A brief reference to the classic writings of Carl von Clausewitz provides another way to capture the limitations of conditional war.

Vietnam, Clausewitz, and Conditional War

In *On War,* Clausewitz defines war as "an act of violence intended to compel our opponent to fulfill our will." Both the "we" and the "they" in the statement are states, and the "act of violence" is to be carried out by national armies that are controlled by those states. War, Clausewitz famously argues, is only "the continuation of politics by other means." The preparation for war, the execution of war, even victory and defeat themselves, are part of the broader social process in which states compete for power. Recruiting a fighting force, arming it with weapons, and planning to use this force and its weapons are partly technical but are also rooted fundamentally in the pulls and tugs of the political process. War, state, and society are closely intertwined.

War, according to Clausewitz, contains three distinct analytic levels: political goals, military strategies, and public attitudes. Political leaders as supposed to set the goals to be pursued by armed force. Military leaders establish the fighting force and develop the strategy designed to achieve those goals. And the public must provide support if the goals and strategies are to be pursued effectively. Successful coordination of the three levels occurs when political goals, military strategy, and popular support are both clear and mutually reinforcing. In "abstract war" state interests, military force, and public "passions and sentiments" are bound together in an effective package. (As a German political philosopher, Clausewitz thought that something that was "becoming abstract" was also something that was becoming perfect.)

Writing shortly after Napoleon introduced France to conscription, and the consequent use of citizen-soldiers rather than a smaller, purely professional force, Clausewitz underscored the central importance of public attitudes if a war is to be prosecuted effectively. As he wrote about the impact of popular sentiments: "The more violent the excitement which precedes the War, by so much the nearer will the War approach to its abstract form, so much the more will it be directed to the destruction of the enemy, so much the nearer will the military and political ends coincide, so the more purely military and less political the War appears to be."[5]

The "excitement" which precedes war gives political and military leaders greater flexibility to formulate goals and develop strategies. The conduct of the war appears "purely military" and less made up of political calculations. Public emotions and sentiments are thus central to Clausewitz and, in his view, focusing them in support is absolutely necessary to achieve abstract war. The problem now facing Washington is that the tendency of Americans to become more peaceful has made it more difficult (but not impossible) to get the public excited. And, even where war management is able to stimulate public passions, it has become more difficult to keep the excitement alive.

Clausewitz then proceeds to compare abstract war to "real war." The latter contains "fog" or "friction," which arises from the imperfect coordination among goals, strategy, and public attitudes. Friction can happen where there is a failure to establish clear political goals. In this situation, developing an effective military strategy becomes difficult because no one fully understands what it is that the military is supposed to do. Friction may also exist when the goals are clear but military strategy is ineffective because of inadequate planning or poor communication between different fighting units. Bureaucratic irrationalities and insufficient logistical support can also add problems. A striking example came during the U.S. invasion of Grenada: An army officer already on the island wanted to call in a barrage of Navy artillery but found that his radio was limited to frequencies that made it impossible to communicate with ships offshore. To get the message through, the officer ended up using a personal credit card to place a long-distance call to the Pentagon, which relayed the request back down to the ships in the Caribbean, which in turn directed munitions to the location indicated by the officer on the ground. More recently, in Afghanistan, a U.S. soldier on the ground was in the midst of calling in an air strike against a nearby target. At one point during the operation he changed the batteries on his communication set. He did not realize that this step automatically recycled the signals emitted by the device back to the default coordinates. Unfortunately, these coordinates were the device itself. The munitions that the soldier requested were precision guided and landed exactly where they were aimed: his own position.

The war in Iraq provided several other examples of "friendly fire" in which U.S. troops erroneously targeted each other or their allies, or mistakenly sent cruise missiles and other munitions onto empty bunkers, Iraqi families that supported the United States, or wedding parties out in the desert. In Afghanistan, Pat Tillman, a National Football League player for the Arizona Cardinals, was killed by others in his own company in tragic circumstances that were hidden by the Pentagon from his own family and the rest of the public. The history of war offers many other examples of how the military can, at times, be its own worst enemy. Much planning, not all of it successful, is devoted to reducing these uncertainties.

When the fog is really thick, military strategy and political goals work at cross-purposes. In Vietnam, which became just about as good an example of a compromised real war as one could ever hope to find, the military felt that the political goals of the intervention were never clearly defined. As General Norman Schwarzkopf, commander of U.S. forces during the first Gulf War, later said about Vietnam: "When you commit military forces, you ought to know what you want that force to do. You can't kind of say 'Go out and pacify the entire countryside.' There has to be a more specific definition of exactly what you want the force to accomplish. . . . But when I harken back to Vietnam, I have never been able to find anywhere in precise terms what the ultimate objectives of our military were."[6] The strategy became one of attrition in which massive airpower and search-and-destroy missions were applied with uneven success against revolutionary forces. The bombing had little or no impact on the logistical capacity and morale of the Vietnamese forces, who also controlled the timing and location of most of the fighting. This strategy was also totally at odds with the parallel political campaign to win the hearts and minds of the local population. Bombing, ground sweeps, forced pacification, and "free-fire zones" backfired and ended up encouraging the South Vietnamese population to join the National Liberation Front rather than support the Saigon government.

In the meantime, support from the U.S. public continued to trickle away, creating yet a third source of friction: a reduction in will to continue the fight. As Clausewitz observes about the loss of support: "The weaker the motives and the tensions [of public sentiments], so much the less will the natural direction of the military element—that is, force—be coincident with the direction, which the political element indicates; so much the more must, therefore, the War become diverted from its natural direction, the political object diverge from the aim of an ideal War, and the War appear to become political."[7] Conditional war would be, in Clausewitz's terms, either permanently "political" or on the verge of becoming so.

Objectively, the United States continues to have a huge military advantage over every other country in the world. No other nation has the airlift capacity, quality of weapons, or communications capability. Allowing for all forms of official and unofficial outlays, Washington's recent defense expenditures are approximately equal to those of the rest of the world combined. But even this large lead in dollars fails to capture the true advantage. Take, as one example, aircraft carriers, which are really floating, mobile air bases. A single one, the USS *Enterprise*, has a crew of 3,200 to run the ship and another 2,400 to pilot and service the seventy aircraft onboard.[8] The ship is normally accompanied by an Aegis-class cruiser designed to intercept incoming missiles, a fleet of frigates and destroyers to protect it from submarines, and a variety of supply vessels. Helicopters and assault troops are also included in the fleet. The total cost of this flotilla is well over $20 billion. A few other countries also have aircraft carriers but none has a carrier task force capable of projecting the range and power of the USS *Enterprise* and its accompanying fleet. Currently, the United States has twelve such carriers. But this technical and fiscal prowess needs to be considered in the context of public reservations about war and the underlying tension between the ways that Washington will want to use force and the reluctance of the public to support that use of force.

Despite the tendency of Americans to become more peaceful, it is still possible for Washington to commit military force in support of political goals. The military can still be used in pursuit of traditional geopolitical goals such as protecting markets, preserving a favorable distribution of power, and supporting governments favored by Washington. The public may be less inclined to accept the costs of war but support can be managed within the framework of conditional war. At the same time, the result is often the more compromised political dimensions of Clausewitz's real war than clear-cut military victory. Abstract war remains elusive even though Washington continues to try to rely on military force.

Circumventing War Constraints

Political and military leaders in the United States have four methods of shaping and using force to blunt underlying public opposition to war. Where successful, this strategic management limits criticism to Type I opposition. Type II opposition remains beneath the political surface.

The first method of circumventing the public's reluctance to accept high-cost war is through the so-called revolution in military affairs (RMA), or the use of recent advances in information technology to improve the accuracy of many weapons, increase the visibility of the battlefield, and enhance communication among fighting units. Supporters claim that RMA not only improves U.S. ground, air, and sea operations but also transforms the nature of battle so that conventional fighting forces play a significantly smaller role. The promise is to use technology to "deter or defeat traditional military threats at relatively low cost."[9] RMA has helped develop precision-guided munitions, which raise the possibility of fighting wars by hitting strategic targets with great accuracy. The proponents of RMA hold that wars can be fought with few casualties on either side and that the opposition's leadership can be "decapitated" without causing undue collateral damage to the other side's army or civilian population. Force can be delivered by remote means, dramatically changing the face of battle to the U.S. public. One advocate claims that RMA underscores "the best aspects of the Western Way of Warfare, encouraging tendencies towards efficiency, discrimination in the use of weapons, and low casualties."[10]

In some circumstances, the revolution in military affairs probably does allow the Pentagon to use military force without provoking underlying public unease. This is especially true where airpower alone seems to have a significant strategic impact. One much-cited example was Kosovo, where the United States and NATO were able to bomb Milosevic's forces without suffering a single casualty to its own forces and without significant domestic opposition—at least in the United States.

The application of information technology and precision-guided munitions was also on dramatic display during early periods of the

Afghanistan and Iraq wars, which produced the overthrow of the Taliban and of Saddam's regime in short order. Supporters of RMA again claimed that the traditional reliance on ground troops had been reversed and that airpower would either succeed alone or play a much larger role. But in each of these cases, RMA delivered far less than originally claimed. Both Afghanistan and Iraq have required a long commitment of ground troops. And while the failures in Iraq have commanded the most attention, the political goals of military intervention in Kosovo and Afghanistan have also proved to be elusive. NATO's 1999 bombing minimized the loss of U.S. and European soldiers but did little to stop Milosevic's policy of forcing Albanians out of Kosovo. Indeed, the flow of refugees actually increased during the bombing campaign and eventually reached more than seven hundred thousand. Following the NATO bombing campaign, Washington's ally, the Kosovo Liberation Army (KLA), moved still deeper into organized crime and the trafficking of drugs and women. Similarly, airpower might have been successful in the quick overthrow of the Taliban in Afghanistan but a longer review of the situation, including the continued fighting over several years, fails to sustain the argument that precision-guided bombing could by itself promote long-term security and stability.

Advocates of RMA also tend to ignore a parallel "revolution" in the lethality of so-called light arms, which can be carried by one or two combatants and which under some circumstances can thwart the superior technology of more advanced weapons systems. No fighting force in the world has even a remote chance of defeating the United States directly. But light arms such as the Kalashnikov rifle, rocket-propelled grenades, and handheld surface-to-air missiles can frustrate and limit the effectiveness of U.S. forces. Helicopters are particularly vulnerable, and in Iraq the United States was forced to adjust its tactics after several helicopters were shot down. The conflict in Iraq has also demonstrated that improvised explosive devices are also extremely deadly. The modern U.S. military on the ground may have sophisticated nightscopes and communications gear but in other respects not much has changed. As one national security official observed in an interview:

> The one place where "transformation"—the advancement in sensors, the precision, and all the rest—hasn't worked is in infantry close combat. We still do that in the same way. If marines in Haiti in the early part of the twentieth century were to see modern American troopers, they would recognize most of what they are carrying. In close combat, many of the technical advances that we enjoy go away. What's more, it is always possible for nations, no matter how poor, to put together decent units at the low combat level.

The same official went on to make the following observation about the difficulty of defeating a committed resistance force:

> It requires the occupied country to have the political soundness and loyalty of the population to pull it off. That was the achievement of the Vietnamese. You have to be highly motivated to be a guerrilla because the chances of getting killed are pretty high. It's an extraordinarily arduous life and you never stop running. One could take some comfort in the fact that while it would be an effective response to U.S. military forces, it wouldn't be a particularly easy one to mount. But, having seen one mounted in Iraq, I see no clear answer to it. Everyone I talk to sees no clear answer to it.

In certain circumstances, the revolution in military affairs might be able to successfully manage public perceptions of the face of war. But since many conflicts have required actual "boots on the ground," and since this type of fighting has not been fundamentally transformed, the possibility for stronger Type II opposition remains.

A second way for war managers to circumvent the tendency of Americans to become more peaceful is to rely more on special operations forces. These überprofessional soldiers possess multiple skills ranging from familiarity with many types of weapons to training in medicine, negotiation, and police instruction. They are part Rambo, part civil servant. But their real advantage is their comparative ease of deployment. Stationed in Fort Bragg, North Carolina, soldiers in the special forces have typically been deployed in many countries but with less visibility than conventional military units. Media coverage is governed by unique rules and the president is not currently required to notify Congress before authorizing an overseas mission.

While the size of the armed forces shrank after the cold war, the special forces actually increased and now total more than forty-seven thousand troops. While their budget is classified, expenditures have increased as well, especially following the role of the special forces in the early stages of the fighting in Afghanistan and Iraq.[11] Recent revisions to the military's organizational structure have given the special operations forces their own command with little direct oversight from Congress and civilian secretaries who monitor the other divisions in the Pentagon. After receiving political flack from some army officers about his plans for the war in Iraq, Secretary of Defense Donald Rumsfeld brought former special forces commander General Peter Schoomaker out of retirement to be named army chief of staff, and chose Thomas O'Connell, who served in the Phoenix program in Vietnam, as the new civilian assistant secretary for special operations. These appointments signal an augmented role for the special forces.

A third possible method of circumventing public constraints on the use of force is through the use of surrogates or proxy armies. In recent years, the two most prominent examples are the KLA and the Northern Alliance in Afghanistan. In both cases, the combination of airpower and local substitutes for U.S. infantry were effective against weak foes and did not raise the risk that a significant number of U.S. troops would be killed in ground action. But weak opposition is a significant part of the equation and the Taliban hardly measured up as an effective military force. Kamal Matinubim, a retired Pakistani general, later called the United States' foe "a ramshackle people who've been given some weapons. They've had a little training, like jumping over some obstacle logs or digging ditches, but strategy and tactics are way beyond them."[12] Similarly, former NATO commander General Wesley Clark found the Taliban to be the "most incompetent adversary the United States has fought since the Barbary pirates."[13] Yet, as one observer of security affairs noted approvingly:

> If America's political and military leadership remains casualty-phobic, and if advances in military technology permit the use of force with little risk—then a combination of airpower, small supporting specialty ground force contingents (backed by regular ground forces held in reserve), and indigenous proxies is likely to become the U.S. model for waging future war. . . . [This model] permits a casualty-phobic political and military leadership to wage war effectively without paying the blood price traditionally associated with attainment of those effects.[14]

At the same time, the seeming success of surrogate forces is complicated by the tendency of local armies to have their own agendas, which may conflict with Washington's priorities—and very often collide with human rights. This was certainly true in the case of the KLA, which used its alliance with Washington to further its own illicit interests. The Northern Alliance also proved itself an unreliable partner in the pro-West government established in Kabul following the overthrow of the Taliban. The Northern Alliance was also involved in the massacre of Taliban prisoners during an uprising in Mazar-e-Sharif, which prompted Amnesty International to call for an international investigation. Other warlords who had been bribed by the CIA to fight against the Taliban were more interested in regaining control over their traditional fiefdoms, including the cultivation of opium poppies, than in hunting down al Qaeda. In fact, Osama bin Laden may have been able to escape into Pakistan because Washington was reluctant to commit its own troops to a potentially costly cave-by-cave search in the Tora Bora complex. The local substitute forces were not up to the task. Finally, opposition to the United States that initially appears weak and thus appears potentially controlled by U.S.-supported proxy armies can also gain in strength and strategic sophistication, thereby thwarting the substitute forces and requiring more direct Pentagon involvement. The Taliban may not have been able to stand up in a direct fight against the Pentagon but, four years later, its forces are still frustrating the U.S. military's efforts to control all of Afghanistan.

Another danger associated with the use of proxy armies is the possibility of "blowback," or a pattern in which fighting units initially supported by Washington end up reversing their loyalties and using deadly force against the United States. Two examples are Osama bin Laden, who received support from the United States during the 1980s as a surrogate fighting against the Soviet Union in Afghanistan but ended up sponsoring the terrorist attack on September 11, 2001; and Saddam Hussein, whom Washington supported during the 1980s, despite his abysmal treatment of the Kurds and other opponents, because he was seen as a counterweight against revolutionary Iran. Still another potential danger with surrogate armies is that they may actually encourage military action when to do so appears to be cost free.

Subcontracting is a fourth way that Washington can try to use military force without encountering a public reaction. One of the best examples is provided by Military Professional Resources Incorporated (MPRI), which was founded in 1987 and led by General Carl Vuono, a former army chief of staff. MPRI consists almost entirely of retired U.S. military personnel who are pledged to remain loyal to U.S. foreign policy goals and who only work on contracts that have the approval of the U.S. government. Indeed, MPRI executives maintain close contact with officers still in government.[15] MPRI has operated in many countries including Colombia, Bosnia, and Nigeria and claims that it has every military skill possessed by the Pentagon, which is located only a short distance way. Its Web site maintains that it is able to "perform any task or accomplish any mission requiring military skills (or generalized skills acquired through military service) short of combat operations."

MPRI played a particularly important role in the Balkans. The first Bush and the Clinton administrations had regarded the region through the normal geopolitical prism, which did not identify significant national interests in the region. As a result, they did little in response to Milosevic's policies of ethnic cleansing. Clinton had come to office promising that he would do more, but his generals and Congress did not support direct forms of intervention and Europe was unwilling to make a commitment without U.S. leadership. The solution was found in a proxy army, the Croats, and proxy advisers,

MPRI. MPRI helped the Croatian army formulate strategy and may have even assisted in the circumvention of the arms embargo that then operated in the region.

In 1995, a force of two hundred thousand Croats quickly overran a smaller number of Serb soldiers who had been occupying Krajina, a region of Croatia where many Serbs had lived. More than a hundred thousand Serbs fled the region for Serb-dominated areas of Bosnia and Serbia itself. The Croatian offensive served the foreign policy interests of Washington, which then successfully exerted political pressure on Serb leader Milosevic to negotiate a settlement in the Balkans. "We didn't want this to happen, we didn't urge it," said Secretary of State Warren Christopher in response to the situation in Krajina, but "the facts may possibly give rise to a new strategic situation that may turn out to be to our advantage." In U.S. negotiator Richard Holbrooke's realpolitik assessment, "the success of the Croatian ... offensive was a classic illustration of the fact that the shape of the diplomatic landscape will usually reflect the balance of forces on the ground."[16]

The operation carried significant human costs. The Helsinki Federation Fact-Finding Mission reported it had found "evidence of systematic destruction and looting of Serbian homes and community buildings by the Croatian Army (HV), Croatian Civil Police, civilians, and 'arson teams' ... and conflicting claims from Croatian authorities concerning civilian casualties, missing persons, and summary executions."[17] The international war crimes tribunal in The Hague investigated summary executions and the role of the Croat military in killing civilians, creating new refugees, and committing other human rights violations.[18] Of particular concern was the initial assault, in which three thousand shells fell on the city of Knin over forty-eight hours; the shelling appeared to be aimed indiscriminately and certainly killed many civilians. All of these actions were carried out by the Croatian military but in the immediate background was MPRI playing a surrogate role for the United States.

Subcontracting has increased in many areas and the Pentagon has signed more than three thousand contracts with private military firms over the last ten years.[19] In Iraq, in 2005, more than sixty firms employed more than 20,000 to perform functions that used to be carried out by military personnel. This figure is roughly equal to the presence of the UK and all other coalition partners combined. With an estimated 175 deaths and almost 1,000 wounded, they have suffered in proportion. Halliburton's annual contract in Iraq is more than twice what the United States paid to fight the entire 1991 Gulf War. These companies are involved in many activities including providing security for key individuals and facilities, providing supplies for troops, maintaining key equipment, transporting sophisticated weapons systems, translating, and escorting convoys. Even some of the interrogators in Abu Ghraib prison were contractors. Their activities help the Pentagon to compensate at least partially for smaller-than-necessary troop deployments and help disguise the scale of the overall commitment. But as P. W. Singer notes, private military firms "allow governments to carry out actions that would not otherwise be possible, such as those that would not gain legislative or public approval. Sometimes, such freedom can be beneficial: it can allow countries to fill unrecognized or unpopular strategic needs. But it also disconnects the public from its foreign policy, removing certain activities from popular oversight."[20] Private military firms can lower the political cost (although not the economic price) of military intervention and may make it possible for the White House to circumvent limits imposed by congressional legislation on overt military deployment. Many of the firms' activities are not subject to the same scrutiny and accountability as government operations and thus reduce transparency.

Strengthening the Tendency of Americans to Become More Peaceful

I have been discussing different methods by which Washington might directly or indirectly use force and at the same time reduce the chances that the U.S. military itself would incur costs. The most important implication is that war can only be waged by taking into account a collection of constraints that also carry enormous potential for the development of stronger opposition to war. While its adherents still are a minority of the population, principled Type I opposition to war is significant. Type II opposition is also crucial but unlikely by itself to convert Washington's policies so that they embody a principled peace program. Constraints stemming from the nonacceptance of war coexist with traditional enablers that make it possible to generate war support. The strength of Type II opposition, left to itself, will continue to oscillate, underscoring a fluidity that at times weighs against war but at other times can be shaped into support for war. The fundamental question becomes this: what are the possibilities of developing a set of genuinely peaceful policies that reflect and strengthen the already existing but uneven tendency of Americans to become more peaceful?

Looking over the entire landscape of post-Vietnam U.S. military involvement, one point stands out. The still incomplete process in which Americans are disconnecting from war is all the more remarkable because it is taking place without a political party, a prominent public leader, or even a mass-circulation magazine capable of challenging the premises of the war system. Other than through some churches, a small number of peace programs in universities and colleges, a few political magazines with relatively small circulation, and the organized peace movement itself, there are relatively few opportunities to offer a counterframe to the established way of thinking about the necessity of war. Newspaper columnists and op-ed writers who are critical of the Pentagon can be found, but the mainstream press and media do not—and probably cannot—offer a substitute framework for war. Even more importantly, there is no politician in the United States who has been able to articulate a systematic, consistent, and accessible alternative to the practices of both the Republican and Democratic parties. "Security" still means something that should be pursued primarily through military force. "Force" and "power" are still equated with imposing one's will. Peace is still best guaranteed by "preparing for war." Few have a clear picture of—or even think about—what it might mean to ensure peace by "preparing for peace." Yet a counterframe is essential to begin the transition from the system of organized violence. A majority of the public either think that the war system is broken or harbor many hesitations about its effectiveness. But they don't know how to replace it or create a better way.

By mid-2004, the true dimensions of the Iraq debacle began to become clear to more people. Not only the antiwar movement, dissident intellectuals, and doves but also a significant majority of the population had turned against the war. In an illustration of how Type II opposition can percolate throughout the population, even many conservatives and mainstream security analysts began to voice their opposition. Republican congressman Walter Jones of North Carolina, infamous among antiwar activists for renaming the side dish that goes with hamburgers "freedom fries" after the French were reluctant to go along with the Bush administration's policy, appeared at an antiwar caucus chaired by liberal Democrat Lynn Woolsey of California. Jones's constituency, located far from the more conventional sources of dove support on the coasts, was now firmly against the war. Nebraska senator Chuck Hagel became increasingly critical of the war, and his stance was increasingly seen as the Republican equivalent of Democratic senator William Fulbright's opposition to President Lyndon Johnson on Vietnam. In early 2006, the opposition within the armed forces, from both officers and enlisted personnel, that has already been documented deepened still further with criticism focused in particular on Secretary of Defense Rumsfeld. The "realist" school of thought within international relations is normally associated with recognition of the need for force in international affairs yet many from that persuasion also voiced their doubts.[21] Even Jeffrey Record, professor of strategy at the Air War College and member of the revisionist reading of the public's willingness to take casualties, offered the following strong assessment: "I see no ray of light on the horizon at all. The worst case has become true. There's no analogy whatsoever between the situation in Iraq and the advantages we had after the second world war in Germany and Japan."[22]

Given the recognition of the mounting costs and the range and depth of oppositional voices, the failure of the Democratic Party to offer a clear alternative to the logic of the war is particularly striking. In early 2006, mainstream Democrats attempted to gather behind a broad "strategic redeployment" plan authored by former Reagan administration defense secretary Lawrence Kolb, which would take most U.S. troops out of Iraq by the end of 2007. All reservists and National Guard members would return to the States but a major military presence would remain in the region, presumably to possibly reenter Iraq or fight terrorism elsewhere in the region. This redeployment was intended to protect the Democrats from Republican charges that they had "cut and run." Senator Jack Reed of Rhode Island said, "It's important to note that it's not withdrawal—it's redeployment." Similarly, Representative John Murtha's well-publicized call for withdrawal retained the capacity for a quick-strike force. (A White House spokesperson still called the proposal a "surrender to the terrorists.")

Most Democrats continue to try to win office by capitalizing on the failure of the Republicans rather than by offering a clear alternative approach to war and peace. In the 2006 congressional elections, more than fifty veterans ran as Democrats. Many called for more troops and a tough military stance toward Iran and North Korea and thus reflected the belief that winning congressional and national elections continued to rest on a willingness to use U.S. military strength.[23] Not wishing to be out of step with presumed beliefs of the mainstream public, centrist organizations such as the Progressive Policy Institute called for more, better-applied military force rather than rethinking the basic need for such force. "Having the strongest military in the world is the first step," said Senator Hillary Clinton at a meeting of the similarly centrist Democratic Leadership Council, "but we also have to have a strong commitment to using our military in smart ways that further peace, stability, and security around the world."[24] And yet it was these arguments that were out of step with the views of the public. The reluctance to redefine the need for military force had less to do with the public and more to do with retaining "credibility," the rationale employed by Richard Nixon and Henry Kissinger as they renewed the commitment in Vietnam long after it was clear that the war could not be won. Keeping credibility, avoiding the label of losing after making a commitment, cost the lives of the thirty thousand American soldiers and at least 1 million Vietnamese who died after Nixon assumed office. And it did not alter the outcome of the war. "Credibility" can be understood only via reference to the structure of power within the United States, not to the presumed views of the public. The public suffers in not having a reference point that could gather all of its multiple doubts and hesitations about war and put them together in a coherent, persuasive perspective that sustains a movement toward peace.

Media coverage is a crucial side of the tension between war management and the becoming more peaceful process. Transparency is an especially important goal, for it is increasingly difficult for military operations to stand the light of day. Important constraints are created when journalists just perform their job of providing accurate information and closely scrutinizing the rationales offered by government officials. The public should be able to expect a full accounting of the impact of war, measured not only in casualties and dollars, but also in its impact on women, the environment, family life, and conditions in the war zone itself. The "impact statement" includes psychological as well as physical wounds and morale within the military. To some degree a more independent media voice has emerged during the war in Iraq, although we will know that there has been a significant change only when the major networks begin to hire "peace" experts to go along with the retired military personnel they feature as commentators. The Internet and international news sources have been an important source of information for those with the time and resources to pursue them. There is also a need to develop further the promising beginnings of progressive media outlets on radio, blogs, and perhaps even on television. Activists can certainly expect a more sympathetic ear to the demand to review the evidence for going to war more thoroughly.

One of the strongest constraints against war is the reluctance of most Americans to serve in the armed forces. Until Iraq, the Pentagon has done reasonably well with a professional force and there is some justification to their overall assessment that those who want to make a career in the military will be happier and better soldiers than those conscripted against their will. But the citizen-soldier is essential to democracy and to the decision to commit forces to battle. There is a fundamental injustice when elites and the middle class so consistently have someone else do the fighting for them. If the country cannot accept the standard of going to war premised on everyone having a theoretically equal chance of fighting in it, then perhaps it is not worth fighting in the first place. At the every least, everyone should perform some type of national service.

Honor has also been one of the most important themes running throughout this book. It is an extremely important resource. Honor is a commonality among those who serve their country in the military and among those who feel that military operations and accompanying practices such as those seen at Abu Ghraib and Guantánamo Bay have been a major violation of honor. Honor provides a moral voice. In Vietnam, Nixon said that we was seeking "peace with honor." By that he meant that the United States should prevent the revolutionary forces from determining the political future of their country. That was a major distortion of meaning. But peace policies should have a strong sense of honor, especially in upholding one of the most powerful self-perceptions of Americans, namely, that their country is a force for good. Most Americans want their country to have an active global role, make the world a better place, and, where necessary, engage and defeat evil. That engagement need not be violent but it should be strong and powerful. It is culturally and psychologically important to see good come from one's work.

Ultimately, we return to the powerful story lines provided by war and especially to the continuous comparisons to the heroic "good fight" of World War II and the disastrous quagmire of Vietnam. The country is stuck on Vietnam and has yet to create a suitable public forum to review what happened there. Current politicians tend to look the other way and tell the public that there is nothing positive to be gained from "refighting the war." The Bush-Kerry presidential campaign managed to reduce Vietnam to an unsatisfying debate over the candidates' respective military records rather than over the war itself. If shaping the future depends in part on how one reads the past, a review of Vietnam is long overdue.

In the long run, the development of more explicit, principled peace policies must engage the entire set of domestic inequalities and other problems of American society. More proactive visions of peace must be broader than "just" preventing war. Recognition of the multiple negative impacts of organized violence and its alternatives must be linked to health care for all; reductions in poverty; a different energy policy; modified rules for globalization; a rights agenda that also includes sex, race, and class; and a reclamation of the sense that government can do some good. Dismantling and replacing the war system will need many allies, not just peace activists. There is more potential here than most realize.

The transition from mobilized to conditional war means that we are in the midst of a long, slow, and contradictory process in which war as an acceptable policy is becoming dismantled. The situation can be compared to Jenga, a game in which players start with a structure of beams and pillars and then take turns trying to pull out individual pieces while trying to keep the structure from toppling. The game ends when the piece is removed that causes the entire edifice to collapse. The structure is the war system; the individual pieces are popular beliefs, national policies, and institutional practices that provide war support. Some types of support for the war system, such as conscription, have been removed. Others, such as the influence of enemy images, are still present but are becoming weaker. Still other props for the war system, such as equating support for the troops as support for the policy that placed the troops in harm's way, are particularly difficult to remove. The fact that some elements of the war system are being removed does not prevent more powerful players from putting supporting pieces such as fear back into the structure. Some war managers are inventive and will try to construct entirely new types of sustaining devices such as embedded reporting. The war system has yet to crumble. Washington is able to—and does—go to war. But in some ways the structure looks weakest when a war is taking place. The remaining pieces rock and shake in the spaces left by the withdrawn war enablers. War may remain but its structure is no longer so solid. At what point do we realize that our security is dependent upon playing a new game?

Notes

Notes to Chapter One

1. Estimating the size of antiwar movements is especially difficult. In his definitive study of the movement against the Vietnam War, Charles DeBenedetti states that "several million" were involved by 1969. See *An American Ordeal: The Antiwar Movement of the Vietnam Era* (Syracuse, N.Y.: Syracuse University Press, 1990), 389. The largest Vietnam-era national demonstrations had 250,000 participants. At least that many gathered in Washington, D.C., and New York City prior to the 2003 start of the war in Iraq, and many towns and larger cities also staged their own rallies. While it is difficult to estimate its scale with precision, another significant form of opposition to the 2003 war was Internet activism.

2. "What We Do Now," *Nation*, April 21, 2003.

3. I explore the impact of the movement against the Vietnam War in "Direct and Indirect Effects of the Movement against the Vietnam War," in *The Vietnam War: Vietnamese and American Perspectives*, ed. Jayne Werner and Luu Doan Huynh (Armonk, N.Y.: M. E. Sharpe, 1993); and the impact of the nuclear freeze movement in *Peace Politics: The United States between the Old and New World Orders* (Philadelphia: Temple University Press, 1993).

4. Peter Feaver and Christopher Gelpi use polling data to divide the public into four groups: "solid doves"; "solid hawks"; a "casualty-phobic" group, which is sensitive to casualties; and a "defeat-phobic" group, which reacts to perceived success and failure. I prefer a larger middle group that is pulled in different directions by war sensitivities and war support. The size of their "doves" and "hawks" groups and the sum of the "casualty-phobic" and "defeat-phobic" groups correspond to my estimates for my categories. See their *Choosing Your Battles: American Civil-Military Relations and the Use of Force* (Princeton, N.J.: Princeton University Press, 2004).

5. Michael Mann, *States, War, and Capitalism* (Oxford: Blackwell, 1988), 124.

6. C. Wright Mills, *The Power Elite* (New York: Oxford University Press, 1956). See esp. chap. 8, "The Warlords."

7. White House, "The National Security Strategy of the United States of America," September 2002.

8. Frances Fox Piven, *The War at Home* (New York: New Press, 2004); Noam Chomsky, *Hegemony or Survival* (New York: Henry Holt, 2003); Chalmers Johnson, *The Sorrows of Empire* (New York: Henry Holt, 2004); Michael Klare, *Blood and Oil* (New York: Henry Holt, 2004); Benjamin Barber, *Fear's Empire* (New York: W. W. Norton, 2003).

9. Andrew Bacevich, *The New American Militarism: How Americans Are Seduced by War* (New York: Oxford University Press, 2005).

10. Quoted by John Judis, *The Folly of Empire* (New York: Scribner, 2004), 14.

11. Quoted by Bacevich, *New American Militarism,* 12–13.

12. See Cassio Furtado, "37 Percent of College Students Would Evade the Draft," *Miami Herald,* June 21, 2002; Frank Luntz, "College Students Speak Out," survey conducted for Americans for Victory over Terrorism, May 2–12, 2002, http://www.avot.org.

13. Robert Burns, "Rumsfeld Apologizes, Calls Draft Remarks Misconstrued," *Boston Globe,* January 23, 2003, 4.

14. The structure and implication of the gap between the military and civilian society is explored at length in Peter Feaver and Richard Kohn, eds., *Soldiers and Civilians: The Civil-Military Gap and American National Security* (Cambridge, Mass.: MIT Press, 2001).

15. See esp. Sam Keen, *Faces of the Enemy: Reflections of the Hostile Imagination* (San Francisco: Harper & Row, 1991).

16. For details, see Wesley Clark, *Waging Modern War* (New York: Public Affairs, 2001).

17. See http://www.iraqbodycount.net.

18. Confusing Pentagon accounting practices have also made it difficult to track the precise allocation of these funds. Government audits found that it was not possible to account for at least $20 billion in war-related spending. See Bryan Bender, "Oversight of War Spending Is Faulted," *Boston Globe,* December 4, 2005, 1, 26.

19. Bryan Bender, "$120b More Is Sought for War Efforts," *Boston Globe,* February 3, 2006.

20. The study, prepared by Joseph Stiglitz and Linda Bilmes, is summarized in "Economists Say Cost of War Could Top $2 Trillion," *Boston Globe,* January 8, 2006.

21. For more examples of "trade-offs" between military and civilian spending, see http://www.warresisters.org.

22. See P. W. Singer, *Corporate Warriors: The Rise of the Privatized Military Industry* (Ithaca, N.Y.: Cornell University Press, 2003); and "Outsourcing War," *Foreign Affairs,* March/April, 2005.

23. Michael Ignatieff, *Virtual War: Kosovo and Beyond* (New York: Henry Holt, 2000), 3–4.

24. Colin McInnes, *Spectator-Sport War: The West and Contemporary Conflict* (Boulder, Colo.: Lynne Rienner, 2002), 148.

25. Jean Baudrillard, "La Guerre de Golfe n'a pas eu lieu," *Libération,* March 29, 1991.

26. For details, see Samantha Power, *A Problem from Hell* (New York: Basic Books, 2002), 373–77.

27. For an example of how the United States could develop a civilian intervention capability, see Jeffrey Garten, "Wanted: A U.S. Colonial Service," *Foreign Policy,* September/October 2003, 63–67.

28. An interesting, complex treatment of the contributions and limitations of the role of the Special Forces during peacekeeping operations in Haiti can be found

in Bob Shacochis, *The Immaculate Invasion* (New York: Penguin, 1999). Ultimately, Shacochis focuses more on the limitations than the contributions. With respect to Kosovo, a similar description of limitations of militarized peacekeeping, despite the positive intentions of those carrying out the operation, can be found in Dana Priest, *The Mission* (New York: W. W. Norton, 2003).

29. Patrick Condon, "Sign on Iraq's Toll Stokes Anger," *Boston Globe*, January 3, 2006, 3.

30. Jerry Lembcke, *The Spitting Image: Myth, Memory, and the Legacy of Vietnam* (New York: New York University Press, 1998).

31. Zinni also appeared on *60 Minutes* (May 23, 2004) to explain his views and coauthored a book with Tom Clancy (*Battle Ready* [New York: G. P. Putnam, 2004]), which also provided a scathing indictment of the Pentagon and the war in Iraq.

Notes to Chapter Two

1. Barry Glassner, *Culture of Fear: Why Americans Are Afraid of the Wrong Things* (New York: Basic Books, 1999), xi.

2. Glassner, *Culture of Fear*, xxi.

3. Charles Pierce, "What's Next? How the SARS Scare Played into America's Culture of Panic," *Boston Globe Magazine*, June 1, 2003.

4. Bill Dedman, "Racial Profiling Is Confirmed, *Boston Globe*, May 4, 2004, B1, 4.

5. Study summarized by Tom Incantalupo, "Study Ties Phones to Auto Accidents," *Newsday*, July 12, 2005, 42.

6. George Grey and David Ropeik, *Risk: A Practical Guide for Deciding What's Really Safe and What's Really Dangerous in the World around You* (Boston: Houghton Mifflin, 2002).

7. Pew Research Center for the People and the Press, Pew Global Attitudes Project, *What the World Thinks in 2002* (Washington, D.C.: Pew Research Center, 2002), 53.

8. "Remarks by the President after Two Planes Crash into World Trade Center," Emma Booker Elementary School, Sarasota, Fla., September 11, 2001, http://www.whitehouse.gov/news/releases/2001/09/20010911.html.

9. "Statement by the President in His Address to the Nation," September 11, 2001, http://www.whitehouse.gov/news/releases/2001/09/20010911–16.html.

10. Excerpts quoted by Neil Mackay, "Bush Planned Iraq 'Regime Change' before Becoming President," *Sunday Herald* (Glasgow, Scotland), September 23, 2002.

11. See Sandra Silverstein, *War of Words: Language, Politics, and 9/11* (London: Routledge, 2002), 15–17.

12. Silverstein, *War of Words*, 26.

13. Quoted by John Stauber and Sheldon Rampton, "The Fog of War Talk," July 28, 2003, http://www.alternet.org.

14. Quoted by William Lutz, "The Rhetoric of Fear; Unraveling the Message behind the President's Pronouncements since the Terrorist Attacks," *Newsday*, September 7, 2003, A32.

15. Claudia Deane and Dana Milbank, "Hussein Link to 9/11 Lingers in Many Minds," *Washington Post*, September 6, 2003.

16. The Iraqi intelligence officer in question, Ahmed Khalil Ibrahim Samir al Ani, now in U.S. custody, has told interrogators that he had never met Atta. See Warren Strobel, Jonathan Landay, and John Walcott, "Doubts Cast on Efforts to Link Saddam, al-Qaida," Knight-Ridder publications, March 4, 2004.

17. Renana Brooks, "A Nation of Victims," *Nation*, June 30, 2003.

18. Quoted by Eliot Weinberger, "What I Heard about Iraq in 2005," *London Review of Books*, January 5, 2006.

19. Independent Sector, *Giving and Volunteering in the United States, 2001* (Washington, D.C.: Independent Sector, 2001).

20. All findings are drawn from National Opinion Research Center (NORC), *America Recovers: A Follow-up to a National Study of Public Response to the September 11th Terrorist Attacks* (Chicago: University of Chicago, August 7, 2002).

21. Robert Putnam, "Bowling Together," *American Prospect*, February 2002, 20–22.

22. Greenberg Quinlan Rosner Research, "Report on Post–September 11th Women's Survey," November 2001, http://www.greenbergresearch.com.

23. Theda Skocpol, "Will 9/11 and the War of Terror Revitalize American Civic Democracy?" *PS*, September 2002, 537–40.

24. NORC, *America Recovers*.

25. William Schlenger et al. "Psychological Reactions to Terrorist Attacks: Findings from the National Study of Americans' Reactions to September 11," *JAMA*, August 7, 2002.

26. Ellen Barry, "TV Viewing after 9/11 Is Linked to Distress," *Boston Globe*, August 7, 2002. It may also be possible that those who watched more television were already distressed and that the additional viewing habits served more as a coping mechanism than as a source of symptoms.

27. Frank Phillips, "Jump in Cigarette Sales Tied to Sept. 11 Attacks," *Boston Globe*, January 24, 2002, B1, 6.

28. http://www.StopSmokingDoctors.com.

29. Mathew Bars, e-mail communication, August 13, 2003. Bars is director, Fire Department of New York Bureau of Health Services.

30. Marc Magee and Will Marshall, "Breaking the Silence on AmeriCorps Funding," *Christian Science Monitor*, August 11, 2003.

31. Advertising quoted by Skocpol, "Will 9/11 Revitalize American Democracy?" 538.

32. Quoted by Silverstein, *War of Words*, 124.

33. Pew Research Center, news release, "Bush Approval Slips—Fix Economy, Say Voters" (Washington, D.C., August 7, 2003), 2.

34. Bureau of Transportation Statistics, *BTS: Airline Traffic*. Data available from http://www.bts.gov/programs/airline_information/airline_traffic_data/press_releases/index.html; Department of State, *Passport Statistics*, available from http://travel.state.gov/passport/services/stats/stats_890.html. Much of the data in this paragraph was collected by Matthew Weinberg, a student in my fall 2004 Windows on Research seminar.

35. Theme-park attendance figures can be found at http://www.solarius.com/dvd/wdw/attendance_figures.htm. Data from national parks is drawn from Public Use Statistics Office, 2004, http://www2.nature.nps.gov/stats/.

36. Jessica Mathews, "September 11, One Year Later: A World of Change" (Policy Brief, Special Edition 18, Carnegie Endowment for International Peace, Washington, D.C., 2002).

37. Zogby International, February 17–20, 2003.

38. Fox News / Opinion Dynamics, February 11–12, 2003.

39. The most notorious incident came in 1982 when T. K. Jones, a technical assistant to Reagan administration official Paul Nitze, told a reporter that in case of a nuclear attack, Americans "should dig a hole, cover it with a couple of doors and then throw three feet of dirt on top.... If there are enough shovels to go around, everybody's going to make it" (Fred Kaplan, *The Wizards of Armageddon* [New York:

Simon & Schuster, 1983], 388). For the most part, the public considered such efforts to be nonsense. Fewer than 10 percent, for example, ever constructed their own shelters.

40. CBS/*New York Times* poll, September 8, 2003. Some of the polling discussed in this section was collected by Ketan Gajria, a student in my fall 2004 Windows on Research seminar.

41. Gallup Poll, March 3–5, 2003.

42. Of course, September 11 was a tragedy for the families and loved ones of those who died. Their reactions to the attacks are intensely personal and follow a different path than the reactions of the vast majority of the public.

Notes to Chapter Three

1. *New York Times*/CBS News Poll. February 10–12, 2003.

2. Gallup/CNN/*USA Today* Poll, March 29–30, 2003.

3. ABC News/*Washington Post*, April 27–30, 2003.

4. Janet Elder and Patrick Tyler, "Poll Shows Most Want War Delay," *New York Times*, February 14, 2003.

5. In Bryan Bender and Michael Kranish, "Bush Backs Cheney on Assertion Linking Hussein, al Qaeda," *Boston Globe*, June 16, 2004.

6. Program on International Policy Attitudes (PIPA), *Misperceptions, the Media, and the Iraq War* (Center for International and Security Studies at the University of Maryland, College Park, Md., October 2, 2003).

7. William Rivers Pitt, "The Sins of September 11," http://truthout.org/docs_03/101303A.shtml.

8. "Reflections in the Evening Land," *Guardian* (UK), December 17, 2005.

9. Markus Prior, "Political Knowledge after September 11," *PS*, September 2002, 523–29.

10. National Annenberg Election Survey, September 21–26, 2004.

11. Minxin Pei, "The Paradoxes of American Nationalism," *Foreign Policy*, May/June 2003, 31–37.

12. Simon Schama, "The Nation: Mourning in America; A Whiff of Dread for the Land of Hope," *New York Times*, September 15, 2002.

13. John Keane, *Reflections on Violence* (London: Verso, 1996), 6.

14. Sheldon Wolin, "Inverted Totalitarianism," *Nation*, May 19, 2003.

15. Nina Eliasoph, "Political Culture and the Presentation of a Political Self," *Theory and Society* 19 (1990): 465–94.

16. The independent "educative" impact of Michael Moore's *Fahrenheit 9/11* is difficult to assess. The movie, which offers a highly critical review of the Bush administration, was the largest-grossing documentary ever produced, and many reviewers raised the possibility that the film would provide a substitute public "text" that would compensate for the failures of more establishment journalism. A Gallup Poll conducted in July 2004 found that more than half of all Americans had either seen the film or expected to see it. But the same poll found these intentions closely related to party affiliation, thus raising the possibility that the information in the film had already been seen by viewers who were already opposed to the war, or was entirely missing from the factual universe of those who decided that they would not see the movie. At any rate, fewer than a quarter of the Republicans who saw *Fahrenheit 9/11* gave it a favorable rating.

17. Bob Woodward, *Plan of Attack* (New York: Simon & Schuster, 2004), 261.

18. The document was leaked to the *Times* of London and was published on May 1, 2005. The reaction of the U.S. press is discussed in the next chapter.

19. Woodward, *Plan of Attack*, 1.

20. The Wolfowitz interview was published in *Vanity Fair.* This quotation is drawn from Mark Curtis, "Psychological Warfare against the Public: Iraq and Beyond," in *Tell Me Lies: Propaganda and Media Distortion in the Attack on Iraq,* ed. David Miller et al. (London: Pluto, 2004), 75.

21. See Nicolas Kristof, "Save Our Spooks," *New York Times,* May 20, 2003.

22. Veteran Intelligence Professionals for Sanity, "Memorandum for Confused Americans: Cooking Intelligence for War," *Counterpunch,* March 15, 2003, http://www.counterpunch.org/vips03152003.html.

23. Dana Milbank and Claudia Deane, "Hussein Link to 9/11 Lingers in Many Minds," *Washington Post,* September 6, 2003.

24. Bryan Bender and Michael Kranish, "Bush Backs Cheney on Assertion Linking Hussein, al Qaeda," *Boston Globe,* June 16, 2004.

25. Quoted in Anne Kornblut, "Bush Firm on Iraq, Qaeda Link," *Boston Globe,* June 18, 2004, A32.

26. A sampling of editorial opinion after the June interim report includes the following (quotations collected by Stephen Stromberg, "The View from the Editorial Pages," *Salt Lake Tribune,* June 18, 2004):

New York Times: "It's hard to imagine how the commission investigating the 2001 terrorist attacks could have put it more clearly yesterday: there was never any evidence of a link between Iraq and al Qaeda, between Saddam Hussein and September 11. Now President Bush should apologize to the American people, who were led to believe something different."

Miami Herald: "As long as the administration insists on the 9/11 connection, its solution to the Iraqi problem will be based on false assumptions. The 9/11 panel's report, based on the findings of U.S. intelligence and unencumbered by political considerations, should be the last word on the subject."

Salt Lake Tribune: "No matter what the Bush administration did or did not say about it, it is now clear that Saddam Hussein was not involved in the terrorist attacks of September 11, 2001, and that any support for the Iraqi war based on the assumption that he was involved was misplaced. Misplaced, widely held and, most disturbingly, still given life by the president himself."

27. Derrick Jackson, "Cheney-Speak," *Boston Globe,* June 23, 2004.

28. Kornblut, "Bush Firm on Iraq, Qaeda Link."

29. John Mueller, quoted in Milbank and Deane, "Hussein Link to 9/11 Lingers."

30. Brian Whitaker and Michael White, "British 'Intelligence' Lifted from Academic Articles," *Guardian* (UK), February 7, 2003.

31. Woodward, *Plan of Attack,* 311.

32. Andrew Grise and David Usborne, "The Niger Connection: Tony Blair, Forged Documents, and the Case for War." *Independent* (UK), June 5, 2003.

33. Joseph Cirincione, Jessica Mathews, and George Perkovich, *Weapons of Mass Destruction in Iraq: Evidence and Implications* (Washington, D.C.: Carnegie Endowment for International Peace, January 2004).

34. Woodward, *Plan of Attack,* 354.

35. *Washington Post,* March 3, 1999, quoted in Fairness and Accuracy in Reporting (FAIR), "Spying on Iraq: From Fact to Allegation," *Action Alert,* September 24, 2002.

36. *New York Times,* January 7, 1999, quoted in FAIR, "Spying on Iraq."

37. FAIR, "Spying on Iraq."

38. For the "stenographer" reference, see Bill Moyers, "Take Public Broadcasting Back" (speech, National Conference for Media Reform, St. Louis, May 15, 2005), http://wwwfreepress.net.

39. James Moore, "How Chalabi and the White House Held the Front Page," *Guardian* (UK), May 29, 2004.

40. PIPA, *Misperceptions, Media, and Iraq War*, 1.

41. About a third had no misperceptions, another third held one mistaken belief, 20 percent had two misperceptions, and just under 10 percent believed all three.

42. The notion that NPR contains a liberal bias is an article of faith among many conservatives but such a charge is unsupported by the evidence. FAIR studied the guest list of four news shows, *All Things Considered, Morning Edition, Weekend Edition Saturday,* and *Weekend Edition Sunday,* finding that among those with a direct partisan affiliation, Republicans outnumbered Democrats by more than three to two. Representatives of think tanks to the right of center outnumbered those to the left of center by more than four to one. These numbers do not confirm a presumed bias but certainly can be compared with Fox's *Special Report with Brit Hume,* where of 101 guests appearing over twenty-five weeks, Republicans outnumbered Democrats by five to one. Furthermore, the majority of the Democrats were centrist while most of the Republicans were ideological conservatives. See Steve Rendall and Daniel Butterworth, "How Public Is Public Radio?" *Extra!* (FAIR), May/June 2004.

43. Description drawn from Peter Canellos, "Support for War Has Not Erased Doubt," *Boston Globe,* April 12, 2003.

44. Adam Levy, a student in my Windows on Research class, was of great assistance in the preparation of the polling results in this section.

45. Richard Morin and Dan Balz, "Survey Finds Most Support Staying in Iraq; Public Skeptical about Gains against Insurgents," *Washington Post,* June 28, 2005, 1.

46. Stephan Lewandowsky et al., "Memory for Fact, Fiction, and Misinformation: The Iraq War 2003," *Psychological Science* 16, no. 3 (2005): 190–95. My summary also relies on Sharon Begley, "People Believe a 'Fact' That Fits Their Views Even If It's Clearly False," *Wall Street Journal,* February 4, 2005, B1.

47. The survey was conducted by PIPA and is summarized in Jim Lobe, "Three of Four Bush Supporters Still Believe in Iraqi WMD, al Qaeda Ties," OneWorld.net. October 22, 2004, http://www.commondreams.org/headlines04/1022–01.htm.

Notes to Chapter Four

1. This account relies on the description provided by Tom Engelhardt, *The End of Victory Culture* (New York: Basic Books, 1995), 187–93.

2. David Perlmutter, *Visions of War: Picturing Warfare from the Stone Age to the Cyber Age* (New York: St. Martin's, 1999).

3. In Dennis Chiu and John Zaller, "Government's Little Helper: U.S. Press Coverage of Foreign Policy Crises, 1946–1999," in *Decisionmaking in a Glass House: Mass Media, Public Opinion, and American and European Foreign Policy in the Twenty-first Century,* ed. Brigitte Nacos, Robert Shapiro, and Pierangelo Isernia (Lanham, Md.: Rowman & Littlefield, 2000).

4. Walter Cronkite, "Mired in Stalemate," in *Major Problems in the History of the Vietnam War,* ed. Robert McMahon, 2nd ed. (Lexington, Mass.: D. C. Heath, 1995), 528–29.

5. Quotations from Chester Pach Jr., "The War on Television: TV News, the Johnson Administration, and Vietnam," in *A Companion to the Vietnam War,* ed. Marilyn Young and Robert Buzzanco (Oxford: Blackwell Publishers, 2002), 452–53.

6. Daniel Hallin, "Television and Vietnam," in *War and Photography: A Cultural History,* ed. Caroline Brothers (London: Routledge, 1997), 203.

7. For further development of this perspective, see Daniel Hallin, *The "Uncensored War": The Media and Vietnam* (New York: Oxford University Press, 1986).

8. Peter Braestrup, *Big Story: How the American Press and Television Reported and Interpreted the Crisis of Tet 1968 in Vietnam and Washington* (Garden City, N.Y.: Doubleday, 1978).

9. Douglas Kinnard, *The War Managers* (Hanover, N.H.: University Press of New England, 1977).

10. The issues are detailed and complex, but generally Westmoreland insisted that intelligence assessments of the size of the opposing Vietnamese forces be kept low in order to support the argument that Washington was winning the war of attrition. An "A to Z" internal policy review conducted by new secretary of defense Clark Clifford following the Tet Offensive considered significantly higher estimates that had been supplied by the CIA and made it more difficult to argue that the United States was winning.

11. For accounts of the trial, see Renata Adler, *Reckless Disregard* (New York: Alfred Knopf, 1986); and Bob Brewin and Sydney Shaw, *Vietnam on Trial, Westmoreland vs. CBS* (New York: Atheneum, 1987).

12. For examples, see Judith Raine Baroody, *Media Access and the Military* (Lanham, Md.: University Press of America, 1998); John Fialka, *Hotel Warriors,* Woodrow Wilson Center Special Studies (Baltimore: Johns Hopkins University Press, 1992); and John MacArthur, *The Second Front: Censorship and Propaganda in the Gulf War* (New York: Hill & Wang, 1992).

13. Ken Auletta, "Fortress Bush: How the White House Keeps the Press under Control," *New Yorker,* January 19, 2004, 54.

14. Auletta, "Fortress Bush."

15. Stanley Hoffman, "The U.S. Marches Backward," *New York Review of Books,* June 12, 2003.

16. Auletta, "Fortress Bush."

17. FAIR, "Is Media Bias Filtering Out Good News from Iraq?" October 28, 2003, http://www.fair.org/press-releases/Iraq-good-news.html.

18. Quoted in Ari Berman, "Newsweek Was Right," *Nation,* May 18, 2005. An action alert by FAIR cites many examples of other press reports throughout the world. See "Newsweek, the Quran, and the 'Green Mushroom,'" *Action Alert,* May 19, 2005.

19. Brent Cunningham, "Rethinking Objectivity," *Columbia Journalism Review,* July/August 2003, 24–32.

20. See esp. Jonathan Mermin, "The Media's Independence Problem," *World Policy Journal* 21, no. 3: 67–72.

21. Data are from the Audit Bureau of Circulation and are reported by Michael Massing, "The End of News?" *New York Review of Books,* December 1, 2005.

22. Ignacio Ramonet, "Final Edition for the Press," *Le Monde Diplomatique,* January 16, 2005.

23. Sarah Secules, "War and the Letters Page: Who's Counting," *Columbia Journalism Review,* May/June 2003, 10.

24. Democracy Now, "Congress Overwhelmed with Anti-War Calls from 'The Silenced Majority,'" September 29, 2002, http://www.democracynow.org/Congress-Calls.htm.

25. Robert Filner, speech to Peace and Justice Studies Association, Georgetown University, Washington, D.C., October 4, 2002. It is also important to note that these are tendencies, not absolutes. Liberal talk shows also exist and conservatives have been known to write a letter to a newspaper or to lobby their Washington representatives.

26. Madeleine Holt, "Is Truth a Victim?" BBC, May 16, 2002, http://news.bbc.co.uk/1/hi/programmes/newsnight/archive/2029634.stm.

27. Michael Massing, "The Unseen War," *New York Review of Books,* May 29, 2003, 18.

28. Nicholas Engstrom, "The Soundtrack for War," *Columbia Journalism Review,* May/June 2003, 46.

29. Engstrom, "Soundtrack for War," 46.

30. Scott Althaus, "American News Consumption during Times of National Crisis," *PS,* September 2002, 517–21.

31. The comparison figures were 21 percent from newspapers, 22 percent from radio, and 17 percent from the Internet. Respondents were able to give two answers. Survey summarized by Terence Smith, "The Real-Time War: Hard Lessons," *Columbia Journalism Review,* May/June 2003, 26–28.

32. Althaus, "American News Consumption."

33. Lawrence Grossman, "War and the Balance Sheet," *Columbia Journalism Review,* May/June 2003, 6.

34. Markus Prior, "Political Knowledge after September 11," *PS,* September 2002, 523–29.

35. FAIR, press release, "Action Alert: In Iraq Crisis, Networks Are Megaphones for Official Views," March 18, 2003; and Steve Rendall and Tara Broughel, "Amplifying Officials, Squelching Dissent: FAIR Study Finds Democracy Poorly Served by War Coverage," *Extra!* May/June 2003.

36. Dave Astor, and Greg Mitchell, "Why Did 'NY Times' Run 2 Accounts of Antiwar Rally?" *Editor and Publisher,* November 1, 2002.

37. Anne Kornblut, "Confronting Iraq: Policy Tactics, Problems of Images and Diplomacy Beset U.S.," *Boston Globe,* March 9, 2003, 25A.

38. FAIR, "Media Advisory: Pentagon Plan Is Undemocratic, Possibly Illegal," February 19, 2002, http://www.fair.org/activism/osi-propaganda.html.

39. Lolita Baldor, "U.S. Describes Program of Planting Stories," *Boston Globe,* December 3, 2005, A8.

40. Eric Schmitt and David Cloud, "The Struggle for Iraq: Propaganda," *New York Times,* December 2, 2005, 10.

41. James Bamford, "The Man Who Sold the War," *Rolling Stone,* December 1, 2005.

42. David Shaw, "Media under Public Barrage over Content of War Coverage," *Los Angeles Times,* November 8, 2001, A8.

43. The military mission could be described in only general terms, and journalists were not permitted to file reports about the details of classified weapons or their exact location. Furthermore, the unit military commanders could block a reporter's access to the satellite connection at any time.

44. Matt Kelley, "Pentagon Considering Making Policy Official," *Boston Globe,* June 18, 2003. It appears that the Clinton administration at least considered embedding reporters during the Kosovo conflict. A member of that administration later said in an interview, "The people who worked with former Secretary of Defense William Cohen tried to convince him to do that. Apparently they did a huge 'I told you so' during the war with Iraq. 'Look at how it works,' they said. 'See what kind of press you get when you place reporters on the front lines. They become part of the mission.'"

45. Brookings Institution, "Assessing Media Coverage of the War in Iraq," (Brookings Iraq Series Briefing, Washington, D.C., June 17, 2003). Transcript available at www.brookings.edu/comm/events/20030617.pdf.

46. Brookings, "Assessing Media Coverage."

47. Brookings, "Assessing Media Coverage."

48. Brookings, "Assessing Media Coverage."

49. Account drawn from Terence Smith, "The Real-Time War: Hard Lessons," *Columbia Journalism Review,* May/June 2003, 2628.

50. Farah Stockman, "Tapes of Explosives under Review," *Boston Globe,* October 29, 2004, 14.

51. BBC, "Correspondent: War Spin," May 18, 2003, http://www.news.bbc.co.uk.

52. BBC, "Correspondent: War Spin."

53. Mark Hosenball, Michael Isikoff, and Evan Thomas, "Cheney's Long Path to War," *Newsweek,* November 17, 2003.

54. For the self-review of the *New York Times,* see "The Times and Iraq," *New York Times,* May 26, 2004.

55. Frank Rich, "It Takes a Potemkin Village," *New York Times,* December 11, 2005.

56. Data provided by the Committee to Protect Journalists and reported by Joanna Weiss and Anne Barnard, "Two ABC Journalists Injured in Iraq," *Boston Globe,* January 30, 2006, 1.

57. H. D. S. Greenway, "The Toll of 'Friendly Fire' on Journalists in Iraq," *Boston Globe,* March 11, 2005.

58. Julia Day, "U.S. Forces 'Out of Control,' says Reuters Chief," *Guardian* (UK), September 28, 2005.

59. Bryan Bender, "Base Bars Media as Wounded Treated," *Boston Globe,* December 6, 2001.

60. Michelle Goldberg, "Now Playing in 2,600 Home Theaters: Bush's Lies about Iraq," http://salon.com/news/feature/2003/12/09/uncovered/index.html.

61. For more on this process, see Lawrence O'Rourke, "Downing Street Memo a Growing Problem for Bush," *Minneapolis–St. Paul Star Tribune,* June 17, 2005; FAIR, media advisory, "Justifying the Silence on Downing Street Memos," June 17, 2005; and Mark Danner, "Secret Way to War: The British Smoking-Gun Memo," http://www.tomdispatch.com/index.mhtml?pid=2486. The June 10, 2005, editorial of the *San Francisco Chronicle* provides a counterexample of a newspaper that did address the implications of the Downing Street memo.

62. Pew Research Center, November 3–6, 2005.

63. For more detail, see Dahr Jamail, "An Eyewitness Account from Inside the U.S. Siege of Falluja," *Nation,* April 12, 2004; and Aaron Glantz, *How America Lost Iraq* (New York, Penguin, 2005).

64. Mustafa Abdel-Halim, "U.S. Forces Want al-Jazeera out of Fallujah," Islam OnLine, April 9, 2004, http://www.islam-online.net/English/News/2004–04/09/article06.shtml.

65. John Burns, "Troops Hold Fire for Negotiations at Iraqi Cities," *New York Times,* April 12, 2004.

66. On April 8, 2003, U.S. forces hit al-Jazeera's Baghdad office with missiles and killed one of the network's correspondents.

Notes to Chapter Five

1. Guernica is often thought to be the site of the first aerial bombing of a civilian population. In fact, small attacks against a number of cities took place during World War I and European nations sometimes launched air attacks against their colonies before the Spanish civil war. England, for example, bombed a number of Iraqi villages in the 1920s. The bombing of Guernica was shocking because it violated the "understanding" that the deliberate targeting of noncombatants might be tolerated outside Europe but should not take place inside the "civilized world."

2. In Susan Sontag, *Regarding the Pain of Others* (New York: Farrar, Straus & Giroux, 2003), 62–63.

3. Sontag, *Regarding the Pain of Others*, 106.

4. This discussion avoids the tricky history of staged wartime photography, which has existed throughout photographic history. Capa's famous photograph is one example where questions of authenticity have been raised. See the extensive discussion of photography during the Spanish civil war provided by Caroline Brothers, *War and Photography: A Cultural History* (London: Routledge, 1997).

5. General William Westmoreland, the commander of U.S. forces in Vietnam during the peak of the fighting, later suggested that the burns suffered by the girl were the result of a portable cooking stove. Brothers, *War and Photography*, 203–4.

6. Peter Howe, *Shooting under Fire: The World of the War Photographer* (New York: Artisan, 2002), 128.

7. Howe, *Shooting under Fire*, 217.

8. George Roeder, *The Censored War* (New Haven: Yale University Press, 1998).

9. David Perlmutter, *Visions of War: Picturing Warfare from the Stone Age to the Cyber Age* (New York: St. Martin's, 1999), 208–9.

10. Nik Gowing, *Real-Time Television Coverage of Armed Conflicts and Diplomatic Crises: Does It Pressure or Distort Foreign Policy Decisions?* Shorenstein Center, JFK School of Government, Harvard University, June 1994, 13–14.

11. John Taylor, *Body Horror: Photojournalism, Catastrophe, and War* (New York: New York University Press, 1998), 181.

12. Howard Zinn, *Terrorism and War* (New York: Seven Stories Press, 2002), 33.

13. For a detailed discussion of the politics of representing Hiroshima and Nagasaki in peace museums in both Japan and the United States, see Greg Mason and Paul Joseph, "Beyond Accusation and Self-Pity: Exhibiting World War II in Japanese and United States Peace Museums," *Peace Review* 14, no. 4 (2002): 465–80.

14. The interview took place in July 2003 in the Washington, D.C., offices of Human Rights Watch.

15. David Perlmutter, *Photojournalism and Foreign Policy: Icons of Outrage in International Crises* (Westport, Conn.: Praeger, 1998), 99.

16. For details, see David Halberstam, *War in a Time of Peace* (New York: Scribner, 2001), 250–51; and Samantha Power, *A Problem from Hell* (New York: Basic Books, 2002), 285–86.

17. Michael Gordon in Perlmutter, *Visions of War*, 180.

18. Perlmutter, *Visions of War*, 190.

19. James Burk, "Public Support for Peacekeeping Operations in Lebanon and Somalia," *Political Science Quarterly* 114, 1999 (Spring): 53–78.

20. In Howe, *Shooting under Fire*, 78–79.

21. Gowing, *Real-Time Television Coverage*, 29.

22. Their actions are described in Halberstam, *War in a Time of Peace*, 283–92.

23. In the case of Kosovo, the credibility of NATO in the face of human rights violations was underscored repeatedly in interviews I conducted with national security officials.

24. Michael Ignatieff, *Virtual War* (New York: Henry Holt, 2000).

25. Wesley Clark, *Waging Modern War* (New York: PublicAffairs, 2001).

26. Martin Shaw, "Media and Public Sphere without Borders? News Coverage and Power from Kurdistan to Kosovo," in *Decisionmaking in a Glass House*, ed. Brigitte Nacos, Robert Shapiro, and Pierangelo Isernia (Lanham, Md.: Rowman & Littlefield, 2000), 33.

27. Christine Chinlund, "Picturing the War Too Clearly?" *Boston Globe,* April 21, 2003, A15.

28. The caption is an important part of the response to the story. The *Globe* later determined that the troops who carried out the looting were not soldiers shown in the picture. The original Associated Press caption said only that the soldiers were "relaxing" after searching the palace. *Globe* staffers mistakenly connected the soldiers in the picture with the day's lead news story, which did discuss inappropriate behavior by some members of the military.

29. Chinlund, "Picturing the War Too Clearly?"

30. This research was assisted by my fall 2004 Windows on Research seminar, which included the following students: Monica Camacho, Alexandra Dunk, Bruni Hirsch, Megan Chang, Michael Rausch, Peter Shaeffer, Adam Levy, Ketan Gajria, Chryssa Rask, and Matthew Weinberg.

31. Two of my students, Megan Chang for the London *Times,* and Michael Rausch for the *New York Post,* coded the pictures that appeared in the two papers. Tabulations are not included here but can be obtained by writing the author.

32. Mark Jurkowitz, "Media Protest Treatment in Iraq," *Boston Globe,* November 13, 2003, 25.

33. Hugh Gusterson quoted in Julian Petley, "Let the Atrocious Images Haunt Us," in *Tell Me Lies,* ed. David Miller (London: Pluto, 2004).

Notes to Chapter Six

1. It is now recognized that psychological trauma can come from the very proximity to violence, and it is thus likely that some nurses deployed overseas during World War II also suffered from "combat fatigue" even if they were not in combat themselves.

2. The figure for Iraq is drawn from Department of Defense records as summarized by Kate Summers of the Miles Foundation in a February 7, 2006, post to H-Minerva@H-Net.msu.edu. The Afghanistan figure is derived from a compilation from USAR (Ret) Noonie Fortin in a June 9, 2005, post to the same discussion group.

3. Mark Grandstaff, "Visions of New Men: The Parsifal Motif and the Heroic Soldier Narrative in American Advertisements during World War II" (paper prepared for the conference on War and Virtual War, Ste. Catherine's College, Oxford, July 2003).

4. Christina Jarvis, *The Male Body at War: American Masculinity during World War II* (DeKalb: University of Northern Illinois Press, 2004), 58.

5. Josephine Callisen Bresnahan, "Dangers in Paradise: The Battle against Combat Fatigue in the Pacific War" (Ph.D. diss., Harvard University, 1999), 34.

6. Bresnahan, "Dangers in Paradise," 158.

7. *Time,* January 4, 1943, 44, cited in Bresnahan, "Dangers in Paradise."

8. Joshua Goldstein, *War and Gender: How Gender Shapes the War System and Vice Versa* (London: Cambridge University Press, 2001), 258.

9. Bresnahan, "Dangers in Paradise," 148.

10. Bresnahan, "Dangers in Paradise," 177.

11. Bresnahan, "Dangers in Paradise," 160.

12. *Life,* September 20, 1943, cited in Bresnahan, "Dangers in Paradise."

13. Charles Pinzon and Bruce Swain, "The Kid in Upper 4," *Journalism History* 28, no. 3 (Fall 2002): 112–20.

14. "By His Deed ... Measure Yours," *Life,* March 15, 1943, 97.

15. See Gallup Polls 312 (February 16, 1944) and 315 (March 15, 1944).

16. For more details, see Karen Anderson, *Women in Wartime: Sex Roles, Family*

Relations and the Status of Women during World War II (London: Greenwood Press 1981.

17. M. C. Bourg and M. W. Segal, "The Impact of Family Supportive Policies and Practices on Organizational Commitment to the Army," *Armed Forces and Society,* 1999.

18. D. R. Segal and M. W. Segal, *Peacekeepers and Their Wives: American Participation in the Multinational Force and Observers* (Westport, Conn.: Greenwood Press, 1993).

19. Dennis Orthner in Gregg Zoroya, "Soldiers' Divorce Rates Up Sharply," *USA Today,* June 6, 2005.

20. Brian Kates, "Army Red-Faced over New Prison Antics," *New York Daily News,* February 5, 2005.

21. For more on the debate, see Ilene Rose Feinman, *Citizenship Rites: Feminist Soldiers and Feminist Antimilitarists* (New York: New York University Press, 2000); Lorry Fenner and Marie deYoung, *Women in Combat? Civic Duty or Military Liability?* (Washington, D.C.: Georgetown University Press, 2001); Linda Bird Francke, *Ground Zero: The Gender Wars in the Military* (New York: Simon & Schuster, 1997); and Laura Miller and John Allen Williams, "Do Military Policies on Gender and Sexuality Undermine Combat Effectiveness?" in *Soldiers and Civilians: The Civil-Military Gap and American National Security,* ed. Peter Feaver and Richard Kohn (Cambridge, Mass.: MIT Press, 2001), 361–402. Also see *Minerva: The Quarterly Report on Women and the Military* and Carol Burke's *Camp All-American, Hanoi Jane, and the High-and-Tight* (Boston: Beacon Press, 2004), which provides an extremely interesting interpretation of the debate.

22. Rowan Scarborough, "Army Agrees No Women in Combat for Now," *Washington Times,* January 13, 2005.

23. Elaine Donnelly, "The Army's Gender War," *National Review Online,* January 7, 2005, http://www.nationalreview.com.

24. Associated Press, "Women in Combat Not a 'Big Deal,'" http://www.cnn.com/2004/WORLD/meast/01/02/sprj.irq.military.women.ap.

25. In Richard Sisk, "The Women of War," *New York Daily News,* December 14, 2004.

26. Michael Moss, "Hard Look at Mission That Ended in Inferno for 3 Women," *New York Times,* December 20, 2005.

27. Stanley Alpern, *Amazons of Black Sparta: The Women Warriors of Dahomey* (New York: New York University Press, 1998), 65. This discussion also relies on Robert Edgerton, *Warrior Women: The Amazons of Dahomey and the Nature of War* (Boulder, Colo.: Westview Press, 2000).

28. Alpern, *Amazons of Black Sparta,* 97.

29. At least some European observers thought that this rule was frequently broken; Goldstein, *War and Gender,* 63. The Amazon corps may have also had female wives, and female prostitutes may have been employed in the palace.

30. R. Law, "The 'Amazons' of Dahomey," *Paideuma* 39 (1993): 245–60.

31. Alpern, *Amazons of Black Sparta,* 54.

32. Melissa Herbert, *Camouflage Isn't Only for Combat: Gender, Sexuality, and Women in the Military* (New York: New York University Press, 1998), 18.

33. Pessimistically, Lorry Fenner suggests that this acceptance has little to do with equality for women in the military and is more an outcome of the devaluing of women in all aspects of life, both military and civilian. She notes that there is no "hue and cry demanding measures to protect women better or to prosecute their tormentors on the home front, nor is there any determined drive to obtain or enforce restraining orders or enforce already weak gun control measures that are associated with elevated violence against women." In Fenner and deYoung, *Women in Combat?* 25.

34. Miller and Williams, "Do Military Policies Undermine Combat Effectiveness?" 369. Female military officers are more supportive of women in combat roles than civilian females (70.4 to 59.6 percent) while male officers are less supportive than civilian males (30.4 to 49.4 percent). The result is a forty-point gender gap within the military on the issue of women serving in combat roles. See James Davis, "Attitudes and Opinions among Senior Military Officers and a U.S. Cross-Section, 1998–99," in Feaver and Kohn, *Soldiers and Civilians*, 116.

35. Miller and Williams, "Do Military Policies Undermine Combat Effectiveness?" 378. A similar pattern of increasing public acceptance of homosexuals in the military but also of continuing conflicting attitudes is traced by Oscar Torres-Reyna and Robert Shapiro, "The Polls—Trends: Women and Sexual Orientation in the Military," *Public Opinion Quarterly* 66, no. 4 (Winter 2002).

36. A more recent study found some easing in these attitudes, with 50 percent of junior enlisted officers saying that gays and lesbians should be allowed to serve openly in the military. See Annenberg National Election Survey 2004, Annenberg Public Policy Center, University of Pennsylvania. October 16, www.naes04.org.

37. Bryan Bender, "Gays' Ouster Seen Leaving a Gap in Military," *Boston Globe,* February 24, 2005.

38. Liz Sidoti, "'Don't Ask' Rule Seen Costing $363.8m," *Boston Globe,* February 14, 2006.

39. Associated Press, "Allegations of Sexual Assault Continue at Air Force Academy," *Boston Globe,* October 25, 2003.

40. Mary Leonard, "Panel Blames Leadership in Air Force Academy Scandal," *Boston Globe,* September 23, 2003.

41. E. J. Graff, "Bring Me Women," *American Prospect,* May 2003.

42. Office of the Inspector General of the Department of Defense, *Report on the Service Academy Sexual Assault and Leadership Survey,* Project 2003C004, March 4, 2005. Available at http://www.dod.gov.

43. Catherine Lutz and Jon Elliston, "Domestic Terror," *Nation,* October 14, 2002; and Maureen Orth, "Fort Bragg's Deadly Summer," *Vanity Fair,* December 2002.

44. In February 2002, the Pentagon allowed the charter of DACOWITS, the Defense Department Advisory Committee on Women in the Services, to expire. DACOWITS advises the military on several issues including the need to respond promptly to charges of sexual assault (see Michael Moss, "Pentagon Faces New Questions on Old Problem," *New York Times,* March 2, 2003, 26.) The panel had played an independent role in reviewing the military's handling of sexual harassment cases and had conducted dozens of private meetings with officers and cadets in many military installations around the country.

45. Amy Herdy and Miles Moffeit, "Female GIs Report Rapes in Iraq War: 37 Seek Aid after Alleging Sex Assaults by U.S. Soldiers," *Denver Post,* January 24, 2004.

46. Kate Summers, "Karpinski Allegations," post to H-Minerva, on H-Net.MSU. edu, February 7, 2006. There is no current Web site for the Miles Foundation, but the foundation may be reached at Milesfdn@aol.com.

47. Eric Schmitt, "Reports of Rape in Pacific Spur Air Force Steps," *New York Times,* March 9, 2004.

48. Eric Schmitt, "Military Women Reporting Rapes by U.S. Soldiers," *New York Times,* February 26, 2004.

49. Chris Shumway, "Sexual Violence against Female Soldiers Going Largely Unpunished," *New Standard,* December 12, 2004.

50. United Nations Foundation, "A Portal on Women, Peace, and Security," http://www.womenwarpeace.org/issues/violence.htm.

51. Center for Gender Equality, "The Impact of Terrorist Attacks on Women," November 11, 2001, http://www/Greenbergresearch.com/publications/.

52. Mary Leonard, "War Gives Laura Bush Her Own Cause," *Boston Globe*, November 29, 2001.

53. Wayne Washington, "Bush Touts Support for Women's Rights," *Boston Globe*, March 13, 2004.

54. Pamela Constable, "Attacks Beset Afghan Girls' Schools," *Washington Post*, September 8, 2003.

55. Kate Allen, "Reality Check," *Guardian* (UK), February 25, 2004.

56. Carlotta Gall, "Karzai Is Urged to Prosecute War Crimes," *New York Times*, January 30, 2005.

57. Thomas Wagner, "Darfur Toll Lowballed, Say British Lawmakers," *Boston Globe*, March 31, 2005.

58. Griff Witte, "Jailing of Afghan Publisher Ignites Debate on Free Speech," *Boston Globe*, December 25, 2005.

59. Media Benjamin, "On International Women's Day, Iraqi Women Have Little to Celebrate," commondreams.org, March 8, 2004.

60. "Sexualized Violence against Iraqi Women by U.S. Occupying Forces" (briefing paper prepared by Kristen McNutt, Association of Humanitarian Lawyers, presented to United Nations Commission on Human Rights, Geneva, March 2005).

61. "U.S. Troops Said to Use Iraqi Wives as Leverage," http://abcnews.go.com/WNT/IraqCoverage/story?id=1552649.

62. Susan Schmidt and Vernon Loeb, "'She Was Fighting to the Death'; Details Emerging of W. Va. Soldier's Capture and Rescue," *Washington Post*, April 3, 2003.

63. Christopher Hanson, "American Idol: The Press Finds the War's True Meaning, " *Columbia Journalism Review*, July/August 2003.

64. Jerry Adler, "Jessica's Liberation," *Newsweek*, April 14, 2003.

65. Melani McAlister, "Saving Private Lynch," *New York Times*, April 6, 2003.

66. Mohammed was later brought to the United States, given citizenship, hired by a Washington, D.C., consulting firm, and offered book and movie deals and a tour on the lecture circuit.

67. Peter Kampfner, "Saving Private Lynch Story 'Flawed,'" BBC News, May 15, 2003, available at http://news.bbc.co.uk/1/hi/programmes/correspondent/3028585.stm.

68. Kampfner, "Lynch Story 'Flawed.'"

69. Lynda Hurst, "From Hero, to Whistle-Blower, to Celebrity," *Toronto Star*, November 16, 2003.

70. David Kirkpatrick, "Jessica Lynch Criticizes U.S. Account of Her Ordeal," *New York Times*, November 7, 2003.

71. The pictures taken by the soldiers themselves have been compared by Susan Sontag to lynching pictures in which subjects in the photographs grin and smile despite the grim evidence that hangs over their shoulders. They can do so only because they are fully confident that their behavior will be approved. See "What Have We Done?" *Guardian* (UK), May 24, 2004.

72. For two analyses of how the torture at Abu Ghraib came from the top leadership at the Pentagon, see Jackson Diehl, "How Torture Came Down from the Top," *Washington Post*, August 27, 2004; and Seymour Hersh, "The Grey Zone: How a Secret Pentagon Program Came to Abu Ghraib," *New Yorker*, May 24, 2004. Principal roles were played by Defense Secretary Donald Rumsfeld, his assistant Stephen Cambone, and Geoffrey Miller, the commander of the Guantánamo Bay prison, who visited Abu Ghraib shortly before the abuse captured in the pictures was conducted. Besides England, Specialists Megan Ambuhl and Sabrina Harman participated in the torture at Abu Ghraib.

73. Paisley Dodds, "Detainee Shaming Detailed," *Boston Globe*, January 28, 2005.

74. Uwe Siemon-Netto, "Women's Role in Abuse Shocks Arabs," *Washington Times*, May 7, 2004.

75. Mary Leonard, "Abuse Raises Gender Issues," *Boston Globe*, May 16, 2004.

76. Frank Rich, "Saving Private England," *New York Times*, May 16, 2004.

77. Zillah Eisenstein, "Sexual Humiliation, Gender Confusion, and the Horrors at Abu Ghraib," June 21, 2004, http://www.portside.org.

78. In 1971, psychologist Philip Zimbardo conducted an experiment at Stanford University in which student volunteers were randomly assigned prisoner and guard roles. Though everyone knew that it was an experiment, within a remarkably short time Zimbardo discovered that young men, selected by the university for their mental health and positive values, could turn abusive. "My guards," Zimbardo wrote, "repeatedly stripped their prisoners naked, hooded them, chained them, denied them food or bedding privileges, put them into solitary confinement, and made them clean toilet bowls with their bare hands." The planned two-week study had to be ended after only six days. The potential for abuse contained in absolute power and the absence of accountability is enormous and seems to affect human beings no matter what their background. See Philip Zimbardo, "Power Turns Good Soldiers into 'Bad Apples,'" *Boston Globe*, May 9, 2004.

79. Joan McAlpine, "Why the Jezebel of Abu Ghraib Is Such Bad News," *Herald* (Glasgow, Scotland), August 5, 2004.

80. The research of Chryssa Rask, a member of my Windows on Research seminar, contributed to the comparison of press reporting about Jessica Lynch and Lynndie England that follows.

81. A Lexis-Nexis search from April to December 2004 found 125 articles focusing on Lynndie England. Of these, every fifth was examined along five criteria: her appearance, pregnancy, social background, attributed motivation, and status as victim or perpetrator.

82. Agencies on Fort Bragg, "Dog Leash Soldier Gives Birth," *Advertiser* (Adelaide, Australia), October 28, 2004.

83. McAlpine, "Jezebel of Abu Ghraib."

84. Maki Becker, "GI in Torture Case Hires Legal Top Gun," *New York Daily News*, May 9, 2004.

85. "Lynndie England," Wikipedia, December 11, 2004, http://en.wikipedia.org/wiki/Lynndie_England.

86. Michael Fuoco and Cindi Lash, "Abu Ghraib's MP's Hearing Postponed," *Pittsburgh Post-Gazette*, June 23, 2004.

87. "Took No Joy from Actions at Prison, England says," *Rocky Mountain News* (Denver), May 13, 2004.

88. Evan Thomas et al. "How Did a Wispy Tomboy Behave like a Monster at Abu Ghraib?" *Newsweek Web Exclusive*, May 15, 2004, http://www.newsweek.msnbc.com.

89. "When Women Abuse Power, Too," Minerva Center, May 16, 2004, http://www.h-net.org/~minerva/.

90. Monica Camacho, a student in my Windows on Research advising unit, assisted with some of the research discussed in this section.

91. C. W. Hoge et al., "Combat Duty in Iraq and Afghanistan, Mental Health Problems, and Barriers to Care," *New England Journal of Medicine* 351, July 2004:13–22. By March 2005, of 250,000 soldiers who had returned from Iraq and Afghanistan, almost 12,500 had been to VA counseling centers for symptoms of psychological distress and other readjustment problems. See also Kirsten Scharnberg, "Female GIs Hard Hit by War Syndrome," *Chicago Tribune*, March 20, 2005.

92. Esther Schrader, "These Unseen Wounds Cut Deep," *Los Angeles Times*, November 14, 2004.

93. Peter Beaumount, "Stress Epidemic Strikes American Forces in Iraq," *Observer* (UK), January 25, 2004.

94. Sara Corbett, "The Permanent Scars of Iraq," *New York Times Magazine*, February 15, 2004.

95. R. R. Ireland, "Suicide Prevention and Suicide Rates," Washington, D.C.: Office of Assistant Secretary of Defense, 2005.

96. Andrew Gumbel, "Is America Sending Battle-Weary, Clinically Stressed Soldiers Back into the Heat of Iraq?" *Independent* (UK), April 3, 2004.

97. Gumbel, "Is America Sending Soldiers?"

98. Wilbur Scott convincingly argues that the acceptance of PTSD as a medical category came only after a protracted political battle that occurred in the context of opposition to the Vietnam War. See "PTSD in DSM-III: A Case in the Politics of Diagnosis and Disease," *Social Problems* 37, no. 3 (August 1990): 294–310.

99. The results of the survey are summarized in Cheryl Reed, "War Stress Heavier on Women: Some Hesitate to Admit They Are Having Problems," *Chicago Sun-Times*, May 8, 2005.

100. For a useful survey, see Arline Kaplan, "Hidden Combat Wounds: Extensive, Deadly, Costly," *Psychiatric Times*, January 1, 2006.

Notes to Chapter Seven

1. This discussion draws upon Duncan Campbell, "'Dixie Sluts' Fight On with Naked Defiance," *Guardian* (UK), April 25, 2003; Steve Morse, "Touring Chicks Don't Duck Controversy," *Boston Globe*, June 18, 2003, and "Dixie Chicks Arrive to Little Dissent, and Thrill Their Fans," *Boston Globe*, June 20, 2003; and Chris Willman, "Stars and Strife," *Entertainment Weekly*, May 2, 2003.

2. See Tim Jones, "Media Giant's Rally Sponsorship Raises Questions," *Chicago Tribune*, March 19, 2003; and Gabriel Rossman, "Elites, Masses, and Media Blacklists: The Dixie Chicks Controversy," *Social Forces* 83, no. 1 (September 2004): 61–78.

3. Willman, "Stars and Strife," 24.

4. James Schubert, Patrick Stewart, and Margaret Ann Curran, "A Defining Presidential Moment: 9/11 and the Rally Effect," *Political Psychology* 23, no. 3 (September 2002): 559–83.

5. Brian Gaines, "Where's the Rally? Approval and Trust of the President, Cabinet, Congress, and Government since September 11," *PS*, September 2002, 531–36.

6. The comparable proportions are: Britain, 49 percent; Denmark, 48 percent; France, 40 percent; Italy, 39 percent; and the Netherlands, 20 percent (World Values Survey conducted in 1999–2000 cited in Minxin Pei, "The Paradoxes of American Nationalism," *Foreign Policy*, May/June 2003, 31–37.) Many non-European nations also exhibit high levels of national identification similar to that found in the United States.

7. The ABC/Washington Post poll is cited in Janny Scott, "The Changing Face of Patriotism," *New York Times Week in Review*, July 6, 2003, 1, 5.

8. Scott, "Changing Face of Patriotism."

9. Strategies that attempt to manage the public through its patriotic sentiments are not always successful. Political commercials in support of President Bush's 2004 reelection campaign that featured firefighters carrying flag-draped stretchers through the debris of the World Trade Center were seen by many as a crass attempt to exploit September 11. The ads were opposed by many citizen groups, including those whose members had lost family members during the attacks; the ads were subsequently withdrawn.

10. Senator Tim Johnson (D-S.Dak.).

11. Some of the research that follows was carried out by Bruni Hirsch, a member of my Windows on Research advising group.

12. Annenberg Public Policy Center, National Election Survey, October 16, 2004, www.naes04.org.

13. AP-Ipsos poll conducted in June 2005 and summarized in Will Lester, "Poll Finds Most Oppose Return to Draft, Wouldn't Encourage Children to Enlist," Associated Press, June 24, 2005.

14. Harvard University Institute of Politics, October 18–27, 2002.

15. BET/CBS News Poll of African American Voters, July 6–15, 2004.

16. All quotations found in Thomas Shanker, "Need for Draft Is Dismissed by Officials at Pentagon," *New York Times,* October 31, 2004.

17. Douglas Belkin, "Struggling for Recruits, Army Relaxes Its Rules," *Boston Globe,* February 20, 2006.

18. Erika Hayasaki, "They're Taking Up Arms," *Los Angeles Times,* April 5, 2005.

19. The report was prepared by Andrew Krepinevich, a retired army officer, and is summarized in Robert Burns, "Missions in Iraq, Afghanistan Straining Army, a Study Warns," *Boston Globe,* January 25, 2006.

20. In Thomas Ricks, "Small Minority Says Draft Could Happen: New Conflict Would Further Strain Troop Levels," *Washington Post,* October 27, 2004, A3.

21. Ron Harris, "African-American Youths Are Rejecting Army, Military Says," *St. Louis Post-Dispatch,* March 14, 2005.

22. Charlie Savage, "Military Recruiters Target Schools Strategically," *Boston Globe,* November 29, 2004.

23. John Gregory Dunne, "The Horror Is Seductive," *New York Review of Books,* May 29, 2003.

24. Charles Rangel (D-N.Y.), press release, "The Vote on the Poll to Reinstate the Draft Is a Political Maneuver to Protect the President," October 5, 2004.

25. Dunne, "The Horror Is Seductive."

26. Deborah Schildkraut, "The More Things Change … American Identity and Mass and Elite Responses to 9/11," *Political Psychology* 23, no. 3 (September 2002): 511–35. The editorial appeared on December 22, 1941.

27. Some of the research in this section was carried out by Alexandra Dunk, a student in my Windows on Research advising unit.

28. Tanya Schevitz, "FBI Sees Leap in Anti-Muslim Hate Crimes: 9/11 Attacks Blamed for Bias—Blacks Still Most Frequent Victims," November 26, 2002, http://sfgate.com.

29. Stephen Kaufman, "U.S. Government Fights Hate Crimes in September 11 Aftermath," U.S. Department of State International Information Programs, December 11, 2002, http://usinfo.state.gov/usa/civilrights.

30. Aziz Haniffa, "Asian Groups Dispute FBI Report on Hate Crimes," *India Abroad,* December 10, 2004.

31. Council on American-Islamic Relations (CAIR), "57% of American-Muslims Experienced Post 9/11 Bias: Poll," October 4, 2002, http://www.cair-net.org.

32. CAIR, "Poll: 1-in-4 Americans Holds Anti-Muslim Views," October 24, 2004, http://www.cair-net.org.

33. Andrea Elliott, "Study Find City's Muslims Growing Closer since 9/11," *New York Times,* October 5, 2004.

34. "CAIR Launches 'Hate Hurts America' Radio Campaign," IslamOnline.net. April 17, 2004, http://www.islamonline.net.

35. Media and Society Research Group (MSRG), "Restrictions on Civil Liberties, Views of Islam, and Muslim Americans," Cornell University, December 2004, www.comm.cornell.edu/msrg/msrg.html.

36. Twenty-seven percent supported requiring all Muslim Americans to register their home address with the federal government, 22 percent favored racial profiling to identify potential terrorists, and 29 percent thought that government agents should infiltrate Muslim organizations in order to monitor their activities and fund-raising efforts.

37. CAIR, "Survey: 44 Percent of Americans Would Curtail Muslim Civil Rights," December 17, 2004, http://www.cair-net.org/asp.

38. Michael Traugott et al., "How Americans Responded: A Study of Public Reactions to 9/11/01," *PS*, September 2002, 511–16.

39. CAIR, "57% of American-Muslims Experienced Post 9/11 Bias: Poll," October 4, 2002.

40. CAIR, "1 in 4 Americans Holds Anti-Muslim Views," October 4, 2004.

41. In Schildkraut, "The More Things Change,"521.

42. CAIR, Action Alert 415, "NY Congressman Calls U.S. Mosque Leaders 'An Enemy Amongst Us,'" February 11, 2004, http://www.cair-net.org.

43. Schildkraut, "The More Things Change."

44. "City Resounds with Support for Muslims," *Portland (Maine) Press Herald,* September 13, 2001.

45. "Events in 30 Cities Mark National Day of Solidarity with Muslim, Arab, and South Asian Immigrants." Refuse and Resist! 2002, http://www.refuseandresist. org.

46. Renee Gadoua, "Diverse Display of Unity; Non-Muslims Show Solidarity with Muslim Community," *Syracuse (N.Y.) Post-Standard,* February 27, 2004.

47. "Islam 101," *Oprah Winfrey Show,* October 5, 2001. http://www.oprah. com/tows/pastshows/tows_past_20011005.jhtml.

48. Arab American Institute, press release, "Golden Globe Winner Mary-Louise Parker Joins Queen Noor as Presenter at Arab American Gala," March 31, 2002, http://www.aaiusa.org.

49. Ad Council, press release,"The Advertising Council, the National Crime Prevention Council, and SHiNE Launch New Public Service Ads with Celebrities to Encourage Americans to 'Stop the Hate,'" January 23, 2002, http://www.adcouncil.org.

Notes to Chapter Eight

1. Scott Sherman, "The Avenger: Sy Hersh, Then and Now," *Columbia Journalism Review,* July/August 2003, 34–44.

2. This is not to imply that any level of casualties is ultimately "acceptable." In this context, "acceptable casualties" is the number that will be tolerated without leading to politically significant objections.

3. *Reporting America at War,* produced by Amanda Pollak and Stephen Ives, Public Broadcasting System, aired November 2003.

4. See James Tobin, *Ernie Pyle's War* (New York: Free Press, 1997), 135–37. The quotation here has been edited from the original and follows the version read by Linda Hunt in the PBS documentary *War Correspondents.*

5. Douglas Kinnard, *The War Managers* (Hanover, N.H.: University Press of New England, 1977), 74–75.

6. See Caspar Weinberger's speech in *Ethics and American Power: Speeches by Caspar W. Weinberger and George P. Shultz* (Washington, D.C.: Ethics and Public Policy Center, 1985).

7. George Shultz, in *Ethics and American Power.*

8. Colin Powell, "U.S. Forces: The Challenges Ahead," *Foreign Affairs,* Winter, 1992.

9. Edward Luttwak, "Where Are the Great Powers? (At Home with the Kids)?" *Foreign Affairs*, July/August 1994.

10. Dana Priest, *The Mission* (New York: W. W. Norton, 2003), 52.

11. For a sampling see James Burk, "Public Support for Peackeeping Operations in Lebanon and Somalia," *Political Science Quarterly* 114 (Spring 1999): 53–78; Steven Kull and Clay Ramsay, "The Myth of the Reactive Public: American Public Attitudes on Military Fatalities in the Post–Cold War Period," in *Public Opinion and the International Use of Force*, ed. Philip Everts and Pierangelo Isernia (London: Routledge, 2001); Eric Larson, *Casualties and Consensus: The Historical Role of Casualties in Domestic Support for US Military Operations* (Santa Monica, Calif.: RAND, 1996); Jeffrey Record, "Collapsed Countries, Casualty Dread, and the New American Way of War," *Parameters*, Summer 2002, 4–20; Peter Feaver and Christopher Gelpi, "Casualty Aversion: How Many Deaths Are Acceptable? A Surprising Answer," *Washington Post*, November 7, 1999, and *Choosing Your Battles: American Civil-Military Relations and the Use of Force* (Princeton, N.J.: Princeton University Press, 2004); and Benjamin Schwarz, *Casualties, Public Opinion, and U.S. Military Intervention* (Santa Monica, Calif.: RAND, 1994).

12. Record, "Collapsed Countries," 9.

13. Drawn from Kull and Ramsay, "Myth of the Reactive Public," 207–11.

14. Feaver and Gelpi, *Choosing Your Battles*.

15. See esp. Burk, "Public Support for Peacekeeping."

16. Nicholas Lemann, "The Next World Order," *New Yorker*, April 1, 2002.

17. See analysis by Richard Eichenberg, "Victory Has Many Friends: The American Public and the Use of Military Force, 1981–2005," *International Security* 30, no. 1 (Summer 2005): 140–77.

18. Philip Everts, "War without Bloodshed? Public Opinion and the Conflict over Kosovo," in Everts and Isernia, *Public Opinion and the International Use of Force*.

19. Many revisionists are quite sophisticated in their handling of polling data. The better studies recognize many of the limitations of polling and the ways that shifting contexts can affect results at different times. Feaver and Gelpi, in *Choosing Your Battles,* have taken pains to register the difficulty of determining the public's definition of an "acceptable casualty" when the prospect of even one death is not welcome.

20. Bruce Jentleson, "The Pretty Prudent Public: Post Post-Vietnam American Opinion on the Use of Military Force," *International Studies Quarterly* 36, no. 1 (March 1992): 49–74; and Bruce Jentleson and Rebecca Britton, "Still Pretty Prudent: Post-Cold War American Public Opinion on the Use of Military Force," *Journal of Conflict Resolution* 42, no. 4 (August 1998): 395–418.

21. Eichenberg, "Victory Has Many Friends."

22. Kull and Ramsay, "Myth of the Reactive Public," 220.

23. Chicago Council on Foreign Relations, "Global Views 2004," 24.

24. Feaver and Gelpi, *Choosing Your Battles*, 119.

25. The Afghanistan and Iraq casualty figures are from the Department of Defense at http://www.defenselink.mil. The other figures are used by Feaver and Gelpi, *Choosing Your Battles;* and Eichenberg, "Victory Has Many Friends."

26. In Eliot Weinberger, "What I Heard about Iraq in 2005," *London Review of Books*, January 5, 2006.

27. John Files, "Pentagon Agrees to Issue Photos of Coffins of Iraq War Dead," *New York Times*, August 5, 2005, 7.

28. Annenberg National Election Survey, Annenberg Public Policy Center, University of Pennsylvania, October 16, 2004, http://www.naes04.org.

29. Regine Labossiere and Eric Slater, "Mother Encourages Photos of Coffins," *Los Angeles Times*, June 28, 2004.

30. An interesting exercise conducted by *Media Matters*, a PBS show, tried to measure public attitudes toward a controversial but Pulitzer Prize–winning photograph by Jean-Marc Bouju of a Nairobi morgue the day after the bombing of the U.S. Embassy in Kenya killed more than two hundred people and injured more than four thousand. Twelve Americans were among the dead. Corpses are shown in the background. The survey asks whether the pictures should be published and 85 percent answer yes. www.pbs.org/wnet/mediamatters/php/poll303.php.

31. Thomas Ricks, "Dissension Grows in Senior Ranks on War Strategy," *Washington Post*, May 9, 2004.

32. Sidney Blumenthal, "Far Graver than Vietnam," *Guardian* (UK), September 16, 2004.

33. John Murtha, "Dear Colleague on Redeployment of Troops in Iraq," December 14, 2005, http://www.house.gov/apps/list/press.

34. The army did not make the report public but did provide a copy to the Associated Press. See Robert Burns, "Missions in Iraq, Afghanistan Straining Army, a Study Warns," *Boston Globe*, January 25, 2006.

35. "Deserters: We Won't Go to Iraq," December 4, 2004. CBS News.com.

36. Le Moyne College / Zogby poll, "U.S. Troops in Iraq: 72% Say End War in 2006," February 28, 2006, http://www.zogby.com/news.

37. Terence Smith, "The Real-Time War: Hard Lessons," *Columbia Journalism Review*, May/June 2003, 28.

38. Carl Conetta, *The Wages of War: Iraqi Combatant and Noncombatant Fatalities in the 2003 Conflict*, Research Monograph 8 (Washington, D.C.: Project on Defense Alternatives, 2003), 45.

39. James Winnefeld, "Interpreting an Unfolding War and Its Humanitarian Consequences: A Dialog" (working paper, Carr Center for Human Rights Policy, John F. Kennedy School of Government, Project on the Means of Intervention, 2004), 201–3.

40. Patrick Tyler, "Powell Says U.S. Will Stay in Iraq 'for Some Months to Come,'" *New York Times*, March 23, 1991.

41. Rick Atkinson, "The Chief Who Said Too Much; General Dugan's Firing Might Bring a Halt to Military Candor," *Washington Post*, September 23, 1990, B1.

42. Jack Kelly, "Estimates of Deaths in First War Still in Dispute," *Pittsburgh Post-Gazette*, February 16, 2003.

43. Helen Thomas, "Who's Counting the Dead in Iraq?" *Miami Herald*, September 5, 2003.

44. Niko Price, "Iraq to Stop Counting Civilian Dead," Associated Press, December 10, 2003, www.wire.ap.org.

45. Bob Woodward, *Plan of Attack* (New York: Simon & Schuster, 2004), 328.

46. The exchange can be found in Oren Dorell, "Bush Puts Deaths of Iraqis at 30,000," *USA Today*, December 12, 2005.

47. Dorell, "Deaths of Iraqis."

48. Bob Woodward provides several examples during the prewar planning of Operation Iraqi Freedom. At one point, U.S. war planners had identified 130 targets with potentially high collateral damage. Later, this list was narrowed to 24 targets. Woodward, *Plan of Attack*, 158, 331.

49. Kelley Beaucar Vlahos, "Military Seeks to Minimize Civilian Casualties," FoxNews.com, November 16, 2004.

50. For examples, see Woodward, *Plan of Attack*, 158, 331, 387.

51. Agence France Presse, "Pakistan Legislators Urge Expulsion of U.S. Envoy," January 23, 2006.

52. These photographs can be found in Thorne Anderson et al., *Unembedded: Four Independent Journalists on the War in Iraq* (White River Junction, Vt.: Chelsea Green Publishing, 2005).

53. Letta Tayler, "Grieving and Angry," *Newsday*, March 7, 2004.

54. "Joint Publication 3–06: Doctrine for Joint Urban Operations," quoted by Eric Schmitt and Thom Shanker, "U.S. Refines Plans for War in Cities," *New York Times*, October 22, 2002, 1, 14.

55. See the remarkable interview on Democracy Now! "Exclusive: Al Jazeera Reporters Give Bloody Firsthand Account of April '04 U.S. Siege of Fallujah," February 22, 2006, http://www.democracynow.org.

56. See special Fallujah folder on the Iraq Body Count Web site, www.iraqbodycount.net. For a useful review of sources on the costs of the Fallujah operation, see David Cromwell, "The Tragic Blindness of the Embedded BBC," *ZNet*, November 28, 2005.

57. Will Dunham, "Pentagon Says It Used Phosphorus in Fallujah in 2004," *Boston Globe*, November 17, 2005. Also see Giuliana Sgrena, "Napalm Raid on Falluja, 73 Charred Bodies—Women and Children—Were Found," November 23, 2004, http//www.ilmanifesto.it/pag/sgrena/en/420dd721e0ff0.html.

58. For more detail, see George Monbiot, "The U.S. Used Chemical Weapons in Iraq—and Then Lied about It," *Guardian* (UK), November 15, 2005.

59. Some of the research in this section was carried out by Peter Shaeffer, a student in my Windows on Research seminar.

60. Anne Barnard, "Death Lurks in Unspent U.S. 'Bomblets,'" *Boston Globe*, May 1, 2003, 32.

61. Human Rights Watch, "Needless Deaths in the Gulf War: Civilian Casualties during the Air Campaign and Violations of the Laws of War," New York, 1991; Conetta, "Wages of War," app. 2, "Iraqi Combatant and Noncombatant Fatalities in the 1991 Gulf War."

62. Kelly, "Estimates of Deaths Still in Dispute." Daponte was first fired and later reinstated in the turmoil that followed her estimates.

63. Beth Osborne Daponte, "A Case Study in Estimating Casualties from War and Its Aftermath: The 1991 Persian Gulf War," *Medicine and Global Survival* 3, no. 2 (1993).

64. Richard Garfield, "Morbidity and Mortality among Iraqi Children from 1990 through 1998: Assessing the Impact of the Gulf War and Economic Sanctions" (Kroc Institute Occasional Paper 16, Notre Dame University, March 1999).

65. Human Rights Watch, "Somalia: Beyond the Warlords: A Need for a Verdict on Human Rights Abuses," Human Rights Report, vol. 5, no. 2 (March 7, 1993); available at http://www.hrw.org/reports/1993/somalia/.

66. Human Rights Watch, "Civilian Deaths in the NATO Air Campaign," Human Rights Report, vol. 12, no. 1(D) (February 2000); available at http://www.hrw.org/reports/2000/nato/.

67. Noam Scheiber, "Counting the Civilian Dead in Yugoslavia," *Slate*, February 9, 2000, http://www.slate.com/id/1004570/.

68. The order was signed by President Clinton. Human Rights Watch, "Civilian Deaths in NATO Air Campaign," cites discussions with U.S. Air Force and Joints Chiefs of Staff officers in October 1999.

69. Richard Lloyd of the UK Consulting Group on Landmines estimates that 440 were either killed or wounded in the year after the bombing ended. See Richard Blystone, "NATO's 'Collateral Damage' Still Takes Toll in Kosovo," April 3, 2000, http://archives.cnn.com/2000/WORLD/europe/04/03/kosovo.damage/.

70. Laura King, "AP Review of Civilian Casualties Suggests Toll in Hundreds; Taliban Inflated Count," *Associated Press*, February 11, 2002.

71. Marc Herold, "A Dossier on Civilian Victims of United States' Aerial Bombing of Afghanistan: A Comprehensive Accounting," database available at www.cursor.org/civilian_deaths.htm. Herold's compilation does not seem to have been updated.

The losses do not include the massacre of civilian and Taliban prisoners by Northern Alliance forces who were allied with the United States. Oliver Moore, "U.S. Bid to Prevent Massacre of Prisoners Fails," *Toronto Globe and Mail*, November 28, 2001.

72. For a discussion of various tactical, strategic, and geographic reasons why this might have been the case, see Carl Conetta, "Operation Enduring Freedom: Why a Higher Rate of Civilian Casualties?" (working paper, Project on Defense Alternatives, Washington D.C., 2002).

73. Dexter Filkins, "Flaws in U.S. Air War Left Hundreds of Civilians Dead," *New York Times*, July 15, 2002.

74. Les Roberts et al.,"Mortality Before and After the 2003 Invasion of Iraq: Cluster Sample Survey," *Lancet*, October 29, 2004, http://image.thelancet.com/extras/04art10342web.pdf. The methodology was quite different from the compilation of individual incidents followed by most other approaches. Instead, the Hopkins group selected thirty-three clusters, or areas of Iraq, interviewed thirty households from each cluster in an effort to determine how many people died in the household in the fourteen months before the invasion of Iraq compared to number who died during the seventeen months after the invasion of Iraq. The mortality rate was 5 per 1,000 before the invasion and 12.3 per 1,000 after the invasion. These results were then extrapolated to the entire country of Iraq. Violent deaths were reported in fifteen of the thirty-three clusters and were mainly attributed to coalition forces. At the 95 percent level of confidence, the range in increased civilian deaths fell between 8,000 and 194,000 people. The midpoint is roughly 100,000.

75. Irwin Arieff, "39,000 Iraqis Killed in Fighting," Reuters, July 11, 2005.

76. Calculations from Iraq Body Count and reported in Luke Baker, "Survey Finds 25,000 Deaths of Civilians since War Began," *Boston Globe*, July 20, 2005.

77. The report is titled "Measuring Stability and Security in Iraq" and was posted on the Department of Defense Web site on October 13, 2005. For more detail and a discussion of factors influencing the estimates, see Sabrina Tavernise, "U.S. Quietly Issues Estimate of Iraqi Civilian Casualties," *New York Times*, October 30, 2005, 10.

78. Jim Krane, "Iraqi War Death Toll Remains Elusive," *Boston Globe*, March 11, 2006.

Notes to Chapter Nine

1. Robert Norris and Hans Kristensen, "US Nuclear Forces, 2006," *Bulletin of the Atomic Scientists*, January/February 2006, 68–71.

2. Program on International Policy Attitudes (PIPA), "Americans on WMD Proliferation" (Center of Policy Attitudes and the Center for International and Security Studies at the University of Maryland, April 15, 2004).

3. PIPA, "Americans on WMD Proliferation," 19.

4. Chicago Council on Foreign Relations, "Global Views 2004: American Public Opinion and Foreign Policy." Findings summarized in this paragraph are supported by data on p. 28, 33, 34, and 36.

5. Carl von Clausewitz, *On War,* ed. Anatol Rapoport (New York: Penguin, 1968), 119–20.

6. Bruce Jentleson, "The Pretty Prudent Public: Post Post-Vietnam American Opinion on the Use of Military Force," *International Studies Quarterly* 36, no. 1 (March 1992): 53–54.

7. Clausewitz, *On War,* 120.

8. This description relies on Paul Kennedy, "The Eagle Has Landed," *Financial Times*, February 2–3, 2002.

9. William Owens and Joseph Nye, "America's Information Edge," *Foreign Affairs*, March/April 1996, 20–36.

10. Lawrence Freedman, "The Revolution in Strategic Affairs," Adelphi Paper 318 (Oxford: Oxford University Press, 1998), 50.

11. Dana Priest, *The Mission* (New York: W. W. Norton, 2003); Seymour Hersh, "'Phoenix' Arises in Iraq," *New Yorker*, December 12, 2003.

12. Jeffrey Record, "Collapsed Countries, Casualty Dread, and the New American Way of War," *Parameters* 32 (Summer 2002), no. 2:7.

13. Michael Gordon, "'New' U.S. War: Commandos, Airstrikes, and Allies on the Ground," *New York Times*, December 29, 2001.

14. Record, "Collapsed Countries."

15. In 2002, MPRI had a local staff in Washington of about forty people with eight hundred deployed in the field. Annual sales had reached the $100 million mark. P. W. Singer, *Corporate Warriors* (Ithaca, N.Y.: Cornell University Press, 2003), 120.

16. Quotations in Mark Danner, "'Operation Storm,'" *New York Review of Books*, October 22, 1998.

17. Danner, "'Operation Storm.'"

18. Raymond Bonner, "War Crimes Panel Finds Croat Troops 'Cleansed' the Serbs," *New York Times*, March 21, 1999.

19. Data drawn from P. W. Singer, "Outsourcing War," *Foreign Affairs*, March/April 2005.

20. Singer, "Outsourcing War."

21. For an example, see Andrew Bacevich, "The Realist Persuasion When It Comes to War and Peace," *Boston Globe*, November 6, 2005.

22. In Sidney Blumenthal, "Iraq War a Disaster, Say Senior U.S. Experts," *Guardian* (UK), September 16, 2004.

23. Rick Klein, "Democrats Embrace Tough Military Stance," *Boston Globe*, August 14, 2005.

24. Klein, "Democrats Embrace Tough Military Stance."

Index